WHY NOT?

BREAKING LIMITS IN SPORT, BUSINESS AND LIFE

MATT FORMSTON

WILEY

First published 2026 by John Wiley & Sons Australia, Ltd

ISBN: 978-1-394-43462-6

A catalogue record for this book is available from the National Library of Australia

Registered Office
John Wiley & Sons Australia, Ltd. Level 4, 600 Bourke Street, Melbourne, VIC 3000, Australia

For details of our global editorial offices, customer services, and more information about Wiley products visit us at www.wiley.com.

Wiley also publishes its books in a variety of electronic formats and by print-on-demand. Some content that appears in standard print versions of this book may not be available in other formats.

Cover design by Wiley
Cover Image: © borchee/Getty Images
Back cover photo: © Lauren Mac

Set in 11.5/16.5 pts and Warnock Pro by Straive, Chennai, India.

For Mum and Dad, who set the standard high enough to matter, and understood long before I did that high standards aren't a burden: they're the greatest gift you can give someone you love.

Contents

Acknowledgements

A book like this doesn't come from one person — it comes from a life built with the right people around you.

To my parents: thank you for the standards, and for never wavering from them. Your consistency and accountability taught me that real love means holding the line, not lowering it. You showed me that standards matter because people matter.

To my wife: you hold me accountable every single day to be the husband you deserve and the man I claim to be. You are the reason I understand that accountability isn't punishment — it's love in action.

To my children: you only know the version of me that made it through. One day, when you're old enough to read this book, you'll meet a version of your father that might be hard to recognise. I'm not proud of everything in these pages, but I am proud of what came after. The standards I ask of you are the same ones I now hold myself to every single day. If you grow up to be good humans with the courage to live by your values, then I'll know I got the most important job right.

To my colleagues at Optus, the boards I've served on, and the leaders I've learned from along the way: thank you for showing me what real leadership looks like. It's been a privilege to work alongside you and to serve the communities and brands that have trusted me.

And to everyone who has sat in the audience and shared their story: this book is for you.

Introduction

Rock Hard, Marshmallow Soft

Blindness was never my biggest fight.

At five years old, a professor of ophthalmology told my parents their son would go blind. My macular dystrophy was progressive and incurable. I would never play sport, never get a decent job, never have many friends. They should lower their expectations — prepare me for a life of dependency. The world, according to medical science, had already written my future.

Four decades later, I've won four world championships in surfing, become a world champion cyclist and world record holder, surfed a 51-foot wave at Nazaré that earned a Guinness World Record, built an executive career across sales, operations and leadership, raised three children, and been awarded the AM: the Member of the Order of Australia.

But none of that was the hard part.

The real battle was internal, not physical. I spent years chasing an identity I didn't understand — a life of partying and violence that nearly ended with me dead or in jail. When sport disappeared from my life after glandular fever took me out of competition, I didn't just lose an outlet — I lost the only place where my identity had been real. Without the footy field, without the ice hockey rink, without an arena where I was measured on contribution rather than perception, I didn't know who I was anymore.

So, I built something else. Not a life — an image.

My new sport became other people's validation. I trained every day, but not to perform: I trained to look good. Heavy weights, speed bag, boxing drills. I wanted an eight pack. I wanted ripped shoulders. I wanted a body that would attract the chicks. I wanted to look like someone you wouldn't mess with.

And it worked. I could pull chicks. I could drink harder than most. I could hold my own in fights. But the pride wasn't coming from inside me. It never was. It was borrowed pride — pride that only existed if someone else said it out loud.

One Christmas Eve, I woke up covered in blood that wasn't mine, with no memory of what I'd done. The next morning I sat at the family table playing the loving son, hoping the police wouldn't knock on the door.

That was rock bottom. Not the wave, not the blindness — the person I'd become when I wasn't holding myself accountable.

Losing yourself is harder than losing your sight. That's the truth this book is built on.

The turning point

The moment everything changed came in a dark apartment in Killara. I was 30 years old, living in my sister Jacqui's spare room after another failed relationship, surrounded by nothing but silence and the sound of other people's lives drifting through the walls.

There was a man living in the building. About 60. Unemployed and living with his mother. Every time I passed him, he'd tell me about the awesome job he used to have. Past tense. His mother made excuses for him constantly. It was the world's fault he was unemployed; it was the world's fault he'd never built a life of his own.

One afternoon, I came inside and thought: *What a loser.*

Then the worse thought hit: *That could be me.*

He had fewer excuses than I did. I was blind. I had a disability. I had discrimination and inaccessible systems. I had excuses that would hold up in any court of public opinion. But they were still excuses. And if this man, with the world at his feet, could waste his life making excuses, then I had even more reason to stop making mine.

That realisation scared me into having what my dad would call 'a good hard look at yourself'. And what I found wasn't pretty. I'd spent years letting my blindness become a ceiling instead of a starting point. Letting other people's low expectations become my excuse to aim low. Letting the difficulties of my disability justify my mediocrity.

It had to stop. I had to take complete responsibility for my standards and my own future. No more blaming my circumstances; no more waiting to be saved; no more accepting excuses — my own or anyone else's.

People ask me all the time what my greatest achievement is. They assume it's being honoured as a Member of the Order of Australia, or the Netflix documentary, or one of my world records or world titles.

But it's none of these.

My greatest achievement is bringing my life back from nearly death or jail. Building a foundation for a successful relationship with my wife. Creating a life that gives my children something solid to stand on. That internal work — the brutal honesty, the raised standards, the refusal to accept excuses — created the platform for everything that followed.

In 2008, I made the decision. In 2010, everything showed up. I met my wife Bex. I was selected to cycle for Australia. I became an executive and was appointed to my first board. I bought my second property. It might sound like a lucky year, but there's nothing lucky about it. I'd done the work. I was finally set up right. The external results followed the internal transformation.

And here's the part no one expects: my life is easier now than it was before. I work harder than ever — training, business, family, all of it — but it feels lighter. Since I committed to these standards, I've won gold medals, broken world records, and won business awards and community awards almost every year. The contrast is stark. Life feels easier now because I'm set up right. I wasn't before.

The proof

Nazaré, in Portugal, is the colosseum of big wave surfing. Fifty-foot walls of water moving with the weight of freight trains: taller than five-storey buildings, wider than a football field. The Portuguese coast gets hammered by Atlantic storms that travel thousands of kilometres across open ocean, gathering power, before funnelling into the underwater Nazaré Canyon, a geological formation that acts like a wave amplifier, turning ordinary swells into moving mountains.

For most surfers in the world, just being there is unthinkable. For most people in the world, the sight of those waves is unbelievable. And for a blind person to step one foot into this water is inconceivable.

Make no mistake: Nazaré is a war zone in the ocean. Every person in the water knows that if we don't do our jobs right — if I miss a cue, if my tow driver misjudges a wave, if my safety team is a second too slow — someone goes home to their family in a body bag. The stakes couldn't be higher. This isn't extreme sports theatre: it's life and death with an audience.

In front of me, Lucas 'Chumbo' Chianca sat on his jet ski, throttle steady, the rope stretched tight between us. He was my eyes out there. Because I'm blind, I don't have access to the visual data stream other surfers rely on — the ability to read wave faces, judge timing, spot escape routes. Lucas interpreted all of that for me and translated it into sound with three blasts of his whistle. The first told me to release the tow rope. The second told me when to bottom turn. The third signalled it's time to kick out. Trust is reduced to sound. My job was to listen and commit.

On the first blow of the whistle, I let go of the rope and dropped straight down the wave face. I could feel the immense size of the wave under my feet.

I couldn't see the wave that would become my Guinness World Record. I couldn't see the face steepening or the lip beginning to throw. What I could feel was the board hammering across the surface at 60 kilometres per hour, then launching into freefall down what resembled a five-storey building. This isn't sliding into a wave; it's dropping through space, the board skipping and chattering as it tries to maintain contact with a wall of water that's nearly vertical.

On the second whistle, I made the bottom turn, cutting into the wave face. My brain filtered the world into ruthless focus. All the noise vanished — the jet ski engines, the roar of whitewater, the radio chatter between safety teams. What remained was only the data I needed: the hum of the rail cutting through water; the rush of ocean beneath me; the pressure of the air across my face; the subtle shift in board vibration that told me whether I was holding my line or about to lose it.

I was having so much fun up there that I stayed too long. By the time I heard the third whistle, I knew it was too late. I jumped off my board, trying to get under the power of the wave, but then the wave detonated. Hundreds of Olympic swimming pools' worth of water came crashing down in a single violent moment. The pressure tries to rip your limbs off. Your shoulders might dislocate; your joints might tear. So, I pulled my arms tight into my chest and crossed my legs to give the ocean less to grab. I'd trained my breath hold to nearly six minutes for this exact scenario. The capability was built. The question was whether I'd need to use it.

Towards the end of my second hold down, something strange happened. I started smiling underwater. Giggling, even. Because I'd surfed 24 waves over three days at Nazaré without a single proper wipeout. I'd built all this capability — the breath hold, the strength, the training — and hadn't actually needed to use it yet. On this, my 25th wave, while getting ragdolled in the impact zone, I finally got to test what I'd prepared for.

That probably seems insane: smiling while being held underwater by an immense wave. But that's what happens when the work is done and the training becomes instinct. Fear loses its grip because preparation has already won.

Guinness World Records measured the wave at 51 feet, the biggest ever surfed by any blind person in history. But for me, it was never about a record. It was about what's possible when you refuse to let your circumstances define your limits.

The forbidden word

I was born into a house where the word 'can't' didn't exist. My brother, my sister, none of the Formston kids were allowed to say, 'I can't.' The fact that I was blind didn't exclude me from that. If you tried it, you'd be shut down immediately — not with anger, but with a question.

'Why can't you?'

My dad was a sales and marketing director. He spent his days in hard negotiations: managing teams, closing deals and having the difficult conversations that most people avoid. He was trained to push through objections. So, when his eight-year-old son said, 'I can't do that,' he didn't accept it. He leaned in.

When you have to explain why you can't do something, something shifts. You stop hiding behind the word; you start describing the actual problem. And the moment you describe the problem, you start finding the solution.

One day, Dad and I were fishing. I was trying to tie a hook on thin line. With most fishing line, and thicker holes, I could feel my way through. But we were using small hooks and thin line. I asked him for help.

'No,' he said. 'You can do it.'

So, I found a process. I ran my fingers up the shaft of the hook and felt the way it was orientated. The hook curves one way, and the hole sits at 90 degrees to the direction of the hook. I pushed the line towards it, felt the hole and threaded the line through, then wove the line around the hook six times, found the hole, pushed back through and pulled tight. All by feel — no sight required.

Dad would talk me through problems rather than showing me or doing it for me. He'd help me break a big problem into small problems. What's the problem with tying the hook? Getting the line through the eye. What's the problem with that? Finding the hole. Okay, so how do you find the hole? At any part of the process, if I got stuck, he would talk me through it, and I found the solution myself.

That's where the whole *Why Not?* philosophy comes from. It's not a slogan. It's not motivational poster rubbish. It's the question that sat underneath every conversation in my childhood home. Dad would ask, 'Why can't you?', then I'd have to explain the actual problem and, in explaining it, I'd find the workaround.

'Can't' is a toxic, dangerous word that stops people in their tracks and removes their opportunity to develop capacity. The moment you say it, you've given yourself an excuse — permission to stop. But if you say, 'I don't know how to yet' or 'I haven't figured out a way,' that's a door that's still open.

I've now gone full circle with that. I don't use the word 'can't'. I don't let my kids use it either. It's a principle that started with a fishing hook and a father who refused to let his blind son accept limitation.

This book is about keeping that door open.

The Hard Standards

Over the years, I've distilled everything I've learned into eight principles. I call them the Hard Standards.

Not frameworks. Not hacks. Not tips. Standards.

A standard is something you hold yourself to. It's non-negotiable. It's what you do when no one's watching. It's the version of you that exists at 3 am when there's no audience, no applause, no one to impress. There's a saying common in special forces: 'You don't rise to the occasion — you fall to the level of your training.' You don't suddenly step up and become superhuman; you default to the discipline you've drilled in the dark when nobody's watching.

Here are the eight Hard Standards, which I will share with you throughout this book:

- **Two Gears, One Engine.** Know when to go fast and when to go slow. You need both gears. The skill is knowing which one the moment demands.
- **Standards Without Consequences Are Just Wishes.** Rules only matter if they're enforced. If you set a standard for yourself and then let it slide, it was never a standard — it was a fuzzy dream. Accountability is everything.
- **The Bullshit Audit.** Brutal self-honesty. Who are you when no one's watching? Strip away the excuses, the stories you tell yourself, the comfortable lies. It's the hardest thing you'll ever do, and the most important.

- **The Hard Way Is the Easy Way.** There are no hacks. People spend their whole lives looking for shortcuts, and all they do is make their lives harder. The work you put in now makes your future self's life easier, as long as it's the right work.
- **The Future Is Already Real.** Declare your goal before you've earned it. Live in the reality of already being what you want to become. It's supposed to feel uncomfortable. That's how you know the dream is big enough.
- **Empathy Is a Superpower.** To lead others — in business, in sport, in family — you need to understand their whole life, not just their KPIs (key performance indicators). What's going on at home? What are they afraid of? What do they actually want? What are their dreams? Real leadership comes from understanding people completely.
- **Own Every Hat.** You're not one thing. You're a parent, a mate, an athlete, an executive, a partner. Each role is a different hat, and each hat deserves your full presence. Be the best version of yourself when wearing each hat.
- **Trust.** The eighth Hard Standard, trust, is the foundation and the amplifier of everything else. My formula for trust takes all the standards in this book and multiplies them into something consistent that lasts. Trust is something we'll build together throughout this book.

These standards didn't arrive in my life in a neat order. Some I learned as a kid. Some I didn't figure out until my thirties. This book won't feed them to you in a tidy sequence. You'll encounter them when they showed up for me: sometimes overlapping, sometimes colliding, always building on each other. By the end, you'll know them — not because I listed them, but because you've experienced them with me, through this book. And then, you will see how they can work for you, too.

The fuel

The Hard Standards are tools, but tools don't work by themselves. You need fuel.

That fuel is 'Why Not?'

People are always asking me why. Why did you surf Nazaré? Why did you play rugby union when you're blind? Why did you play ice hockey when you're blind? Why would you sprint for a world championship finish at over 70 kilometres per hour on a bike you can't steer?

Not how. *Why.*

I find it offensive. The question implies I need to justify choosing to live fully — that blindness should have disqualified me from even trying. That the default assumption is limitation, and anything beyond that requires explanation.

My answer comes from somewhere deep — from the beaches and back streets of Narrabeen, a Northern Sydney beach suburb, in the 1990s, from a childhood where you either backed yourself or got left behind. I might be a senior businessman now — a parent, a husband, someone who knows when to speak carefully and professionally. But at my core, I'm still a rough-around-the-edges Aussie bloke. And my inner dialogue has never changed.

When someone asks why I did something they think I shouldn't have been able to do, my internal response is always the same:

Why the fuck wouldn't I?

Hard and soft

There's one more thing you need to understand before we begin.

This book is for anyone who needs permission to be both hard and soft: to be physically capable, strong, tough, able to endure pain, without being rough or violent; and to be emotionally open, able to feel deeply, to cry when you encounter suffering, to let your heart break, without being physically weak or useless.

The world tells us we have to choose. We don't.

My dad has mesothelioma. Asbestos cancer. He's been put into palliative care. They gave him three options: aged care, living at home with Mum while they send people out when needed, or voluntary death. The man who gave me my frameworks, my philosophies, the standards that are in this book, he'll soon not be on this planet with us anymore.

When my parents told me, I choked up. My eyes filled with water. To hear that your dad — the guy who's given you most of your standards, the principles that have shaped your entire life — is going to die ... it breaks you. The thought of holding his hand as he becomes a frail old man chokes me up when I talk about it. Write about it.

That's the marshmallow soft.

The next morning, I'll get up and do breath holds for longer than most people can focus on a YouTube clip. I'll lift weights to make sure my body can still take a beating from a giant wave. I'll drop into walls of water that can kill me. I'll stand in a boardroom and hold the line in a negotiation that could cost me my job.

That's the rock hard.

Both are true. Both are necessary. You can hold a dying man's hand and weep, then get up the next morning and train until your body screams. That's not contradiction. That's being fully human.

Your move

I work as an executive coach. I lead teams across multiple businesses. And I used to think leadership was about giving people answers, telling them what to do, showing them the way, handing over the solution. I was wrong.

The most powerful coaching tool isn't providing answers — it's asking questions.

This book isn't going to tell you what to do. Instead, in this book I'm going to show you what I did — the mistakes, the wins, the rock bottoms, the breakthroughs. And along the way, I'm going to ask you questions. Hard questions. The kind I had to ask myself when I was sitting on that floor in Killara, realising I didn't deserve the life I was dreaming about.

Who are you? Who do you want to be? And what are you willing to do about it?

Your answers won't be the same as mine. They shouldn't be. You've got your own life, your own challenges, your own version of *Why Not?* But if you engage with the questions honestly, if you really sit with them, you'll find your own path.

That blind kid from Narrabeen who was told at five that his life was basically over is now a blind adult who is a four-time world champion surfer, a world champion cyclist and world record holder, featured in a Netflix documentary, a seasoned board director and business executive, a husband and father of three.

If I can do that, you can do whatever your version of that is.

You've got two choices: keep making excuses and let your dream future starve to death, or do the work, raise your standards and become the person who deserves the life you're imagining.

I know which one I chose.

The question is whether you've got the guts to stop lying to yourself.

So, turn the page. Stop waiting for permission. Stop feeding your excuses while your future starves.

Why the fuck not?

Chapter 1

Different, Not Over

Two Gears, One Engine

> Know when to go fast and when to go slow. My parents taught me this before I could name it. Mum was relentless, always moving, walking so fast through shopping centres that my sister Jacqui and I had to run to keep up. Get it done and move to the next thing. Dad was the opposite: measure twice, cut once; work it out and make a plan before you act. I needed both gears to survive what was coming.

The flat metal electrodes slid under my eyelids like thin strips of cold foil. Even before they turned the machine on, it was painful—itchy, sharp, wrong. I was five years old, sitting rigid in a hospital chair while strangers attached wires to my eyes.

Then came the heavy steel helmet, like something from an old deep-sea-diving movie—the kind you'd expect to see at the bottom of a fish tank, not strapped to a child's head. As it came towards my face, I felt dread. Not fear, exactly—I was resigned to the fact that it was going to happen. Just dread, and a feeling of darkness closing in as the helmet went over my head.

The weight pressed down. My world shrank to blackness and the sound of my own breathing, fast and shallow inside that metal shell.

'Stay still,' they said. Then they flicked the switch.

The electricity pulsed through the electrodes, surging behind my eyes in waves I couldn't control. My eyelids twitched against my will. I gripped the arms of the chair, knuckles white, but I didn't cry.

I don't remember the last time I cried from physical pain. I think it was before I was five. After that, I just stopped. Physical pain would never make me cry again: not broken bones, not stitches, not any of it. Physical toughness was the household standard, with a dad who breathed through the pain and never cried, and an older, rugby-playing brother. But emotional pain was different. I wouldn't allow myself to cry from that either — not until my dog Oscar died when I was in my mid-teens. And after Oscar, I didn't cry again until my friend Andy Mac died. Those were the only two times for years. It would take decades, and a lot of hard work on myself, before I'd have the bravery to let my heart fully open, to feel everything without armour, to cry at the things that moved me rather than just the things that destroyed me. That softness came later. After Bex. After the kids. After I'd finally earned it.

But that's getting ahead of the story.

In that chair, I felt less like a child and more like a crash test dummy — a small body wired to a machine so adults could collect data.

The doctors weren't cruel; they were clinical. That was the problem. No one looked at me like a boy who might be scared. I was an interesting case. A puzzle to solve.

Let me tell you how a five-year-old ended up strapped to that chair.

I was born with perfect sight. I was a healthy baby with no complications, no flags, no indication that anything would ever change. For the first five years of my life, I saw the world the way everyone else did: colours, faces, distance, detail.

I grew up in Narrabeen, in the Northern Beaches region of Sydney. Honestly, it was about as Aussie as it gets. The lake was our backyard. You'd step out the back door, walk 20 metres across patchy grass, and your feet would be in the water. Narrabeen Lake wasn't scenery. It was part of the family.

Stu, my half-brother, was 13 years older than me — more like a young uncle than a sibling in those early years. He introduced me to surfing, and he played high-level rugby union and ice hockey. Jacqui arrived three years after me, close enough to be my partner in crime and sibling frenemy. We were the self-appointed pirates of Narrabeen Lake, using its nearby island as our base — where we would build huts and watch out for 'intruders'. The island had a few acres of bush and was visible from the house, and it sat 50 metres across the water so it was easy to get to.

Before Jacqui came along, Mum and Dad used to swim laps around the island with me hanging on to Dad's neck. I was tiny, just a baby really, but Dad would tuck my arms securely around his neck while they swam the full circuit. Some parents put their kids in prams and pushed them around the block. Mine strapped me to their backs and swam.

There's a story they've told me a thousand times. I was two years old when I just let go of Dad's neck mid-swim. Instead of sinking or panicking, I pushed away from him and started paddling towards the shore of the island while Mum and Dad freaked out behind me. After that, it became a game. I'd stand on the sand watching them swim towards me, then launch myself in and paddle out to meet them. I embraced freedom before I even knew what the word meant. I trusted in my own body before anyone had told me what my body could or couldn't do.

That lake taught me confidence long before sport ever did. Looking back now, I can see how those early experiences planted seeds that would grow into my relationship with the ocean, with cycling, with pushing my body to limits others said were impossible.

The last clear memory

One of the clearest memories from those early years, before I turned five and was legally blind, happened at a Christmas barbecue. All the families from the neighbourhood were gathered in someone's backyard, sausages sizzling, kids running everywhere, adults standing around with beers in hand.

As the sun went down and the sky turned from orange to purple to a deep, velvety black, one of the dads gathered all the kids together on the back lawn. 'Come on,' he said, 'let's see if we can spot Santa in the sky.'

So we all looked up, staring into the night: a bunch of little kids with sticky fingers from the pavlova and wide eyes full of wonder.

And then we saw it. A streak of light shooting across the sky, bright and sharp against the darkness.

In that moment, it was Santa. It was magic. We all gasped. Some of the kids cheered. I just stood there, frozen, watching the sky with my whole heart open.

What makes that memory so powerful now is that it's the last time I remember seeing anything clearly. I can still picture it — thousands of tiny dots, crisp and distinct against the black. Sharp edges. Clear lines. I can still feel the damp grass under my bare feet.

From that point on, everything blurred into everything else. There were no clear lines. The world became like bold cartoon character shapes with fuzzy outlines and no internal detail. When I think about trees, I know they have depth to their leaves, texture on their bark, but I have no memory of ever seeing that. Everything after that Christmas sky became shapes without edges, colours without definition.

The changes to my vision crept up on me during car trips. We used to play I Spy to pass the time — we had no devices back then, and I couldn't read, so games were everything. Jacqui would say, 'I spy with my little eye something beginning with L.' The answer was leaves. But by then I couldn't see a leaf unless it was inches from my face. I had to start imagining what could be out there rather than actually seeing it with my little eyes.

I would often sit there after a game, staring at nothing, thinking about how broken my eyes were. I never compared myself to others. I never felt sorry for myself. But in that moment, I just hated my disability.

Jacqui did what young kids do — she played on the fact that I couldn't see things. She'd pick random stuff I could never imagine. Not leaves, sky, road — the obvious things people use. Specific things, such as 'orange tractor'. And I Spy is one game where you're fucked if someone chooses something you can't see.

I had my memory and it was powerful. I could work out maps and strategies to bridge the gap created by my disability. But playing I Spy exposed the gap every single time.

The picture chart

I didn't know anything was wrong. I was just a kid in kindergarten, more interested in kicking balls around than anything else. But my teacher had started noticing things. She'd draw a duck on the blackboard and I'd tell her I couldn't see it. She thought I was mucking around.

Then one day, a lady walked into the classroom and started taking small groups of students outside for eye tests. Eventually, my name was called and a group of us headed outside. On the back of a door was a picture chart — simple shapes instead of letters. A house at the top, big and clear. Below it, a tree, an elephant, a monkey. Each row got smaller.

The other kids went first. 'House. Tree. Elephant. Monkey. Truck.' They were nailing it.

By the time it was my turn, I'd already adapted. Without even thinking about it, I'd listened to what they said and memorised the pattern. So, when she asked me to read the chart, I proudly called out the answers.

But I wasn't looking anywhere near the chart.

Something shifted in her face. She pointed to a random picture in the middle. 'And what's this one?' I could see only blurry dots, shapes without definition. I guessed. Wrong. She pointed to another. Wrong again.

That moment changed the course of my life. She contacted my parents, urging them to take me to Sydney Eye Hospital.

The diagnosis

I wasn't in the consulting room when my parents received my diagnosis. They sent me out to play in the hallway while the adults talked. I remember feeling mostly confused. Bored. There were other kids out there, and I was thinking about games, about what everyone else was doing while I was stuck at this hospital. I had FOMO before the word existed. I just wanted to get back to playing, to doing what normal kids did. The tests felt like an annoyance more than anything else. I didn't understand their significance.

Inside that room, Mum and Dad sat across from a professor of ophthalmology. His words were clinical, definitive. Macular dystrophy. Progressive. Incurable. He told them I would lose most of my sight. That I would be legally blind. That they should prepare themselves — and prepare me — for a limited life.

By age six, my visual acuity was around 6/120, meaning that if I stood six metres from a stop sign, I would only see what someone with perfect vision could see from 120 metres away. This diagnosis relating to my peripheral vision came as part of my original diagnosis. As a separate point, my central vision has never shown me the middle of anything. When I look directly at an object or a face, the centre vanishes completely. There isn't a black patch or a shadow — there's nothing. To actually 'see' something, I've always had to look out of the sides of my eyes. The images on the next page show the change. The top shows a healthy macula, while the middle photo shows how mine look. The bottom image offer a side-by-side comparison.

At age five, I had five per cent peripheral vision and no central vision. Today, I have less than three per cent peripheral vision.

You can see it in our family photos. Before five, I'd been looking straight at the camera. After five, I was looking everywhere but at it. The diagnosis gave it a name, but the photos had been telling the story for years.

The car ride home was strange. Mum and Dad were talking too much, too brightly, pointing out things through the window like tour guides. 'Look at that dog!' 'Oh, there's the ice cream shop!' I was five; I wasn't stupid. I could feel the weight of what they *weren't* saying pressing against the windows of that car.

Later that day, after trying to hold it together for me during that car ride home, my dad went to a meeting to pitch for a whole-of-business beverage partnership — a major contract he was close to signing. Mid-negotiation, he stood up and walked out with no explanation. As he later said to me, he felt his whole world was falling away beneath him.

Mum and Dad gave me two different things, both essential, and they both run through everything I do. As I navigated my diagnosis, I realised how important these two 'gears' were going to be in my life.

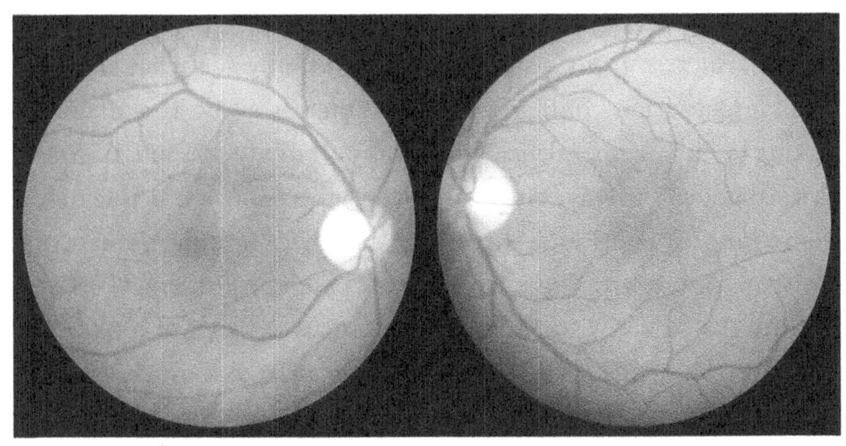

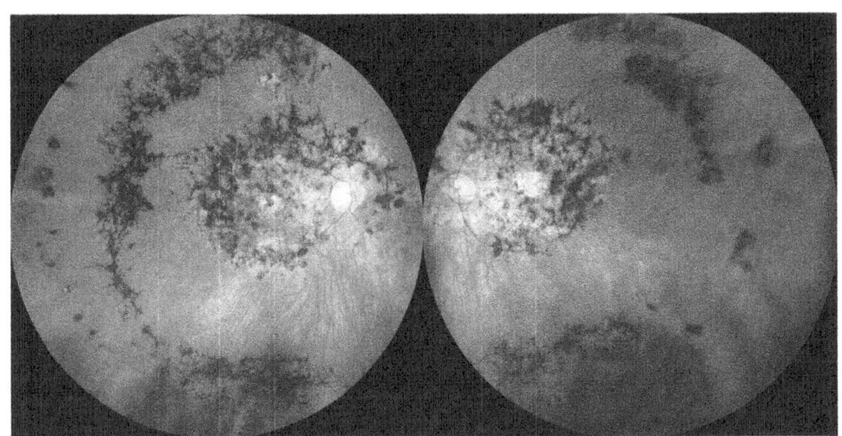

Dad was slow and deliberate. He considered everything carefully. If you were going to do something, you worked it out first, made a plan and then acted. No rushing. No half-arsing anything. He didn't make speeches about it — he lived it. Every job done right or done again. Every commitment honoured. Every shortcut rejected.

He never said, 'I love you.' Not once. He grew up in a different time, when men showed love through presence and provision, not words.

Mum was the opposite. Fast. Relentless. The hardest worker I've ever known. She never stopped. Still hasn't. At 77, she still walks faster than anyone I know. As kids, we'd have to walk then run to keep up with her at the shopping centre. Her legs just kept moving, like time was something you respected by using it. Even now, Jacqui and I still do that half-walk, half-run to keep pace with her. This constant motion taught me that time isn't something you waste. You use it for fun or you use it to create value. But you never just let it pass. That urgency still runs through me, the sense that every minute is building towards something and you need to appreciate it before it's gone.

Mum ran her hairdressing business from home. There was always someone sitting under a dryer, always the sound of women laughing. The house smelled of hairspray and biscuits. And Mum told me she loved me constantly. Without hesitation. Without condition. She'd say it when I left for school, when I came home, before bed — love wasn't something to be earned in her world. It just was.

Dad was the slow gear: process over speed. Mum was the fast gear: get it done, move to the next thing, never stop.

Most people have one gear. They're either careful or they're fast. They're either planners or they're doers. I learned to be both — to use both gears. It meant I could be the executive who can slow down for a critical decision *and* be decisive when momentum matters. The athlete who can be patient in training *and* explosive in competition. Two gears, one engine. That's what my parents gave me.

Between the two of them, I learned that strength and softness weren't opposites. Dad taught me that standards are the backbone of respect — for yourself and others. Mum taught me that love doesn't need to be rationed or earned and that time is a resource you either use or lose. I learned how to shift from slow and deliberate to fast and urgent depending on what the moment demands.

That duality started in a house that smelled of sawdust and hairspray, with a father who taught me to slow down and plan, and a mother who taught me to move fast and never stop.

The drop saw

Dad believed everyone should know how to use tools, including me. My eyesight was fading, but he never once used that as a reason to hold me back.

The drop saw wasn't just another tool in the garage; it was the line between childhood tinkering and real responsibility. Even switched off, it had a presence. Heavy. Solid. Capable of doing real damage if you were careless.

The first time Dad introduced me to it, when I was 13 years old, he didn't sugar-coat anything. 'Alright mate, this one demands respect. It'll cut timber clean ... and it'll cut fingers just as quick if you get sloppy.'

Most parents would've packed the saw away at that point. But Dad wasn't trying to protect me from the challenge — he was preparing me for it.

He flicked the saw on, and the garage filled with the high-pitched whine of the blade. Sawdust hit the air. The vibration travelled through the floorboards into my chest. I couldn't see any of it clearly, but I felt everything.

'So tell me,' he said, 'what's the real danger here?'

'The blade … my hands.'

'Good. And what's not a danger?'

'The sound. Being scared.'

'Exactly. Noise isn't risk. Losing focus is risk.'

Then he taught me the process. The exact one I still use today, thousands of cuts later.

Because I can't rely on sight, everything starts with feel. My right hand finds the measurement point on the timber. I lock my finger there and that finger becomes the marker. Then my left hand drops the saw down until the blade just touches the wood. I slide the timber over until my right finger is resting against the cold edge of the blade itself. The cold edge of that metal against my skin tells me exactly where the cut will happen.

Then I let the saw back up with my left hand. Left hand moves to lock the timber in place. Right hand comes off the wood, moves to the handle, finger near the trigger. I pause. Double-check that I've followed every step. Nothing skipped. Nothing assumed.

Then I pull the trigger.

The motor kicks. There's this jolt — an electrical feeling that shoots up my right hand as the blade spins up. I know now that's just nerves firing, adrenaline responding to the sound and vibration. But as a kid, it felt like the saw was alive.

I drop the blade. The cut happens. Clean.

To this day, I still relish how risky this process is. I take it deadly serious every single time. The sound of the offcut dropping off the right side of the saw can make you jump. A few times it's landed on my foot and almost made me flinch. But I prepare for all of it. That's why I don't make mistakes.

'See?' Dad said to me the first time I made a cut with the drop saw. 'It's not about having perfect vision. It's about having a perfect process. Do it right and you remove the risk. Do it sloppy and you create it.'

Process beats panic. That's what Dad was teaching me. When you can't control what you see, control what you do. When you can't eliminate the danger, build a system that manages it. Step by step, every time. No shortcuts.

While Dad wasn't someone who said 'I love you,' he showed his love for me during that first drop saw lesson. I didn't know it then, but I'd use the framework he taught me that day for the rest of my life. In velodromes. On 50-foot waves. In boardrooms. The specifics change, but the principle never does.

The tinny

The drop saw taught me that danger could be managed with process. The lake taught me that freedom was the reward for earning trust.

After my diagnosis, the one thing that felt jarring was when my parents told me I'd never get a driver's licence. That felt weird at the time. Parents drove cars; kids didn't drive cars. I remember thinking that I didn't really care. But I wouldn't have wanted to lose my freedom on the water.

Dad had bought me a little aluminium tinny when I was five — a small rowboat. I used to row it everywhere with oars. When I was approaching 10 years old, he upgraded the tinny to have a two-horsepower motor. But he didn't just hand over the starting rope. 'The propeller doesn't care if it's water, rope or your arm,' he said. 'Explain to me how you'll manage the risk. Then you can use it.'

Freedom, but tied to responsibility. That was always the deal.

The little motor didn't have a spring recoil, so I had to wind the rope around the top of the motor to get it started. Every time. Wind it tight, brace myself, pull hard. Sometimes it took three or four tries before it coughed to life. But that ritual became part of the process, part of earning the freedom that came after.

The moment the motor fired up, I lost most of my echolocation, which I used to orient myself and stay safe. The constant drone of the motor swallowed the sounds I relied on — the lap of water against the shore, the birds marking distance, the acoustic signatures that told me where I was. All I could do was scan the front of the boat with whatever vision I had. Shapes appeared maybe five metres ahead. That was it.

I was terrified of hitting someone: partly because I didn't want to hurt anyone, but also because I knew that if I ever hurt anyone or hurt myself, Dad would take the boat away. And that boat was my independence — my freedom. The fear of losing it kept me vigilant. Every trip out, I scanned constantly, adjusted my angle, kept the motor low. Process over panic. Just like the drop saw.

The lake became the place where I proved, mostly to myself, that capability was about far more than vision. Capability relied on technique, patience and repetition. The tinny was my first taste of real independence, and I'd earned it by showing I could manage the risk.

Defiance by day, terror by night

The shame of being different started the day of diagnosis and burrowed deep. I did anything I could to hide my blindness: I would disguise it, pretend it wasn't real, ignore it. I refused help. I refused accommodations. I refused to admit I couldn't see what everyone else could see.

But something else was growing alongside that shame. Something harder. More defiant.

I loved climbing trees throughout my childhood. I remember being as young as four or five and climbing trees higher than everyone else — so high it was seriously dangerous. Branches would snap and I'd land on branches beneath me, luckily. My mates would watch from the ground, shaking their heads.

'There's no way you'd climb that high if you could see the ground,' they'd say.

And I'd think: *exactly.*

That was my first way of defying my diagnosis and proving I wasn't blind. If I could climb higher than you, run faster than you, take bigger risks than you, then obviously I wasn't limited. Obviously I wasn't broken. Obviously the professor was wrong.

It was reckless logic. Dangerous, even. But it was also the first spark of something that would define my entire life: the refusal to let anyone else's expectations become my ceiling.

But here's the thing about defiance: it's a daytime emotion.

Every Monday night, around the time I was 10–12 years old, Dad went out. He was the Secretary at the local Rotary Club, and before he left, he'd look at me and say: 'You're the man of the house tonight. Make sure you keep the girls safe.'

He was probably joking — trying to make me feel like an adult, give me a sense of responsibility. But I took it literally.

I'd nod seriously. I was ready. The protector.

Then he'd leave, and I'd lie rigid in bed, barely breathing, cataloguing every sound. The creak of the house settling. The scratch of a branch against the window. The tick of the clock that somehow got louder after dark. I was supposed to protect Mum and Jacqui, but I couldn't see past my own doorway. Every shadow was a threat I couldn't identify. Every noise was evidence of something coming.

In my imagination, the boogeyman lived in my cupboard. He waited outside my window. He existed in every shadow I couldn't see clearly, every sound I couldn't explain.

I never told anyone how scared I was. I was supposed to be protecting the girls. I was the man of the house. But inside, I was a terrified little boy lying rigid in the dark, waiting for the sound of Dad coming home.

Looking back now, as someone who takes professional risks for a living, I understand what those nights were teaching me. The unknown is always the most terrifying thing. The boogeyman in the cupboard is terrifying precisely because he's unknown. Once you have data — once you open the cupboard door and see there's nothing there — the fear dissolves. But a young boy doesn't know what he doesn't know. He just lies there, shaking, waiting for the familiar sound of his dad coming home.

Climbing trees to prove I wasn't broken, then lying awake convinced the darkness was coming for me: that became the pattern that would define my life. I wasn't choosing between hard and soft, but learning to be both.

I didn't know it then, but the duality I kept encountering was the gift. Hard and soft; slow and fast; two gears, one engine.

By the time I was six, I hadn't learned the full meaning of resilience yet — but I was living inside the structure of it. Mum and Dad weren't waiting for the world to adjust to me. They were quietly teaching me how to adjust to the world with grit, creativity and the belief that 'different' was never going to mean 'less'.

Rejecting limitation

After the electrode test — that pulsing, claustrophobic nightmare — Mum later told me something shifted inside her. Not fear. Conviction.

'In that room,' she said, 'watching them wire you up like an experiment, I realised these people saw a case study. I saw my son. And I decided right then that no one would ever write your story but us.'

Dad, normally so calm, had been visibly rattled. He told me years later: 'I knew one thing walking out of that hospital. Advice is one thing. Direction is another. And no one, not even a professor, gets to direct your future.'

They weren't rejecting medicine — they were rejecting limitation. The diagnosis was real. The prognosis was a story and they refused to let someone else write it.

They didn't know what the future held, but they knew it would be my future to forge.

In his garage, with the drop saw, Dad had taught me that process beats panic. He didn't know he was giving me a framework that would carry me through world championships, into corporate boardrooms and across waves that could kill me. He just knew that a blind kid with a reliable process was safer than a sighted kid with none.

That lesson would be tested soon enough. School was about to teach me that not everyone plays by the same rules. Trees don't tease you. Trees don't hold up fingers and laugh when you guess wrong. Trees don't notice that your books are eight times the size of everyone else's.

Kids do.

And they were watching.

The US Navy SEALs have a saying: 'Slow is smooth and smooth is fast.' It's a principle drilled into every operator—the understanding that rushing leads to mistakes, while deliberate action leads to speed. What separates the operators who survive from those who don't isn't raw talent or physical gifts. It's process. The SEALs call it 'front-loading the work'—taking time to build the system so that when the pressure hits, you don't think, you execute. Dad didn't know SEAL methodology. But he was teaching me the same thing in his garage.

• • •

Which gear are you stuck in? And what is it costing you?

Chapter 2

Turn the Wound into the Weapon

The Hard Way Is the Easy Way

> The world tried to tell me what I couldn't do. What looked like defiance — refusing to learn braille, refusing to use a cane or other accessibility tools — allowed me to develop a map of the world around me through pattern recognition, physical navigation, echolocation and memory. This refusal would enable me to develop a world-class skillset that would serve me well decades later. But as a child, the wound of blindness would also become the weapon that made me dangerous.

'Matt, stay back for a moment?'

Six words. That's all it took to strand me.

The teacher meant well. They always did. But they never realised those six words were the worst punishment they could inflict. I usually followed someone out of the classroom to stay connected to my friends, so being held back broke that system. While the teacher talked, my classmates scattered. Chairs scraping, bags zipping, footsteps fading into the playground. The sounds of freedom disappearing.

I'd answer as fast as possible. 'Yes, I understood.' 'No, I don't have questions.' Every second I spent in that classroom was another second my mates got further away.

Then came the wander.

I'd step into the playground and immediately feel the size of it. Hundreds of kids. Dozens of games. Voices overlapping from every direction. And somewhere in that chaos were my friends, if I could find them.

I'd head towards the handball courts, straining to pick out a familiar voice or recognise someone's posture. The shapes all blurred together. Sometimes I'd catch a clue. Most times I wouldn't.

I'd walk up to a group I thought were my mates playing. Get close enough to join in, then realise—wrong kids. Deadly silence. They'd just stare. No laughter, no teasing—just silence. Somehow that was worse. Silence made me feel like I'd walked through a wall into somewhere I didn't belong.

The worst was kiss and catch.

One lunchtime I walked into an area where my friends sometimes played. It sounded like their voices. It looked like their shapes. I joined in, grabbed one of the girls, pulled her towards me and kissed her on the cheek.

I realised I had no idea who she was. Then I realised these kids were in the year above me.

Everyone stopped. Went silent.

I backed away, burning with shame. 'Oh my god, what is he doing?' 'What a freak.' Then, as I walked away: 'That's right, walk away blind boy.' 'He's got no friends; look, he's walking off by himself.'

The worst part was what came after. I couldn't find my friends. So, I sat alone and marinated in the self-hatred of making a mistake that no one who could see would ever make.

The playground was a minefield I had to dodge through every single day. I never told anyone, because telling them would mean admitting I needed help. And asking for help felt like weakness.

A mistake or two in the playground evolved into more isolating, targeted bullying.

'How many fingers am I holding up?'

I heard that question hundreds of times. Maybe thousands. Kids would stand just far enough away that I couldn't see them, hold up their fingers and wait for me to make a wrong guess.

It wasn't one bully. It was everyone and no one. Boys. Girls. Kids I thought were friends. Kids I'd never met. The question followed me everywhere.

At first, I just froze. Sometimes I'd fight back with words. 'At least I don't have red hair.' 'At least I'm not fat.' But I knew I was bringing a pen to a bazooka fight. Whatever I said, they had the perfect counter: 'Okay blind boy, how many fingers now?' And everyone would laugh.

At night, alone in bed, I would shudder thinking about it. The shame would wash through me in waves, physical and cold.

But pain can wire other things too. Determination. Defiance. The slow-burning decision that one day, somehow, I would make it stop.

The giant books

Nothing highlighted my difference more than the books.

In class, at reading time, everyone would take turns reading aloud while the rest followed along in their books. But I couldn't read the book. Everyone knew I couldn't read the book.

The Royal Blind Society asked what size font I could read. Being a competitive six-year-old stitched me up. They showed me a chart, and I pointed to a font size I could barely make out — squinting, straining, desperate to prove I could do it. I thought it was a competition.

That turned out to be size 20-point font.

When the books arrived, they were eight time the size of a normal book. Enormous. Heavy. While everyone else flipped open normal books, I'd haul out something that looked like a poster. It took up half the desk.

But here's the thing I never told anyone: I couldn't even read them.

I could read maybe two or three words at a time. If words had more than four letters, they started swimming together. The books were useless. But I still had to carry them. Every day, lugging around proof of my difference — books I couldn't even use.

Mum would source the books for me — going to enormous lengths to get hold of the books she thought I needed for school. I couldn't bring myself to tell her they were virtually useless.

I should have learned braille. But I was so embarrassed that I refused. Braille meant admitting I was blind in a way I couldn't hide. I still can't read it to this day — not because I couldn't learn, but because I wouldn't. It was too different, too visible — too much of an admission that I wasn't like everyone else.

So, I carried the giant books and pretended.

Two radio stations

Most kids see the social hierarchy. I heard it. I could tell when someone was annoyed by the way they dropped their book. A chair scraping back too fast meant someone was upset. A low murmur between two desks meant gossip I might use later.

In the classroom, survival required splitting my attention in two. I'd listen to the teacher with one ear — hear their instructions, tone, clues about what mattered. With the other ear, I'd track the kids — who was whispering, who was stirring trouble. I'd tune into two conversations at once and pick out the one word that mattered.

It was like running two radio stations at the same time and knowing exactly when to switch frequencies.

That's how I started predicting surprise tests. I'd tell my mates at recess we'd have a test when we went back, and they'd laugh. But time after time, it would happen. Eventually, they stopped laughing and started listening.

Because I couldn't disappear into the background, I leaned into humour as a way of taking control. Humour became my shield — a way to deflect attention from my blindness. But it was also my entry ticket.

The school principal

The queue was nothing special. Just kids lining up for an excursion. I was nine years old. We were going to Botany Bay.

My mate and I arrived at the same time. As little boys do, we started arguing over who was there first. Pushing each other, jostling for position.

He pushed me. I pushed back. He pushed harder. I pushed harder.

Then he just stopped. Stood still. Quiet.

I hadn't seen school principal coming. A scary Catholic sister who could silence a room just by appearing. Every kid in that queue saw her approaching. Every kid went quiet and still.

Except me.

I kept pushing. No one told me. My mate stayed silent and pretended the whole thing was my fault. He'd seen her coming. He didn't say a word.

A hand grabbed my shoulder. I was dragged out of the line.

Three strikes of the cane. Then the sentence: I wouldn't be going on the excursion. I would sit on the steps in front of the Year 6 classroom — a Year 3 student being punished in front of the older kids, visible to everyone — while my entire year group went to Botany Bay without me.

I sat there for hours. Silent. Burning with shame.

The worst part wasn't the cane. It was knowing my disability had caused it. If I could see, I would have stopped the moment the principal appeared. Every other kid did. The only reason I kept going was because I couldn't see her coming. I didn't have the visual data the other kids had.

That shame — the specific shame of knowing your blindness caused your punishment — is different from ordinary shame. In my mind, it wasn't so much that 'I *did* something wrong,' it was more like feeling 'I *am* something wrong.'

Something crystallised that day: trust is the most important ingredient in any relationship, any team, any business. It's a principle I still use. When people break my trust, I don't try to rebuild it. I just move on.

I was still friends with that boy for years. But I never let him close again.

Mapping my world

Mum and Dad bought me a little single-sail catamaran. Just big enough for 10-year-old me and my Cavalier King Charles spaniel, Oscar. I was the captain; he was the first mate. Together, we were the pirates of Narrabeen Lake. Just like the tinny, I had freedom when I was sailing my catamaran.

I didn't just sail — I pushed. I'd angle the catamaran as hard as I could across the wind, chase gusts and lean my body weight into the wind, experimenting until I capsized on purpose. Every mistake made me better.

The lake had its own language. The pull of the sail told me wind direction. The resistance of the rudder told me my turning radius.

The sounds of the shoreline — the reeds, the rocks — had their own acoustic signature. I built a mental map marked with breadcrumbs of sound and sensation.

And there was the sun. I learned to feel its warmth on my face and use it as a compass. At midday, the heat meant north. In the arvo, it meant west. I didn't need to see the sun: I could feel it.

When I was alone on the lake, sometimes adults would approach on kayaks or dinghies. Friendly, probably — but I couldn't see their faces. Most kids use their eyes to assess strangers. They have data to prove the boogeyman isn't real. But I had nothing: just an approaching blur and a voice I couldn't place, which made 'stranger danger' a significant fear.

I think that's where I developed my instinct to stay close. To not let distance become a danger. Because when you can't see what's coming, distance is your enemy.

By age 10, I was navigating through patterns — sound cues, memory, the predictability of objects that never moved. As long as the world stayed still, I could move fast.

Then one day, the world moved.

There was a huge steel skip bin at school. It had lived in the same corner so long it was practically a landmark. I'd built it into my mental map.

But the night before, the garbage truck had taken the old bin and returned with a new one, placing it a few metres from where the previous one had always been.

The next morning, I was sprinting flat-out playing Tip (you may know it as Tap, where whoever gets tapped is 'it'). My friends saw the bin and veered around it. I didn't see anything shift, so I kept running full speed.

And smashed face-first into the steel bin. The impact knocked me out cold.

When I woke up, kids were standing around me. Teachers were running over. And I told them all that I'd tripped.

Even then — concussed, bleeding — my first instinct was to lie. I couldn't admit I hadn't seen the two-metre steel bin everyone else had run around. The shame was so deep that protecting my secret mattered more than the truth.

Without realising it, that was the moment I started experimenting with sound to understand what was happening around me. Clicking my tongue, scraping my shoe, listening for echoes. I didn't know the word echolocation — identifying objects by reflected sounds — but I knew I needed something more reliable than my memory. I was building my own system, because the world doesn't stay still.

Decades later, peer-reviewed research would confirm what my brain had figured out on its own. Studies show that in blind echolocators, the visual cortex — the part of the brain that normally processes sight — activates in response to sound echoes. The brain literally rewires itself through neuroplasticity to use sound as vision. When someone puts noise-cancelling headphones on me, they're not just blocking sound — they're switching off a navigation system that supplements my limited peripheral vision. I'm effectively more blind with headphones on than without them.

More than a target

By age 10, I'd mapped the playground, learned to navigate by sound, built social currency through humour and survived daily humiliation. But the contrast between school and everything else was impossible to ignore.

In class, I was the blind kid. A target.

But outside? I was good at things. Really good.

Handball. Rugby league. I couldn't see the ball until it was a metre away, but I could hear where it hit the ground, read the players' body positions, predict where the ball was going. I was fast. Aggressive. Physical. The footy field made sense in a way the classroom never did.

In the classroom, I was different. On the field, I was just another player. And I was better than most.

So, when a kid at school — nerdy, weak, someone who didn't play footy — said something that cut me, I was ready.

'Santa isn't real.'

I told him to shut his mouth. He said it again.

'Say that again and see what happens.'

He said it again.

I punched him square in the nose. His nose bled all afternoon.

Dad had always taught me not to throw the first punch. This was one of the rare times I broke that rule.

I wasn't defending myself. I was defending Santa. Defending something pure in a life that had become full of shame and humiliation.

But something else had been unlocked. A kid physically weaker than me had tried to stand over me. And I'd realised — right there, with his blood on my knuckles — that I didn't have to accept that. I could fight back.

Words had never protected me. Humour had only gotten me so far. But I realised that my body — the thing I'd been building through competitive sport — *could* make the abuse stop.

My response to the 'How many fingers?' taunts began to evolve.

'How many fingers am I holding up?'

This time, I had an answer.

'How many do you want to keep?'

I'd say it quietly. Calmly. Looking right at them. And I'd let them do the maths.

They'd seen me fight. They'd heard what happened when someone pushed me too far. Suddenly, the question wasn't funny anymore. They had to decide if taunting me was worth it.

Most of them backed off.

I didn't have the words for it yet. But here's what was happening:

- Every night of shame replaying in my head? That was wiring me for hyper-vigilance.
- Every playground wander searching for faces I couldn't see? That was building my ability to read rooms by sound.
- Every 'how many fingers' taunt? That was fuel for a fire I didn't know I was building.

The thing they used to hurt me was becoming the thing that made me dangerous. The wound was becoming the weapon.

It wasn't a healthy lesson. It wasn't the right lesson. But it was the lesson I learned.

The shame didn't disappear. The loneliness didn't end. The taunting kept coming.

But now I had something I didn't have before.

I had fight.

The shame, the humiliation, the moments that made me want to disappear—they weren't just pain. They were raw material.

Toyota's production system is built on a principle they call 'the hard work before the work'. Before a single car rolls off the line, engineers spend months building systems, mapping processes, eliminating inefficiencies. The work looks slow and painful at the start—but it makes everything that follows faster, smoother and more reliable. That's what was happening to me, even though

I couldn't see it yet. Every night of shame, every playground navigation, every fight I shouldn't have had to fight—it was all the hard work before the work. The skills I was being forced to build the hard way would become the very skills that made my career, my sport and my life possible. The hard way was always going to be the easy way. I just didn't know it yet.

• • •

What skill or strength in your life today was built the hard way—through pain, frustration or failure you didn't choose at the time? Now look at what's hard right now—the thing you wish would just go away. What if it's not the obstacle? What if the hard thing you're facing today is building the foundation for who you're about to become?

Chapter 3

Find the Room Where Effort Counts

The Hard Way Is the Easy Way

> There are no hacks. No shortcuts. But here's the thing they don't tell you: the hard way only works if you're in the right room. The same effort that makes you a champion in one environment will crush you in another. Before you commit to the grind, ask one question: 'Does this room reward effort?' If not, find a different room — then give it everything.

The headgear was old and stiff. Leather on the outside, foam padding on the inside that had been compressed by a hundred tackles. Nothing like the soft, flexible headgear players wear today. When I strapped it on that morning, I felt like a warrior putting on armour.

I was 10 years old, and I'd been selected for the Manly Warringah Sea Eagles Catholic Schools representative team — the pathway that fed into the junior ranks of one of the most successful clubs in rugby league.

The journey to that moment had been a rollercoaster. A talent scout had spotted me during a club game at Lake Park, our home ground that sits on the shore of Narrabeen Lake. He'd invited me to try out for the rep team. I showed up nervous, desperate to prove I belonged.

During the set drills — passing, technical work — I felt like I was failing. That stuff wasn't my forte. I couldn't see the targets clearly; I couldn't track the ball the way other kids could. But once we got into open play, I felt like I was at home. Reading the field. Finding gaps. Using instinct instead of sight.

When Dad got the call that I'd made the team, it was a shock: a huge moment in my young life. All those years of adapting, compensating, figuring out how to compete, and here was proof that I could be judged on performance, not perception. My effort could overcome my limitations. It was proof that I belonged.

The weather was good for winter in Australia — a clear sky, cold air, the kind of day where you could see your breath but the sun still warmed your face. I remember being really excited before the first game — I was buzzing with adrenaline, desperate to prove I deserved to be there.

We played the Western Suburbs Magpies first. I played the entire game at hooker — the dummy half, the player who picks up the ball after every tackle and restarts the attack. Every play ran through me. I was at the centre of everything.

Towards the end of the game, I noticed the Magpies' defensive line was light on the blind side — the short side of the field — with just two players there, and their winger was right on his sideline. I picked up the ball and ran straight at him, then I stepped inside him at the last minute and slid over the line.

The winning try. The deciding score of the game.

That became one of my signature moves — attacking the blind side. On the open side, where there was much more space, there was too much going on, too many blobs of blur to track. But the blind side had less detail. I could keep it simple, read the gaps and make the play.

I walked off that field in maroon and white feeling like I'd earned my colours. Manly had won the premiership the year before, in 1987, and scoring that try felt like being one of my heroes in real life.

And then I didn't play for the rest of the tournament. Not for the second match. Not for any of the matches that followed.

It was a one-day round-robin tournament, game after game after game, and I sat on the sideline in full kit — boots laced, mouthguard ready, headgear in my hands.

I held on to that headgear like it was a lifeline: gripping the leather, waiting to be asked to put it back on. The other boys rotated in and out, while I waited for my turn.

It never came.

By the end of the day, they gave us all medals. I held mine and felt nothing. It was empty. I hadn't contributed. I'd already learned from Dad, from Mum and from everything they'd taught me that recognition without effort was worthless. You don't get to feel proud of something you didn't earn.

I assumed it was my fault. Kids always do. I must not have played well enough. Maybe I made mistakes and I didn't realise. Maybe I wasn't as good as I thought I was.

That quiet disappointment stayed with me for years.

The truth about the sideline

It wasn't until my mid-twenties, while having dinner with Mum and Dad, that the story finally came out.

After that first game against the Magpies — after I'd scored the winning try — the head coach for Manly Juniors had found out I was legally blind. He didn't talk to Dad directly. He went to my coaches and told them they had to bench me.

His words were simple: 'I won't allow a legally blind kid to take the field. I don't want to be responsible if he gets injured.'

He benched me — not because of performance, but because of liability.

Dad was furious. When he finally confronted the coach, the argument escalated fast — loud enough that it nearly turned into a punch-up. Dad was defending my right to be treated like every other kid. The coach was defending his fear.

When I heard this over dinner, 15 years after it had happened, something dark rose up in me.

I was angry. Properly angry. The kind of anger that, as a fit and capable man in his mid-twenties, would normally push me towards physical resolution.

An adult had done this to me. A coward who wouldn't even talk to my father directly. Who looked at a 10-year-old boy — a boy who had just scored the winning try — and decided he was too much of a liability to let him play.

And now I had no way of confronting him. As a child, I couldn't defend myself. As an adult, the moment had passed. The injustice just sat there, with nowhere to go.

I was angry at Mum and Dad too, at first. 'Why didn't you tell me?' I asked. 'Why did you let me think it was my fault?'

But even as the anger burned, I knew they were right.

If they'd told me the real reason at 10 years old, it would have rewritten my story. I would have seen myself as broken. Unwelcome. No matter how hard I worked, someone would always find a reason to exclude me. I might have quit playing altogether.

So, they shielded me. They let me believe the disappointment was about performance because performance was something I could improve. Skill was something I could build. But blindness? That was something I couldn't change.

It was one of the wisest things they ever did for me.

Some injustices don't heal. They just scar over.

What I didn't realise at the time, when I was sidelined from playing league, was that my internal voice was already shaping itself around a single principle: don't let your disability let the team down.

Every training session, every game, every moment on the field — that thought ran underneath everything. My blindness was my shortfall. It wasn't the team's fault I couldn't see. But it was my job to make sure they never had to compensate for it.

When I made mistakes — and I did make mistakes — I never admitted they were because of my vision. If I missed a tackle, I'd blame something else: 'Sorry, I wasn't focusing.' 'Sorry, I lost concentration for a second.'

I'd heard lazy players use those excuses. So, when I made a mistake that was absolutely due to my blindness, I'd hide it behind the same words. But for me, it wasn't laziness; it was blindness. And I would never admit that.

The irony was that I was always hyper-focused. I had to be. I couldn't afford to switch off for a second because I was already operating with less information than everyone else.

So I worked harder. Focused more. Made sure I never had to explain myself.

That meant triathlons before school every morning. Hundreds of push-ups to make myself stronger than everyone else on the rugby field. My fitness was my insurance policy — I was going to make mistakes sighted kids wouldn't, so I had to be fitter than all of them to compensate.

I still have that old leather headgear. It lives in a box with my trophies from those days — including my first Best and Fairest from rugby league. My sons laugh every time the headgear comes out. They can't believe anyone ever wore something so uncomfortable. But still, I keep it — it's a cool reminder of my school footy days.

Changing rooms

The contrast between school and sport was becoming impossible to ignore.

At school, I knew I was different. No matter how hard I worked — in maths, in English, in anything academic — I was still the blind kid. I could put in more effort than anyone, build more skill, get better grades, and still get picked on by kids who weren't as intelligent, weren't as fit, weren't as hardworking.

The cruelty wasn't always verbal. Sometimes it was calculated sabotage — and it would happen into my teens. Because I couldn't read normal-sized text, I had a laptop in class when I was 14. I was the only kid in the school who did. It was 1992 — there was no enlargement software, just a screen I couldn't see.

I could touch type, so I'd hammer away without looking at the screen. But that meant I had no idea what was appearing on it.

Kids would lean over and read out loud what I was typing. They'd call out every typo, laughing while I sat there unable to see what they were seeing. Then they'd delete parts of my work — sometimes all of it.

I wouldn't realise until later. Work I'd spent an hour on, gone. I'd have no idea when it happened or who did it.

Every tool became another way to humiliate me.

They didn't pick on the other smart kids. They didn't pick on the other athletic kids. They just picked on me all through school because I had a visible weakness they could exploit.

Take maths. I was good at it — really good. I could build numbers in my head, find patterns, nail calculations with ease. But the moment a question involved a table or a cross-reference, I was lost. The rows and columns blurred together. I couldn't comprehend the question, so I'd get it wrong: not because I couldn't calculate the answer, but because I couldn't access the visual information.

Kids who weren't as smart, who didn't try as hard, would beat me because they could see the table.

At school, I was playing on a different-shaped field. And the goal posts were always moving.

The classroom didn't reward effort. No matter how hard I worked, my difference would always be used against me.

But in footy? Everything was fair.

You made the tackle, or you didn't. You slid over in the defensive line and plugged the gap, or you didn't. My effort was recognised immediately, and when other kids misread plays or didn't plug their gaps, they got the same call-out I did. Exactly the same treatment.

That made me feel normal. Like I was contributing. Like I belonged.

I actually loved being called out for missing a play, because that meant they were holding me to the same standards as the rest of the team. In the classroom, I was never held to the same standards — I was either pitied or targeted, but never treated as equal.

In footy, the boys had my back.

Andy Mac — the big prop who'd become one of my best mates, and who lived on my street — was always there at games, letting the opposition know that if they touched me, they'd have to deal with him. The prop played in the front row of the scrum and was a huge physical presence on the field.

Sometimes when I made a good tackle and someone got hurt at training, they'd lash out. 'Fuck off, blind boy.' It was their way of venting, and my disability was an easy target.

But any time this happened, one of the boys would step in. 'Well, he definitely saw you, he just flattened you.'

It was an unwritten rule. The boys knew that calling me skinny, slow or soft was fair game — they'd call any teammate that. But picking on my blindness was off limits. I think they understood that footy was fair, footy was real, and crossing that line would erode the culture we'd built.

Not once — not a single time — did anyone at footy training say, 'How many fingers am I holding up?'

That was the difference. The culture.

I was the same person, but the culture, and therefore the outcome, was different.

I switched to rugby union from league when I was 11 years old. While training in rugby union, I found my perfect playing position: blindside flanker.

Yes, *blindside* flanker. Literally a position named after my disability (and a setup for my speaking career).

Role clarity gave me belonging. I knew exactly what I contributed to the team. I wasn't 'the blind kid playing rugby': I was the blindside flanker who showed up to every training, who made his tackles, who did his job.

The ruck became my compass. A ruck is what happens after every tackle — the ball hits the ground and both teams pile in over it, competing for possession. The flanker's job is to get there first, every single time. I didn't look for the ball; I *felt* where it had to be. Bodies piling in, pressure building, the moment of release when the ball squirted out one side or the other ... I could read all of it by sound and sensation.

Being the blindside flanker meant operating on the short side of the field — which has less traffic, fewer variables and more predictable patterns. It was the same principle that helped me score that winning try against the Magpies: keep it simple. Read the gaps. Make the play.

Ice hockey was another sport where the culture made all the difference, and effort was rewarded. I started playing around 11 years old. The Narrabeen Ice Rink was just near the beach — it must be the only ice rink in the world that is so close to one of the greatest surf beaches on the planet. For a legally blind kid, ice hockey made strange sense. The puck was black on white ice — high contrast and easy to track. The rink had walls, boundaries, echoes. The game was contained in ways that open-field sports never were. There was no adapted hockey back then — I was playing mainstream competitive ice hockey.

I could hear the scrape of skates, feel the vibration of bodies hitting the boards and sense where players were moving before I could see them clearly. The same skills I'd built in rugby translated directly to ice hockey.

By the time I was a teenager, I'd developed a reputation: not for flashy plays, but as someone who would show up for every training session, who would be there doing the work. Every game, I'd be there putting my body on the line. And if the opposition wanted to get rough with one of my teammates, I'd be there too. I was dependable in every capacity — the kind of teammate you could count on when it got hard.

Nothing was given. Everything was earned. That's how it should be, in sport and in life.

The esky lid

Not every room is easy to read.

One summer, while camping at Seal Rocks, north of Sydney, when I was 11, I met a girl at a bonfire. She surfed stand-up, real boards — serious status for a young girl back then. We talked for hours. I went to sleep thinking the next day might be more of the same.

The next morning, some of the boys told me where she was so I paddled over to say hello. Silence. I tried again. More silence. The same situation I'd faced a hundred times — approaching someone, not being able to confirm who I was talking to, then paddling away with no idea what had just happened.

That night, there was another bonfire. She came over and started talking to me again. Matter of fact. Like nothing had happened.

When I finally asked her, 'Was that you in the surf this morning?' she didn't hesitate.

'Yep. But don't ever fucking talk to me on an esky lid.'

An esky lid. My bodyboard.

In surf culture, bodyboarders were second-class citizens. That was a hierarchy I hadn't learned to read.

But here's the thing: she told me the rule. Directly, with no ambiguity.

The rep team coach never did that. He just benched me and said nothing, letting me think it was my fault. He let me carry that shame for 15 years before I learned the truth.

Both were rejections, but one was honest. The other was cowardice.

I'd rather know the rules and get rejected than be left guessing why I was never given a chance.

That day, I asked my older brother Stu to teach me how to stand up on a fibreglass board. I became obsessed with that goal.

I have no idea who that young lady was. I never saw her again, and I never learned her name. But I have a Guinness World Record, four world titles and some of the most epic experiences of my life to thank her for.

Culture and effort

I didn't have the language for it back then, but I was learning something that would shape every decision I'd make in sport, in business and in life: *culture determines whether you thrive or survive.*

The same person — same effort, same talent, same determination — will flourish in one environment and fail in another. It's rarely about you. It's almost always about the room you're in.

At school, I was surrounded by kids who made excuses for everything, who took accountability for nothing, and who couldn't match my effort or intelligence — and they still had power over me. Because that environment, that culture, rewarded cruelty and punished difference.

The best cultures are built on contribution, not status. Effort was the currency that really mattered. Show up. Work hard. Have your teammates' backs.

Before you try harder, ask: does this room reward effort?

If the answer is no, find a different room. Don't waste your fight on a culture designed to crush you.

I'd found my rooms. Rugby. Ice hockey. Surfing. Places where I could earn respect through what I did, not what I couldn't see.

But those rooms had rules. Serious rules. And the consequences for breaking them were immediate.

That was the next lesson I would learn: once you find the room where effort counts, you realise that standards aren't optional.

They're what keep everyone safe.

The British SAS (Special Air Service) selection process has a 90 per cent failure rate. The candidates who succeed aren't always the fittest or strongest; they're the ones who recognise that selection is a specific environment with specific rules, and they adapt accordingly. SAS psychologists found that candidates who tried to outmuscle the course failed. The ones who read the room—who understood that relentless consistency mattered more than heroic displays—were the ones who earned the beret. Same effort, different application. The hard way only works when you're in the right room.

•••

Are you grinding away in a room that will never reward your effort? Or have you found the place where what you do actually counts? If you are in the right room, are you articulating your value to your team and leaders?

Chapter 4

The Lineup Doesn't Negotiate

Standards Without Consequences Are Just Wishes

> Rules only matter when enforced. The moment you allow a standard to slip without consequence, you've created a new, lower standard. I learned this from my parents before I could surf. I learned it again — harder — in the surf lineup at North Narrabeen. Standards aren't optional. They're what keep everyone safe.

I was 12, staying at my aunty's place in Forster, when a few boys from my rugby team who were camping in the area invited me down to the beach. One of the older guys said the waves were big. Really big. Not playful weekend surf — properly heavy water.

They looked at me and said, 'Are you sure, Matt?'

Mum overheard this as she was passing by, walking back towards the nearby group of adults. Before I could answer, she stepped in: 'Matt, maybe take your bodyboard instead of the surfboard today.'

For whatever reason, I listened. It was one of the best decisions of my life.

Ten of us hit the water, sprinting off the sand and diving straight into walls of whitewater. I couldn't see how big the sets (the groups of waves) were, but I could feel the weight of them — the sound, the rumble, the speed of the water drawing off the bank. They were calling them eight-foot waves, but to my 12-year-old brain they felt like skyscrapers.

I stuck to one of the older boys. Every time he duck-dived, I duck-dived. Every time he angled left or right, I followed. Set after set detonated in front of us until four of us finally punched out the back.

Then one of the older brothers called out: 'Matty! Go for this one!'

When an older surfer calls you in, you don't question it. It's a moment when someone who owes you nothing says, 'You belong here.'

I turned, kicked hard and felt the wave pick me up. It was a big left-hander running off a headland. I was going so fast — I just remember how fun it was. Trimming across the face, body low, heart hammering. For a few seconds I felt weightless, as if I was flying.

Then the whole thing drew up under me and imploded.

The instant I went under, I knew: the more I fought it, the more it would hurt. I don't open my eyes underwater — never have — so there was nothing to see. Just violence: the ocean ragdolling me, spinning me, pushing me into the darkness where there's no up or down.

But the fear wasn't about drowning. The fear was about my wrist rope.

I hadn't been riding the bodyboard much lately; I'd been surfing on my stand-up fibreglass board. So, I knew the rope might be sun-affected, weakened. If the rope snapped now, in this water, everything would change.

With the rope, I stayed close to the surface. With the rope, when I came up, I could get on top of my board and ride the whitewater to safety. Without the rope, I'd have to swim. And with that much water moving, swimming in could take forever. I might end up on the rocks. And I couldn't see the rocks.

I let the rope pull on me, but I tried not to yank it back too hard. I focused on one thing: don't let the wrist rope break.

Finally, the wave let me go. I popped up, gasping.

When I hit the beach, the boys who couldn't get out were all waiting.

'Oh my god, Matty. I can't believe you went out.'

The ego spike was immediate. It was the validation I'd been chasing: the proof that I wasn't blind, I wasn't different, I wasn't less than them.

I didn't tell them how scared I'd been. I didn't tell them about the wrist rope. I just stood there on the sand, chest heaving, playing it cool. Like it was all good.

Being accountable

Before I was ever allowed to walk to the beach on my own, Mum and Dad made one thing absolutely clear: freedom only exists when accountability comes first.

The rules were simple, strict, and enforced with zero wiggle room: cross only at the lights. Same route every time. Tell us exactly when you're leaving. Tell us exactly when you'll be home. Be on time — not roughly on time, not 'close enough', but on time.

If I said I'd be home at 5 pm and walked in the door at 5.05 pm, that wasn't a 'near miss'. That was a breach. And there were consequences to being late: I'd lose the privilege of walking to the beach alone.

It didn't matter if I had a good excuse — and 'the surf was pumping' definitely wouldn't cut it. Excuses weren't accepted. Time was time. Accountability was accountability.

Standards without consequences are wishes. The moment you allow a standard to slip without consequence, you've created a new, lower standard.

That's one of the strongest lessons Mum and Dad ever taught me — stronger than anything I learned in a classroom.

Friday nights

For most kids on the Northern Beaches, Friday nights meant video stores or hanging around the shops. For us, Friday nights meant the Narrabeen Ice Rink.

Inside the rink was another world. Cold air, bright lights and hot chips drowning in vinegar, with Roxette, INXS and Guns N' Roses blasting loud enough to shake the boards. We'd do ice limbo competitions, skating under a bar that got lower and lower until only the most flexible kids were left.

And then there were the ice shows.

The figure skating team put on a full *Phantom of the Opera on Ice* performance. Jacqui had her own solo piece. And Jacqui and I also did a duet together — a proper pairs routine with lifts and choreography.

Picture it: Jacqui, nine years old, in her beautiful white figure skates, gliding across the ice like she belonged there. She was as graceful on the ice as she was full of ferocious energy off the ice. And me beside her in my black Bauer ice hockey skates (because I couldn't skate in figure skates), doing all the tricks and lifts in gear designed for checking people into boards, not for dancing to Andrew Lloyd Webber.

I could see the red boards against the white ice, which provided a good contrast. The painted circles on the ice provided more clues to my position on the rink, while Jacqui was my anchor. As long as I stayed in contact with Jacqui, I could complete the routine.

Jacqui still tells the story: I never got the lifts right in training. Not once. But on performance night, I nailed every single one. Something about the pressure, the audience, the moment, brought out a version of me that training couldn't. Looking back, I got lucky. These days I believe you need to get it perfect in training to get it almost perfect in competition. But that night, the adrenaline carried me through

Those Friday nights weren't just entertainment. They created community. The ice rink was a place where the whole Northern Beaches came together — surfers, hockey players, families — all skating together while 'The Final Countdown' echoed off the ice.

Navigating the lineup

Sighted surfers look ahead to read what's coming; I feel what's directly underneath me with my front foot, much like using a cane, and I use my back foot to steer. The ocean has a pattern — the period between swells tells me when a set is coming. When a bigger wave approaches, that rhythm changes slightly. I'm also aware of what other surfers are doing — if they paddle out, a set is coming; if they are drifting in a certain direction, the waves will be there. I'm just using different data to find them.

My brain now makes the call instinctively, using knowledge built from tens of thousands of waves. Ask me to explain it and it's like asking you to explain how you walk. I just do it.

When I started surfing, I had more than the waves themselves to contend with.

In the late '80s and early '90s, North Narrabeen — Northy, as it's known to locals — wasn't just a surf break. It was a hierarchy, a culture and a law unto itself.

Respect wasn't polite. Respect was survival.

Mum had surfed North Narrabeen in the '60s, one of the first women ever to paddle out there, but I never for a second thought that gave me anything. She put it bluntly: 'Just because I surfed there in the sixties doesn't mean anyone owes you a thing. North Narrabeen has never worked on favours. You earn your place or you don't.'

I didn't expect a shortcut. I wanted to earn my place in the lineup — the order in which you could catch a wave — in the only way North Narrabeen respects: through performance and conduct. I navigated the lineup entirely without help from my mid-teens until my mid-thirties.

The hardcore Northy locals sat deepest in the lineup. The experienced crew sat just inside them. The grommets — young surfers still learning the pecking order — orbited around the edges. The tourists and blow-ins were tolerated ... until they weren't.

The consequences for breaking the rules were immediate and physical.

It happened once, right in front of me. A guy dropped in on one of the heaviest Northy locals. The local followed him to the inside and paddled straight up to him.

'Fuck off. Get out of the water. Never come back to Northy.'

The guy turned around and said, 'Oh yeah? You can fuck off, mate.'

What happened next took about five seconds.

The local paddled straight at him, punched him in the face, grabbed his hair, pushed his head underwater and held it there. Then he grabbed the guy's board, punched the fins sideways and snapped them clean off.

Quick. Swift. Consequences.

The guy paddled in, broken board under his arm, blood on his face. As far as I could tell, he never surfed at North Narrabeen again.

I got my own lesson not long after.

I accidentally dropped in on a local. I didn't see him paddling in on the inside—my vision didn't pick him up until it was too late. I realised straight away and kicked out of the wave, but the damage was done.

As he was paddling back out, he came straight at me. 'Watch it, mate. Stay the fuck away from my waves.'

I was stupid enough to mumble something under my breath.

He grabbed my hair, pushed my head underwater and held it there. When he let me up, nothing else needed to be said. I took my medicine and learned my lesson. I would never have admitted my eyesight got me into that situation. That wasn't an excuse anyone would accept—and I didn't want it to be.

The lineup gave me identity. And the culture taught me the most important truth of those years: respect is earned daily.

Years later, I was on the other side of it.

A guy with a Kiwi accent paddled out and kept pushing further up the lineup. As a Northy local, it felt disrespectful to let him paddle inside me. So I told him to fuck off and have some respect.

'It's a free ocean, mate,' he said. 'You can't tell me where to sit.'

I pushed him off his board. When he came up, he swung at me with a punch. I punched him straight in the face and then punched a hole through his board.

When he surfaced, I told him to paddle in or I'd finish the job.

He left.

You might read this and judge. But it was a different time. The standards existed for a reason: they kept order, they kept people safe, and they made surfing better for everyone who earned their place. The order and the swift consequences meant no one dropped in and fewer people ran each other over.

The lineup taught me something I'd carry into every environment I ever entered: rules exist for a reason. And when the rules aren't enforced, chaos follows. This is reflected in the world's surf lineups now — it's chaos because there are no consequences for bad behaviour.

Immoveable objects

I was 16 when my rugby team travelled to Fiji — my first sporting trip overseas. Even with only five per cent peripheral vision, I could still see contrast, and in Fiji contrast was everywhere: the blackest skin against the whitest teeth, the colour of the water, the brightness of the sun.

The real lesson of the trip didn't come from a scoreboard. It came from a palm tree.

We were playing one of the regional teams on a rough paddock that, by Australian standards, would never be used for a match. I had no idea there were palm trees standing in the middle of the playing space. No one told me, and why would they? For everyone else, the trees were obvious.

During the game, I was in full flanker mode, sprinting from one breakdown to the next. A breakdown is what happens after every tackle — the ball hits the ground and both teams contest for possession. As a flanker, my job was to get there first, every single time.

Halfway across the field, everything went black.

I'd run head first, full speed, straight into a palm tree. And palm trees do not move.

When I came to, the boys were standing around me, half-concerned and half-laughing.

'Mate ... you tried to tackle a palm tree.'

A few days later, on another paddock, I did it again. This time I saw the second palm tree at the very last moment. Just soon enough to drop my shoulder. I avoided knocking myself out, but I smashed my shoulder badly.

Two games. Two trees. Two unforgettable hits.

The boys thought it was hilarious. And honestly? So did I. Sometimes the only way to deal with your limitations is to laugh at them before anyone else can.

Those palm trees taught me something: nature does not negotiate. Palm trees don't care that you only have five per cent peripheral vision. They're immovable, unforgiving and indifferent—just like reefs, rocks, mountains and heavy surf. This rugby field was not like any other rugby field I'd played on.

New environments present new obstacles—and there can be consequences to making assumptions about new places, even if they should follow a known layout. Nature doesn't always follow the rules.

Proving I wasn't blind

By my mid-teens, every minute of life was soaked in movement—sprinting, skating, paddling, wrestling, lifting, grinding. And threaded through all of it was a deeper, unspoken truth: every test was a chance to prove I wasn't blind.

Every sprint I won, every tackle I dominated, every wave I caught... in my teenage mind, it was evidence that I didn't have a disability. I didn't just want to keep up. I wanted to overpower, outwork and outrun everyone, because in my confused young mind I thought that if I could beat you, it meant I wasn't disabled.

It was a deranged barometer. But it became my fuel.

And instead of shying away from danger, I stepped forward. Not because I loved violence, but because my single greatest fear wasn't getting hurt — it was being seen as different. If you could handle yourself in a fight, you weren't seen as weak, or blind.

That fear, the fear of being 'less', outweighed every physical danger in front of me. It made me work harder, train harder, fight harder and hold my space in environments where losing ground meant losing respect.

It wasn't healthy. It wasn't sustainable. But it forged me.

Another thing that forged me is something I've never told anyone.

I had my motor-boat — the 12-foot tinny with a six-horsepower Yamaha outboard that Dad had upgraded for me when I was 12 (my first tinny had a smaller motor). I'd promised I would never hurt anyone. I could scan with my eyes because I could see blurs within about five metres of the boat; the contrast against the flat water gave me enough data to make decisions. When I had mates with me, I'd get them to tell me if there was anyone further ahead.

One afternoon, when I was 17, I was driving alone across Narrabeen Lake to a park on the far side. There was a barbecue happening, and a girl would be there who I wanted to see.

I was driving straight into the sunset, which meant I was even more blind than usual. The glare turned everything into white nothing.

I came around the corner of one of the islands, about 50 metres from shore, when my boat just started going up something, like I was going up a ramp. I was planing, moving fast, and then I was lifting ... and then I came to a complete stop.

I'd run over a guy on his kayak.

He started screaming. Rightly so. He'd just been run over while out on his arvo paddle. I hadn't seen him at all.

I reversed back to make sure I hadn't actually run over his body. The kayak was sinking. It was smashed, basically snapped the whole way through just behind his seat.

'Sorry, sorry, sorry, sorry. Are you okay?' I asked.

He told me he was okay but his kayak was destroyed.

And then I made a decision I've carried with me ever since.

I knew this would take hours to sort out. I knew it might end with me losing the use of the boat. I knew there was a girl waiting at that barbecue.

So I fled.

I left that poor guy there in the water with his smashed kayak. He was yelling angrily as I left. I went to that barbecue and never told a soul.

I've never told anyone about this until now.

That's who I was in my mid-teens: desperate to prove I wasn't blind. Desperate to fit in. And willing to do things — reckless things, selfish things, dangerous things — to protect that image.

The lineup had taught me that rules exist for a reason. That consequences keep everyone safe. That standards matter. And I already knew that standards without consequences are just wishes.

The ocean didn't care about my story. The lineup didn't care about my excuses. The guy on the kayak didn't care that I couldn't see into the sunset.

The world doesn't adjust to you. You adjust to it, or you hurt people along the way.

I was still learning that lesson. The hard way.

Harvard research on organisational behaviour found that teams with clear, enforced standards outperform those with vague or unenforced rules by a factor of three. Here's the part most people miss: it's not the standards themselves that create performance, it's the consistency of the consequences when you cross a line. When people know exactly what will happen if someone crosses that line, and they see it happen every time, then behaviour changes. The lineup at North Narrabeen wasn't sophisticated, but it was consistent. Everyone knew the rules. Everyone knew the consequences. And everyone adjusted accordingly.

• • •

What standard have you let slip? And what would change if you enforced it, starting today?

Chapter 5

When Your Only Thing Disappears

Standards Without Consequences Are Just Wishes

Standards only hold when something enforces them. For most of my childhood, I had two systems of accountability. My parents: who banned the word 'can't', enforced every rule with zero wiggle room and held a line so consistent I never questioned it. And sport: consequences were immediate, physical and non-negotiable on the footy field, at the ice rink and in the surf lineup. Between them, I had structure. I had standards. I had something to fall back on. Then both disappeared at once. Glandular fever took sport. My friend Andy Mac's death shattered everything else. And my parents — the people who had held the hardest line my whole life — eased off on me. Not because they stopped caring, but because they were terrified. They had just watched their son's best mate take his own life. They were genuinely scared that if they kept pushing, if they held the hard line on standards with a grieving, angry teenager

> who was visibly falling apart, they might lose their son the same way Andy's parents lost theirs. That fear changed everything. The two people who had never let a standard slip in my entire childhood suddenly couldn't bring themselves to enforce them. Without consequences, standards collapse. Without standards, identity collapses. This is what that looked like.

There was a tree in my street where I used to go when I needed to disappear.

It was a huge tree with a fork in the trunk where you could sit hidden by the canopy. No one could see you up there. A car would go past every now and then, and you could hear if someone was walking down the street. I couldn't see anything from up there, but as there was only one way up, which was up the trunk, I knew I'd have no unwelcome, unexpected visitors.

The week my friend Andy Mac died, I went and sat in that tree every day.

I don't remember who told me. It might have been my parents. It might have been my friend Andy Kannard, who also lived on our street. What I remember is the feeling — as if my organs and skeleton had been removed from inside my body and there was just a cavity left. No air. No nothing. Just a vacuum that made me feel like I needed to eat something, or breathe or drink something to fill the void. But I didn't feel like doing any of it.

Andy Mac. One of my best mates since childhood. He'd lived on my street. The big prop who was always my security guard on the rugby field. The guy who sat on the motor of his tinny — not on the seat, on the actual motor — driving around Narrabeen Lake like a silhouette everyone recognised. The guy who introduced me to the Red Hot Chili Peppers, blasting *Blood Sugar Sex Magik* from a boombox in his room until they became my favourite band for life.

Gone. Not an accident. Not a close call. A deliberate ending.

One day I sat in that tree for a couple of hours. Just sitting there. In silence.

If you know me, you know how unthinkable that is. I never stop. I'm always moving, always doing things. But after Andy died, I just sat there.

I thought about the meaning of life. What does it all mean? How can people be so mean?

I'd gone to a Catholic primary school and high school. I'd learned about the Christian Bible, heard all the stories. And sitting in that tree, I couldn't understand — if there was a God, how could he allow so much injustice and pain in the world he apparently created? How could he let Andy suffer like that? I didn't have an answer. I wouldn't find one for years.

Andy had been bullied at school, which had been a factor. The final outcome was him taking his life. I was bullied too, and it all felt really shit.

But sitting in that tree, I just kept coming back to one question: why? Why did he do that?

I never found an answer. I'm not sure there is one.

Before

Let me take you back to who we were before that day.

By age 12, Kannard, Andy Mac and I were camping on the island any weekend we could. We'd load an aluminium rowboat with a tent, sleeping bags, sausages, a frypan, fishing gear and, most importantly, the portable tape player. Guns N' Roses, Bon Jovi and Michael Jackson would echo off the water as we paddled across like miniature explorers.

My sister Jacqui and my friend Phil Shanley would often be there too. Phil had been my mate since preschool. He was one of those mates who was just always there. Phil and I would go all the way through primary and high school together, play rugby union together for the Narrabeen Tigers, and eventually stand in each other's bridal parties.

The first time we camped there, we terrified ourselves with ghost stories, panicked the moment the sun went down, and paddled home in the dark. But we kept going back — catching prawns at night under the moon, cooking everything on the fire, exploring the island like it was our own world — even though home was literally 50 metres away.

Those days weren't just adventures. They were the best days of my childhood.

At around the same time as our island adventures, rollerblading became our thing. It wasn't cool compared to skateboarding or surfing — far from it! But it was perfect for ice hockey cross training.

One afternoon, me, Jacqui and Kannard were rollerblading through Narrabeen's Caravan Park after checking the surf. At a T-section, we had to choose left or right. Jacqui and Kannard chose left — the zig-zag route through the caravans. I chose to bomb straight down the centre road past reception and out the main entrance. With my five per cent peripheral vision, fewer variables always meant more speed.

Naturally, a race was declared.

As I approached reception, that internal alarm — the one I still use today surfing big waves — kicked in. A blur of horizontal contrast, a faint metallic vibration.

A boom gate. New. Closed.

I bent my knees, dropped my weight, braced for the hit ... and hit it full speed.

Normally, impacts threw me backwards. But the boom gate flexed. And flexed. And kept flexing until it snapped clean off.

Suddenly, I was rollerblading down the road with an entire boom gate in my hands like some kind of Olympic jouster. I rolled another 20 metres in total disbelief before bursting into hysterical laughter — right before the 'oh shit' realisation kicked in.

I ditched the gate in the bushes — I'm definitely not proud of that — and we all tore around the lake at full speed towards home.

That was us. That was who we were. Before everything changed.

An unfair fight

My friendships with Andy Mac and Andy Kannard lived on our street, in our neighbourhood. They went to different schools to me, so we didn't see each other there.

By the time I turned 15, school had become combat.

The bullying hadn't faded — it had evolved. Kids would run just ahead of me and duck under low branches, leaving me to smash face-first into them. A perfectly timed ambush: engineered humiliation.

And then came the sunglasses. I wore them because the glare burned my eyes. Doctor's orders. But in a school of 800 boys, being the only kid in sunglasses made me a target wrapped in neon tape.

Dad and Stu's voices rang through every reaction I had. 'One day you'll have to protect your wife. One day you'll have kids. You'll need to defend them.' The message was clear: if I couldn't handle myself against some punk at school, how would I ever protect the people I loved?

I stopped mucking around with grapples or bent fingers. If someone targeted me, I went straight to punching — fast, hard, decisive.

Then came the day three of them decided to jump me.

Two of them grabbed my arms from behind. The third started punching me in the stomach and ribs. Then one of them punched me from behind.

First came shock. Then it turned quickly to emotional rage — that someone had decided to do this over some banter in a classroom.

Everything I knew — Dad, Stu, my friends, Northy surf culture, the footy code — told me this was not how real men behave. Three on one is coward shit.

And because it was unfair, something snapped within me.

I put two of them down quickly. The third started backing away, saying 'Calm down, you psycho.'

But it was too late: he'd released the psycho. I put him on the ground and gave him extra punches while he was down there. For good measure.

Violence had clarity. Violence had rules. Violence worked.

Psychologists have a term for what I was experiencing: death by a thousand cuts. Research from Columbia University shows that small, repeated slights — each one individually dismissible, each one met with 'I was just joking' or 'It's not that bad' — are cumulative and energy-depleting. They create what researchers call 'battle fatigue'. The recipient can't call out any single incident without looking like the problem. Teachers told me it wasn't that bad; the bullies would laugh it off. But the thousand cuts were drowning me. Every day: another nick, another comment, another reminder that I was different and they had power over me. No single one was enough to act on, but together they were crushing. Violence was the only circuit-breaker that worked. One real consequence — one moment where the cost of targeting me became physical and immediate — did more to stop the bullying than years of telling teachers, years of ignoring it, years of trying to laugh it off. Even now, as an adult who has managed large teams and navigated corporate politics, I know that was my only option. The alternative was to accept it and be slowly crushed by the years of relentless, invisible abuse.

When the arena disappears

When I was 16, glandular fever took sport from me. Sport was a space where there was no bullying, where I could be recognised and given a positive focus for training, and then just like that it was gone.

I missed an entire season of rugby. When I came back, I felt slower. I'd gone from understanding all the plays, reading everything almost in futuristic terms — anticipating what was coming and then confirming it as it happened — to missing plays, feeling slow and making errors.

I knew it was over in a game against Manly. There were some big players in their team, and the biggest played number eight. Every single time there was a scrum near our tryline, he would come out of the back 100 per cent of the time and run the blind side. It was only me between him and the tryline.

I had known he was coming for years. It was terrifying — he was like a man-child even when we were 12 — but I knew it was my job and so I'd take him down. Every time.

But after I came back from glandular fever, he just smashed past me. I physically couldn't stop him. The gap in our strength had grown too wide while I was sick, and I'd lost the technical skill in my tackling. Reading a footy field using sound and memory is a skill, and like most skills, it's use it or lose it. I hadn't used it for a whole year.

The kick-offs would inevitably come straight to me. If you have a player on the other team with a busted knee, you tackle him on that knee. If you find out a player is legally blind, you send every kick-off straight at him. That's the game.

I started feeling like more and more of a liability rather than one of the major contributors on the field.

And here's the thing I couldn't admit then: if I had just told my team what I could and couldn't see, I might have been able to save my footy career. They could have made adjustments. We could have found solutions.

But I was too stubborn. Too proud. I wouldn't admit what my biggest challenge was.

I basically self-sabotaged with my pride.

The same thing happened in ice hockey: I just couldn't tell them. And so sport, the thing that had been everything to me — the thing that proved I wasn't blind, I was where I belonged, I was valuable — slipped away from me.

When you've built your entire identity on one thing, losing that thing doesn't just hurt. It erases you.

The funeral

The funeral felt like a violation.

There were so many people there. Andy lived in my street for my entire life until we lost him. He was my big prop security guard. As a blindside flanker, my job was to agitate and create disruption — getting under big forwards' noses, making late tackles to take their focus away from the game. That made me a target. But no matter how big or angry opposition players got, Andy was always there.

But when I arrived at that funeral, the crowd overwhelmed me.

In environments like that — crowded, noisy, unfamiliar — I'm lost. My echolocation is useless. My memory maps don't exist. I can't see faces. I can't read the room. Once I'm in a group of more than 15 people, it becomes a logistical and mental nightmare to work out who everyone is.

So there I was, at the funeral of one of my best mates, sad and depressed and angry — and completely isolated. I couldn't grieve with other people unless they came up to me. I couldn't see people to go and talk to them easily — my blindness had created a wall between me and everyone else I knew there.

I did speak to his parents and his brother. I was sad, but I couldn't say what I wanted to say. I couldn't tell them how much he meant to me, how much I'd miss him, how angry I was that he was gone. The words wouldn't come.

And what I heard around me disgusted me.

Girls' voices everywhere, some giggling. A lot sobbing — loudly, performatively, making sure everyone knew they were there. It all felt bolted on. Fake. Like grief was a costume they'd put on for the day.

To this day, I don't go to funerals. That experience left a scar so deep I'll never get over it.

Filling the void

Into the void came partying.

Not because I wanted it. Not because it was meaningful. But because it was the only place I still felt included.

Before glandular fever, I'd been one of the fittest, toughest, most disruptive players in every team I joined. But missing a whole season had wrecked everything. That loss of identity, followed by losing Andy, left a hole, and parties filled it easily.

Drinking didn't require fitness. Partying didn't require discipline. Fitting into the group didn't require excellence. This new world rewarded chaos, not structure.

I'd been playing guitar for years — my Opa, my Dutch grandfather who escaped Nazi training camps on multiple occasions because he refused to fight for them, had given me my first one. After the war, he immigrated to Australia and became head guitar teacher at the Sydney Conservatorium of Music. I learned to play music by ear and memory. He tried to teach me the proper way — jazz scales, the principles of sight reading (not that I could have read the music), classical form — but I wanted Nirvana. I wanted Silverchair.

By 17, that guitar had become my new superpower.

One night at a party, I picked up a guitar and started playing. Within minutes, girls were sitting next to me, giving me song requests, singing along. It was the first time in my life that girls came over to me. I couldn't make eye contact across a room. I couldn't tell if someone was smiling at me. But give me a guitar and suddenly the whole dynamic flipped.

But it wasn't enough to fill the void Andy left.

I was angry. Not just at the world — at everything. The years of bullying. The years of being different. The years of lying in bed at night feeling the shame of my disability. The loss of sport. The frustration of always being the only person like me, everywhere I went. I was isolated and lost and didn't know who I was anymore.

I'd always lived according to standards that came from Mum and Dad, but after Andy they became worried that if they kept holding the hard line with me, they might push me down the same path. They were genuinely frightened they could lose me. The two people who had never let a standard slip during my entire childhood suddenly stopped enforcing them. So, I started to lose my own standards.

And then, when I was 17, I nearly came to blows with my dad.

I don't even remember what started it, which makes it even worse. It was probably something like me going out too much or having to clean my room before I left. Something stupid. Something that didn't matter.

My dad is an intimidating man. Anyone who knows him will tell you that. You back down to him. That's just what people do.

But I'd been fighting so much at parties and pubs by then that I was used to physical confrontation, used to things escalating quickly. So, when he started saying the usual things that would make me back down, I didn't. I stepped up.

I literally stepped into his face, about an inch away from him. I was taller than him by then, so I was standing over him.

'What are you going to do about it?'

He backed down. Took a step back. I think he said something like, 'I hope you're proud.'

I wasn't proud. I was immediately, completely ashamed.

I remember exactly where we were standing. In the middle of our house, in front of a door that went into where Mum had her hairdressing salon set up. And I remember what went through my head in that moment: I was going to put him through the door.

That's what my crazy, angry, confused brain was calculating. How to hurt the man who had spent almost two decades driving me from footy games to ice hockey games. The man who had done everything for me.

I don't really regret many things in my life. I look back at most of my mistakes as childhood mistakes.

But that moment — stepping up to my father, looking down at him, knowing that if he'd thrown a punch I would have hurt him — that's something I regret, something I'd love to delete from my history.

I realised how far I'd fallen.

What Andy gave me

Here's something I've never said out loud: I think Andy's death might have saved me.

There were times — for several years after he died — when I got really low, to the point where I might have considered ending it all.

Andy had done that. I knew how it felt to go through that as one of his best mates. I knew the vacuum it left — the rage, the confusion, the floating in space with no ground beneath me.

I would never have done that to someone else.

His death didn't stop the darkness from coming, but it stopped me from acting on it. I knew what it did to the people left behind.

What I didn't know then was that I was drifting into the darkest years of my life. I didn't know that this identity built from grief, confusion and the loss of purpose would nearly destroy me more than once.

All I knew was that Andy was gone. Sport was gone. And I was trying to fill the void with anything that made me feel something or, to be honest, anything that could numb me enough so that I felt nothing.

I wasn't building a life. I was constructing a disguise.

If I'd had the courage to run the No-BS Doco on myself back then — no fancy editing, no slow motion, no fast forward, just the raw footage — I would have seen the truth. But I wasn't ready to watch that yet.

I had built my entire identity on proving I wasn't the blind kid. When that was taken away, I had nothing left to stand on.

And underneath it all, in moments I never showed anyone, I was drowning too.

In the late 1970s, Canadian psychologist Bruce Alexander ran an experiment that changed how we understand destructive behaviour. The prevailing theory was that addiction was about the substance — that drugs were so powerful they hijacked the brain. Alexander suspected something different. He built two environments for laboratory rats. One was a bare, isolated cage—no stimulation, no community, no structure. The other, which he called Rat Park, was an enriched environment with space, companionship, activities and connection. Both groups had access to morphine-laced water. The rats in the isolated cages drank heavily. The rats in Rat Park largely ignored it. The finding was striking: it wasn't the substance that created the addiction. It was the absence of meaningful structure, connection and accountability. Remove the environment that holds you together, and destructive behaviour fills the vacuum. That's what happened to me. Sport was my structure. My parents were my accountability. My mates were my community. When all three cracked at once—glandular fever taking sport, Andy's death breaking my world, and my parents too terrified of losing me to hold the line—the cage was bare. And I filled it with anything that numbed the emptiness.

• • •

What structures are holding your standards in place right now? And if they disappeared tomorrow, would you hold the line on your own?

Chapter 6

The Collapse

The Bullshit Audit

> Most of us live on a highlight reel. The best moments, the sharpest angles, the version of ourselves we'd choose if we could choose. We share it, perform it and, after a while, we start to believe it. The No-BS Doco is something different. Imagine your life played back as raw documentary footage. No director. No editor. No slow motion on the good stuff and no fast forward through the rest. Every scene included. Every moment in real time — the ones you're proud of and the ones you've buried. No filters. No missing clips. Just the uncut version of who you actually are. That footage is your true baseline. It's not who you want to be, or who you tell people you are. It's who you actually are — when no one's watching, when nothing's being rewarded, when the cameras you perform for aren't there. Most people never watch it. It's too uncomfortable. It's easier to keep running the highlight reel. The Bullshit Audit starts the moment you press play on the real thing.

The collapse didn't arrive as a single moment. It crept in quietly, disguised as confidence.

When sport disappeared, I didn't just lose an outlet — I lost the one place where my identity had been real. Sport had been the only arena where I had felt included, welcomed and measured on my contribution rather than any preconceived perceptions. In rugby, my role was simple and powerful: nobody got through the blind side, and every halfback knew that if they bent down to pick up the ball, I'd be all over them.

Without sport, I didn't know who I was.

So I built something else, over the course of a decade, starting when I was 18. Not a life — an image.

My new sport became generating other people's reactions.

I trained every day, but not to perform. For this sport, I trained to look good.

Heavy weights, speed bag, heavy bag, boxing drills. Hours and hours focused on aesthetics and intimidation. I wanted an eight-pack. I wanted ripped shoulders and arms. I wanted to look like someone you wouldn't mess with.

And it worked.

One day, a mate's girlfriend told him she'd driven past me with a friend while I was working as a labourer, shirt off in the heat. The friend said, 'Oh my god, do you know who that guy is? How good are his abs?' My mate's girlfriend had responded: 'That's Formo. Don't go there. He's a bastard.'

A compliment on the one hand; a reflection of the reality of my behaviour at the time on the other.

But the pride in the result of my efforts wasn't coming from inside me. It was borrowed pride — pride that only existed if someone else said it out loud. If no one was watching, if no one was impressed, there was no reward for me. It was all surface, nothing deeper.

I couldn't see any detail in the mirror, so it was always about others' perceptions. I was forever asking my mates about my body. Are my abs good? Do my arms look ripped? I was so insecure.

It seems so ridiculous and embarrassing to even acknowledge now, but that external recognition became my oxygen.

Fighting ghosts

Kickboxing showed up for the same reasons as the gym. I wasn't training to compete. I was training for the pubs I knew I'd end up in, the fights I knew I'd step into.

One of the guys I had studied health science with had grown up in the western suburbs of Sydney. He was a professional cage fighter, and he started teaching me in a way that made sense for someone who couldn't rely on their sight.

He taught me to read bodies, not faces. Hands were too small and too quick for me to track visually, but shoulders always gave the story away — how they load before a strike, how the torso rotates, how intent broadcasts through the upper body long before a fist launches.

My style became a mix of grappling and strikes: grab, punch, control the body, submit. I could never let a fight stay standing for long. I couldn't see any strikes coming, just shoulders and the blur of an outline. And once contact was made, I'd close the space, drag the person into my world and finish it fast. A rear naked chokehold to make them submit. That's how most of my fights ended.

But here's the truth: I wasn't fighting good men. The only fights that happened were with men who wanted to fight — the angry ones, the volatile ones, the insecure ones who saw someone who looked 'weaker' and went after them. In reality, they were cowards with unresolved trauma.

Just like me.

A bump in a bar felt like a deliberate shoulder-check in a school hallway. Someone pushing in at the bar felt like fingers being held up in my face: 'How many fingers, blind boy?' Someone cutting in on a girl who was talking to or dancing with me felt like the anonymous jeers across the oval.

I was fighting ghosts, not strangers.

Dancing on empty

Under the strobes and shifting lights of a nightclub, I could see shapes and lines, nothing more. It was a sensory nightmare. Some areas were so dark I was completely blind. I had to follow someone else until I'd memorised the layout — the stairs, the walls, where the toilets were.

But I never asked for help. I was still too proud.

The unspoken metric in those clubs was simple: who could dance with the hottest girl? And because I couldn't see faces — especially under nightclub lights — I relied on my mates to tell me the 'score'.

The old 'how many fingers am I holding up?' question from school evolved into a nightclub-ready version. A mate would flash their fingers at me, inches from my face, as part of their dancing — four fingers meant she was a 4 out of 10. Nine meant a 9 out of 10. Most of the time I couldn't see anything, so they'd lean in and whisper the number.

That whisper mattered more to me than it should have. Way more. Because that number told me I was acceptable. It told me I belonged. It told me I wasn't the blind kid from school anymore.

One night at a nightclub on Sydney's Northern Beaches, I was dancing with three girls. My mate yelled 'Right!' while holding eight fingers in front of my face; 'Left!' with four fingers right in my face. When he said 'Middle', he simply added 'No.'

I'd been grinding with the girl on the left. But because my mate had rated her a 4, I moved to chase the 8 instead.

As I started dancing with her, I could feel she was nowhere near as fit as the other girl. She was moving with less grace. I'd been stitched up. He'd taken the fox and sent me hunting for the wildebeest.

I realise now how disgusting that whole system was. I have more shame about behaving this way with women than I have about the fighting that also became a part of my life during this time. Those girls deserved to be treated the way Dad brought me up to treat women.

But I was lost. And I was so far from my core values.

Deep down, what I really wanted was a girl who understood me and would accept me for who I was. But if I couldn't even accept myself, how could I ask someone else to accept me?

I kept people at arm's length so I didn't have to deal with the softness underneath — the part I wanted to let come out but was too scared to show. So, I hid it under a tough shell.

What I didn't understand then was that I wasn't becoming tougher — I was becoming emptier.

Sophie

The clearest sign that I'd lost myself came with Sophie.

She was a really nice girl from a good family — nothing like the girls I was meeting in pubs and clubs. We had a genuine emotional connection. It felt like it could be something real.

I went away on a trip with my family. I was in my late teens, still desperate for credibility and status from my mates. I thought picking up chicks would make me look cool, so I kissed a couple of girls while I was up there. And I bragged about it to my mates.

When she found out, she confronted me in person. I had to sit there with her and hear the hurt in her voice, and I couldn't defend myself. I didn't want to defend my actions because I was never aligned with them in the first place.

She did the right thing — the thing that good people with good values do when they're not treated right. She broke up with me.

I was heartbroken.

I hadn't wanted to cheat on her. I didn't even like the other girls I'd kissed. I only did it because I thought it would make me look cool with my mates. That's how small the reason was. It had been the first and only time in my life I had ever cheated at anything, and it was for applause from boys I don't even talk to anymore.

The shame I felt was one of the rock-bottom moments of my life: not because I got caught, but because I'd betrayed who I actually was. Every value I'd held since childhood — don't steal, don't cheat, don't hurt people who trust you — I'd thrown away for nothing. All for a story to tell at a party.

I'd never cheated as an athlete. Never cheated on a test. Never cheated at anything in my life. Until Sophie.

From that time on, I never even looked at another girl when I was in a relationship. I never cheated at anything again. I learned it early. And while it was awful at the time, I'm glad I never had to learn that lesson when it really counted.

Christmas Eve

Then came the Christmas Eve that forced everything into focus.

I'd been drinking at The Newport Arms Hotel earlier that night. I'd snuck in with a full bottle of vodka stuffed down my pants — straight past the bouncers. Me and the boys drank that bottle, plus whatever else we ordered from the bar. We were all out of control.

Then, everything went dark.

I regained consciousness at a bus stop in Mona Vale. Around 2.30 am.

It had been a really hot day, but I woke up cold. I'd obviously been sitting still for some time, unconscious from the amount I'd drunk. And then I felt it. Wet but dry. That strange sensation of something thicker than water.

Blood. Sticky blood.

I couldn't see it in the dark, but I could feel it everywhere. The hairs on my right arm — the arm I would have wrapped around someone's neck for a rear naked choke — were matted and stiff, pulling at my skin when I moved. Dried blood had pooled in the crook of my elbow, cracking like old paint when I bent my arm. My old vintage shirt from Vinnies was ripped open at the front. It had gone rigid where the blood had soaked through and dried. It had the texture of stiff cardboard instead of soft cotton.

I checked myself. My hands were bruised and swollen.

But there were no cuts. No real pain. No injury.

None of the blood was mine, which meant someone else had taken the damage. Maybe badly.

To this day, I don't know who they were. I have no memory of the fight. Nothing. Just a blackout, a bus stop and someone else's blood drying on my body.

The next morning, I was seriously hungover. I made sure the bloody clothes didn't go in the wash. I scrunched them into a plastic bag and buried them in the bin.

Then I sat at the Christmas table with my family. Presents. Food. Laughter. And I performed. I smiled when I was supposed to smile, said thank you for gifts I couldn't focus on, pulled crackers and wore a paper crown while my knuckles throbbed under the table.

I spent Christmas Day with the family, living a lie. Pretending everything was fine, while in reality, I was hoping the police wouldn't knock on the door.

I thought about that other guy, whoever he was, waking up bloody and bruised, walking into Christmas Day with his family. I hoped he wasn't dead. I hoped he wasn't permanently injured. I hoped he hadn't acquired a permanent disability because of me.

It was the first time I realised that if I kept going the way I was going, I might kill someone. Or get killed.

Dad had said to me once: 'If you hit someone and they land with their head on the ground, they might die.' That thought wouldn't leave my head.

That Christmas morning was probably the first time I had a shred of thinking about how I could become someone I was proud of.

That Christmas Eve wasn't the night that saved me. But it was the night that made me want to save myself.

Restraint versus toughness

The illusion that I knew who I was didn't fully break in a pub or a street. It broke on a bus.

One night I was with a mate — a volatile guy who loved arguing. He started picking on another friend, and I stepped between them, expecting him to back down. Instead, he shoved me hard in the chest.

I flinched. Every instinct surged forward. I could've destroyed him.

But somewhere in me, something new flickered.

Instead of stepping forward, I stepped back. Twice.

I sat down on the bus, shaking with anger, adrenaline burning, furious at myself for not reacting and yet strangely proud that I hadn't. One of my favourite Red Hot Chili Peppers songs at the time was

'Pea'. There's a line where Flea calls himself a pacifist, but then he says what he can do to fuck you up anyway. That contradiction kept running through my head as the bus rattled home. I thought, *That's who I am in my heart. A pacifist. But I've become this guy who wants to fuck everyone's shit up.* The contrast hit me hard.

It took me the entire ride home to understand that restraint didn't make me weak. It made me someone who could preserve a relationship.

Then came another incident with a different so-called friend. We'd walked out of a club, and he sucker-punched me in the stomach — taking advantage of my blindness, knowing I couldn't see it coming. Rage erupted in me. I grabbed for him, but two bouncers tackled me. I was so wound up I levered both of them off me, using my elbows as fulcrums and ripping the skin clean off on the concrete.

My mates got between us. I stopped and I actually listened. I walked away.

The next morning in the surf, my elbows were raw and stinging, but I hadn't hurt anyone. That mattered. I had scars on both elbows for almost 10 years after that night. I still have faint white patches where the skin was ground off. That's how hard I pushed those bouncers off me. That's how close I came to losing control completely.

The bus incident and the incident outside the nightclub forced a truth I couldn't ignore: fighting wasn't strength anymore. It was habit. It was damage. It was a choice, and not a good one.

For the first time, I realised I didn't have to fight. I could walk away.

Real toughness has nothing to do with what other people think. It requires restraint. It involves setting standards. You need to live your life as who you are when no one is watching and nothing is being rewarded.

Who are you?

The drinking and the fighting were symptoms of the collapse I experienced, but the real problem was that I'd stopped caring about who I was; instead, I'd started caring obsessively about who I *appeared* to be.

I'd spent my childhood being bullied, tricked and excluded. Sport had saved me because it didn't care about optics — it cared about contribution. When sport disappeared, I went looking for acceptance anywhere I could find it. And I found it in applause that faded fast.

The Bullshit Audit starts with one question: who are you when no one's watching?

I didn't have an answer. Not yet. But at least I was finally asking the question.

During this time, the only real relief I found was in the ocean.

Surfing didn't judge me. The ocean didn't care how many beers I'd had the night before. It didn't care about status, bravado or the persona I was performing. When everything on land felt chaotic, blurry and unpredictable, the water gave me something simple and honest: movement, rhythm and space to breathe.

I realised I needed to get out of Sydney. I needed to escape the patterns, the people and the version of myself I'd become.

I was 21 years old. The collapse was complete. But climbing out of it — learning to care about who I was instead of who I appeared to be — that would take another decade.

The Bullshit Audit had begun. The rebuild was coming.

The French Foreign Legion has a tradition called 'anonymat'. When you join, you're given a new name and a new identity—your past is erased. The purpose isn't to help you escape who you were. It's to force you to confront who you actually are without the story you've been telling yourself. Stripped of your history, your excuses and your carefully constructed image, you have to face the raw truth of the person underneath. The Legion understands something most of us avoid our entire lives: you can't build something real on a foundation of bullshit. First, you have to tear down the lie.

• • •

Run the No-BS Doco on your last 12 months: no fancy editing, no slow motion, no fast forward—just the raw, uncomfortable footage in real time. What does it reveal?

Chapter 7

The Reset

The Bullshit Audit

> Sometimes you have to retreat to move forward. The bravest thing isn't standing there and taking the punches—it's stepping back, regrouping and deciding to become someone worth fighting for. The Bullshit Audit asks who you are when no one's watching. The reset is where you find out—stripped of the noise, the crowds and the persona you've been performing.

I was heading towards death or jail. I could feel it in my bones—the same way you feel a wave building behind you before it breaks. The trajectory was clear. The only question was which one would get me first.

I was 21. By this time, I had a massage therapy and personal training business that was limping along, and a lifestyle that was systematically dismantling everything I'd built. My rental apartment near the beach looked good on the surface. Underneath, everything was collapsing.

Every Monday night, I'd go to Andy Mac's parents' house for dinner. That was probably my best meal of the week. Mrs McGuinness would pile my plate high—roast lamb, vegetables, all sorts of delicious food—and I'd eat like I hadn't seen food in days.

Andy had taken his own life. His parents had lost their son. Now they were helping me — feeding me when I wasn't feeding myself, giving me something stable when nothing else was.

Then my girlfriend at the time, Theresa, ended our relationship. We'd been together for about a year. Her family was great. She was great. But I was too loose. Too wild. Too much of everything she didn't need. The breakup wasn't the reason I left Sydney, but it was the catalyst. It made me see what I'd been refusing to look at: everything was fucked, and I was the common denominator.

Retreat

Mum and Dad had left Narrabeen a few years earlier. They'd settled on a property in Nabiac, 115 acres of farmland with about a kilometre of water frontage. When I called them, the conversation was short. I asked if I could come stay for a while. They said yes.

The shame was crushing. Leaving the apartment — giving up the pretence of the life I'd been building — and retreating to live with my parents in the middle of nowhere made me feel as if everything I'd been trying to prove about myself was a lie. At 21 years old, I should have been on top of things. Instead, I was moving backwards.

As a blind person, starting over somewhere completely new wasn't really an option. I knew Narrabeen — every street, every curb. It was my mental map. The only other place I knew well enough to navigate was the farm. Going somewhere else — trying to reset in a suburb or region where I'd have to learn everything from scratch, when I was already broken — was a step too far.

I thought about it in fighting terms. I was way down, taking punches from every direction — financial, relationship, identity — and I couldn't even get my hands up to defend myself anymore. I had a choice: keep standing there and copping hits until one of them put me down for good, or retreat, regroup and come back stronger.

I chose retreat. It felt like failure. But it was also a path to survival.

The motorbike

The farm wasn't all quiet contemplation. I was still reckless. Still convinced I was invincible.

The motorbike taught me something about adaptation.

I couldn't see the track, so I learned to feel it. Blue sand under the wheels felt different to dirt. Roots had a rhythm. I could sense the camber, the way the terrain leaned. I'd ride a trail slowly at first, memorising every detail through feel — straight section, bend to the left, rutted section with roots, veer right, gradient change where the descent started.

I only ever did this on two trails. Everything else was walking pace. But those two trails I memorised so well that I could even beat my mates in a race — with five per cent peripheral vision, I could beat sighted guys on a motorbike because I'd learned the track through feel while they were still relying on sight.

Then there was a windstorm one night. The next day, I was flying around the memorised trail. I hit the jump I knew so well at full speed — but halfway across, something looked different. The horizon had changed shape.

A tree had come down in the storm. I landed in the middle of it.

Somehow, I pushed the handlebars down and rolled over the top, through a branch, and landed on the other side. The bike was destroyed — forks bent, frame wrecked. I walked away with scratches.

Each close call was a data point. Each stupid decision that almost cost me something important was a lesson, even if I wasn't fully learning it yet.

Loyalty and partnership

My best mate on the farm was Lucky, the kelpie. I'd chuck him on the front of the motorbike — back paws sitting on the tank, front paws looped over the handlebars, his face up in front of mine. We'd ride around the property together, ears flapping in the wind, him living his best dog life while I tried to figure out how to live any kind of life at all.

When your best mate is a dog, it can seem like things aren't going that well. But Lucky helped me through a difficult time. He was always there. No judgement, no expectations — just presence.

The other thing that saved me was the calves. Bottle-feeding them, making sure they were okay — it gave me a reason to get up in the morning. At that point in my life, I'm not sure what else would have.

One of them was sick at that time. He was a little male calf with a respiratory thing that had him struggling for every breath. We'd keep him warm with blankets and feed him with a bottle to try and get him through each night.

There's something about caring for a vulnerable animal that strips away the bullshit. You can't fake it. You can't perform for them. They either live or die based on whether or not you show up and do the work.

I showed up. I did the work. And, slowly, he got better. It was probably the first time in months I'd felt actually useful. Not performing as useful — actually needed.

There was also a mare called Tara on the property. She was someone else's horse, but she became mine in every way that mattered. And it was while riding Tara that one of the biggest lessons of my life emerged.

I learned to read her energy through feel: the posture of her neck and ears; the way her gait would change — from a comfortable trot to something tighter when she sensed danger ahead. Sometimes she'd let me steer, following my lead across a paddock. But if there was something in the way — a fence I couldn't see, or something left on the path — she'd pull against me and refuse to go where I was pointing.

I ran her into a few fences before I began to understand that she'd worked out I was blind, and from then on she started looking out for me. Once she trusted that I'd keep her calm, she started protecting me from the things I couldn't see.

At the same time, she was reading my energy as much as I was reading hers. If I started getting worried about things, she'd pick up on it immediately. She'd get jittery, which was dangerous for us both.

While riding Tara, I realised that I'd become a 'fight' animal. I wanted to fight everything — people, circumstances, my own limitations. Tara was a 'flight' animal. Her instinct was to run from danger, not towards it. Somewhere in the middle of all that, we had to find a partnership. I learned flight from her. She may have learned a bit of fight from me.

That's a skill I still use today — in boardrooms, in sales meetings, in any room where energy matters. There are times you have to take the reins and lead. And there are times you need to let someone else lead, then pull them back on track when they drift.

Lucky and Tara both taught me things about relationships and about business.

Lucky taught me about unconditional loyalty. He was there no matter what. If I was having a bad day or a good day, if I was hungover or angry, it didn't matter. He showed up.

Tara taught me about conditional partnership. She was only there for me if I delivered for her. If I kept her calm, if I earned her trust, if I showed up properly, then we had a partnership. If I didn't deliver what she needed, she'd throw me off or refuse to move.

Conditional partnership drives how business works; honestly, it drives most relationships. No one's there forever just because they say they will be. They're there for as long as it works. The moment it stops working, the partnership ends.

Both of these lessons—about unconditional loyalty and conditional partnership—would shape everything that came next.

Isolation and relapse

The nights on the farm were long.

Everyone around me was old. Retirees. Not a single person my age for miles. I couldn't message my mates; I couldn't see text messages well enough to read them. I'd call them sometimes, but those conversations made it worse.

They'd be busy, living their lives. I'd hear the energy in their voices, the background noise of bars or parties. Then they'd have to go. And I'd be standing there with the phone in my hand, in the silence of the farm, more alone than before I'd called.

One time, Mum and Dad went away for a couple of nights, leaving me alone on the property. I was sitting on the deck during the day, listening to the sounds of the bush, when I heard a car coming down the driveway. The engine noise grew louder... and then it stopped. The car turned around and drove away.

I couldn't see what kind of car it was. Couldn't see who was driving. Friend or foe—I had no idea. And in that moment, I felt something I hadn't felt in a long time: fear. But I wasn't afraid of whoever was in that car. I was in fear of myself. I was afraid about what I would do if there was a confrontation and I had to handle it alone, with no one to pull me back.

I was still the fighter. The violence was still in me, coiled up, waiting. The farm gave me space to see that clearly, maybe for the first time.

Retreating to the farm was helping me realise a lot about my life, but I had a way to go before the reset was complete. I still wanted to reconnect with my life and my mates back in Sydney. Every few weeks I'd make the trip down, telling myself I'd be sensible this time ... but I was never sensible.

One weekend, I went down for a mate's girlfriend's 21st birthday. I'd been on the farm for about nine months by then, eating properly and lifting weights again. I thought I had myself under control.

The party ended around one. Everyone else went home. But because I'd been storing up all that energy with nowhere to put it, I partied harder than anyone. The night stretched into something formless and desperate.

The sun came up, and I was still there, sitting with two guys I'd known for years but suddenly saw clearly. They weren't going anywhere. They didn't have plans or goals. They were just floating. And I was floating right alongside them.

The trip back was brutal. Two hours on the train to Newcastle, my brain fried. Mum and Dad picked me up from the station, then we drove another two hours in the car. Sitting there, I felt like the biggest loser on the planet: 21 years old and being driven home by my parents as if I was a teenager who'd broken curfew.

But something was different this time. The guilt hit harder. Every time I went back to Sydney, I was getting more allergic to it. The chaos I used to seek out was starting to taste wrong.

And somewhere in the fog of that hangover, two questions started forming. Who did I want to be? And what did I actually want from this life?

September 11

I used to strap a little battery-powered radio to the back of Tara's saddle. We'd ride for hours, just the two of us, cruising around the bush while I listened to whatever was on.

One day, I was about 15 kilometres from the house when the program changed. John Laws was talking about something happening in New York. People were calling in — confused, scared. Then more information started coming through. A plane. Then another plane. Towers collapsing. A terrorist attack.

September 11, 2001. I heard it all unfold while sitting on a horse in the middle of the Australian bush, completely alone.

There was all this chaos and destruction — people choosing destruction and killing innocent strangers for reasons I couldn't comprehend, while I was out on the farm doing my own sort of healing. I was trying to figure out my purpose, how to build something.

While I was riding Tara, hearing about people dying in buildings, I started really thinking: *What were my standards? What did I believe in? What was I willing to stand up for?*

The question

I stayed on the farm for about six months. Time moved differently there — it was slower, thicker. But eventually, I knew I had to go back. The farm was healing, but it wasn't a destination. It was a reset.

The farm had healed me enough to function, but not enough to live. I had regained stability, but not direction; strength, but not meaning; routine, but not identity.

The thing I couldn't escape was the question of who I was. My whole life, my identity had been built on sport. When I'd lost sport, I'd lost myself. I'd replaced it with being the party guy — the crazy one who'd go harder than anyone else. But that wasn't an identity. That was just destruction dressed up as a personality.

On the farm, stripped of all that, I was forced to sit with the emptiness. I had no sport to define me. No party scene to lose myself in. No fights to prove I wasn't weak. It was just me and the main question I kept circling back to: what did I actually want?

I knew what I didn't want. I didn't want to end up like those guys I'd been sitting with when the sun came up. I didn't want to look back at 40 and realise I'd never done anything worth remembering.

And somewhere underneath all the confusion, I knew what I really wanted: what I'd grown up seeing in my parents. A partnership. A family. Kids. Someone to build something with. A life that meant something beyond the next party, the next fight, the next moment of chaos.

But I wasn't ready for any of that. I wasn't the kind of person who deserved it yet. That was the uncomfortable truth the farm kept showing me.

If I'd run the No-BS Doco on myself right then, I would have seen someone halfway between who he was and who he wanted to become. I wasn't there yet, but I was finally moving in the right direction.

Stanford psychologist Carol Dweck spent decades studying what separates people who grow from people who stay stuck. Her conclusion: it comes down to belief. People with a 'fixed mindset' believe they are who they are—their intelligence, their personality, their patterns are permanent. People with a 'growth mindset' believe they can change through effort and reflection. The difference isn't just philosophical—it predicts outcomes. People who believe they can change actually do change. The farm didn't fix me. But it did something more important: it made me believe I could be fixed. It showed me that I didn't always have to be the violent, chaotic person I'd become. That belief—that I could change—was the first step towards actually changing.

• • •

What story have you been telling yourself about who you are? And what if that story is wrong?

Chapter 8

The War on Shame

The Bullshit Audit

> Shame is a liar. It tells you that the thing you're hiding is the thing that will destroy you. But often, it's the opposite: the thing you're most afraid of is often the thing that will set you free. The Bullshit Audit forced me to see who I really was. My decade-long war on shame forced me to stop hiding it.

From the moment I began working at age 12 — washing cars and delivering the *Manly Daily* — work had always been part of my identity. I'd never had a phase of life where I wasn't doing something.

Throughout my teens and during my early twenties, I'd collected more jobs than most people do in a decade. Assembling satellite dishes after school. Managing a small team packing commercial kitchen equipment into crates. Busking. Playing in a band. Coaching Under 11s rugby union. Mowing lawns and doing removals.

By the time I was ready to leave the farm and return to Sydney, I'd racked up a patchwork of experience. But when I looked at all of it together, something hit me hard: every job I had ever done relied entirely on my body.

Landscaping, satellite dishes, packing crates, massage therapy, personal training — every one of these jobs required physical strength or hands-on interaction. My body was the tool. The engine. The access point.

This realisation terrified me, because if anything ever happened — an injury, an accident, even just age — I'd have nothing to fall back on. I couldn't be a checkout operator. I couldn't work retail. I couldn't drive a taxi. Office work required reading and writing, which were both inaccessible to me at the time. Technology for blind people was almost non-existent back then. And trying to get an office job meant exposing my blindness — something I was still deeply ashamed of and desperate to hide.

Making the sale

My first proper job after returning from the farm was at a tile shop on the Northern Beaches. It was my first and last ever retail job.

The boss pulled me aside on day one and said, 'Mate, remember this — the man makes the decision. Sell him on durability. Women care about colours, but the bloke chooses in the end.'

But the truth revealed itself within days. When I'd show customers the samples on the wall, the person who got excited was almost always the wife. I could hear the commitment in her tone. So instead of talking quality, I'd get her emotionally invested in appearance — how it matched other things in her house, how it felt, how it looked. Once she was invested, the sale was complete.

I was hitting my sales target and beating most of the guys on the floor — not because I knew tiles, but because I ignored outdated assumptions and paid attention to real behaviour.

Then a redback spider ended it. I was running a personal training session at Narrabeen Lake — doing commando crawls along the ground with clients — when something bit my shoulder. Within hours

I was delirious, stumbling towards Manly Hospital. My arm swelled up like a balloon. A doctor lanced the infection — a spray of pus and blood shot across the room.

I was better within 10 days, but I never went back to that job — the manager and I weren't a good fit, so it seemed the right time to move on. Within two weeks of recovering, I had a new one.

The cane

My next job was pure hustle: door-to-door electricity sales.

Low vision and doorknocking don't mix. I couldn't see where the gates were. I'd walk into shrubs, fishponds, front-yard ornaments. One time I fell completely into a pond — it had lilies floating on top, the whole thing. My pants were soaked. I took public transport home, dripping wet in my business clothes.

The rejections cut deep. One woman looked at me, then looked over her shoulder to where my eyes were actually pointing, and said, 'Who are you talking to?' There was no one else there.

Another said it straight: 'You can't even look at me, so you're obviously a con man.'

That landed like a fist to the chest. She wasn't wrong to be suspicious, but I couldn't change the reason why she distrusted me. It was something I was born with. Something I was already ashamed of.

I was hitting my numbers, but the complaints kept coming. Customers felt uncomfortable because I wasn't making eye contact. My manager finally sat me down.

'Mate, customers don't know you're legally blind. You need to get a cane.'

I'd never used one. Not once. I felt too much shame. I was too stubborn. I was too much in fear of being seen as 'disabled'.

But he made it clear: no cane, no job.

So, I bought my first white cane.

I remember putting the cane in my bag and feeling like I was carrying contraband. I treated it like something that would poison me if I let it out.

The first time I unfolded it was in Frenchs Forest, at about 10 am, while standing at a stranger's gate. I felt like I was holding a loaded weapon, something that was going to blow up in my hand and hurt me. I was terrified: not of the cane itself, but of what it meant. I was afraid of being seen.

And even then, I couldn't fully commit. I'd walk along the street with the cane folded up, tucked under my arm like a shameful secret. Only at a customer's gate would I unfold it. It was a costume I put on for the performance, then immediately removed.

The irony wasn't lost on me. The moment I unfolded that cane, finding things became so much easier. I could feel the path, the steps, the obstacles. The tool I was so ashamed of was a tool that actually helped.

And overnight, my sales tripled.

I was using the same pitch, the same script, the same tone. But suddenly people were saying yes.

And instead of feeling proud, I felt sick. Were they signing because of the product and my pitch? Or because they felt sorry for the blind guy at the door?

One day I walked into a Tupperware party in Belrose. Twelve women were gathered in a lounge room. They let me in, they were all keen, and I think they wanted to help me. I gave my pitch, and they all signed up. I signed up 12 contracts in 30 minutes. I walked out feeling like a superstar.

I was 300 metres down the road, when the sinking feeling hit me. I'd left my cane inside.

I went back and knocked politely. The original lady answered. They hadn't even noticed I'd left the cane behind — it was just sitting on a table. She had to go back inside and ask: 'Has anyone seen Matt's cane?' You could hear the doubt in their voices, as if they had been tricked into their contracts. She brought it back to me at the door, and I could feel the warmth had gone.

The shame of that moment was enormous. They confirmed what I had already feared: that the cane was selling more than I was. That my success wasn't real. That I was a fraud propped up by pity.

If I'd run the No-BS Doco on myself right then, I would have seen a man so terrified of being seen as disabled that he'd rather fail authentically than succeed with help. That's not integrity — that's pride dressed up as principle.

I quit that same afternoon. Using the cane didn't feel authentic to me then. I'd never had one until that point so, as I reasoned with myself, 'Why would I get one just for a job?' It would be a while before I could see past the shame I felt.

There were two lessons in that cane, and it took me years to untangle them. The first was about shame — my refusal to be seen as disabled, to accept a tool that genuinely helped me. That was pride, and I'd wrestle with it for decades before making peace with it. The second was about integrity — I wasn't comfortable using my disability as a commercial lever to close sales. Those are different decisions about the same object, and both of them were real.

Still, the job taught me something that shaped my entire future: integrity over convenience. Credibility over shortcuts. Honesty over winning.

Corporate clashes

Landing a consumer sales role in pay TV felt like a real step into the corporate world. I was 24 by this time.

During the interview, the hiring manager walked me to a window: 'Look at that view — Sydney Harbour Bridge, the Opera House ...'

I'd told them I was visually impaired, but not how bad. So, instead of focusing on one point, which might be the sky or something completely random, I did a sweep. My eyes moved across everything so it looked like I was appreciating the view.

'Oh, that's amazing. Beautiful,' I said. I saw nothing.

Once I got the job, I disclosed just enough to function — that I'd need screen enlargement. Each letter was a couple of inches tall. My face would be two inches from the monitor just to read anything. Despite my denial, it was obvious to anyone watching that I was significantly vision-impaired.

The selling itself wasn't the problem. I closed deals well above my targets. Years of navigating the world blind had trained me to read tone, detect hesitation and sense genuine interest. These weren't corporate skills; they were life skills, ones I'd perfected over decades.

But the screen enlargement clashed with the company's computer systems — freezing fields, crashing forms, blocking contract submissions. When my system crashed, I didn't just lose my commission — I lost the multipliers that would have doubled it. It cost me thousands.

Eventually, I reached out to a solicitor. They prepared a letter for me, pro bono. The company paid out around $20 000. I felt terrible, like I'd threatened to sue the company I worked for. Within a few weeks, I moved to a different role in the company — government account operations.

The new role suited me: high-value clients, fewer transactions, bigger stakes. Less screen time, more relationship-building. For the first time since sport, my abilities mattered more than my limitations.

But not everything was smooth.

One day during a major customer outage, a senior operations manager stood right behind me and said, loudly enough for half the room to hear: 'No wonder we can't resolve customer issues, we've got a blind guy running things.'

It wasn't just the words. It was the voice: jeering, laughing, sinister, like he was performing cruelty for an audience.

The rage was instant — primal and familiar. I wanted to get up and put his head through a window.

But I stayed in my seat. I focused on my breathing. I didn't turn around. Because I knew myself. If I had stood up, if I had even opened my mouth, I would have hurt him. And then I'd have been fired. And he would've won.

I focused on the problem. Rallied my team. We fixed the issue and delivered a result that spoke louder than his insult.

That manager probably doesn't even remember saying it. It was probably a throwaway comment to him. But I thought about it for weeks. It planted a seed about the kind of leader I would one day become: one who never used sarcasm, shame or belittling as a tool.

The skill I couldn't practice

I didn't just fight the war on shame at work. I was fighting it in my personal life too.

She was into appearances — the right clothes, expensive high heels, flash dinners.

One night, I could tell she was frustrated. I asked what was wrong.

She told me the truth.

She couldn't be intimate with me because I couldn't make eye contact.

I was completely blindsided. The way she said it — like it was a reasonable comment — felt like someone had reached into my chest and ripped something out. I didn't feel pain exactly; instead, I felt empty, hollow, deflated and unworthy.

There was nothing I could do to change it. If it were a skill I could practise, I would have done so. If it were about improving my fitness,

I could have trained harder. But making eye contact? This was something I was born with, which was tied to the deepest shame I carried.

And I couldn't leave. She was sleeping over. So I just rolled over and lay there next to her, marinating in the shame. Hours of it. It was the longest night of my life, and I was trapped in my own bed with my own shame.

She ended up dating someone else, choosing appearances and status over substance. That hurt more than the original rejection. But it also gave me clarity. I needed to choose partners based on values such as depth, kindness and alignment — not appearances, not performance, not proximity.

That lesson would eventually guide me to Bex. But I wasn't ready for her yet.

Strategic accounts

When I moved into strategic accounts at 30 years old, it wasn't just a role shift — it was a return to my natural arena: high-value, high-stakes relationships involving some of the most recognisable organisations in the world, where decisions affected thousands of staff and millions of customers.

And I thrived.

Within my first year, our team signed PepsiCo as a new logo — a multi-product, whole-of-business deal.

The PepsiCo deal taught me a lesson I've never forgotten.

It was our final meeting. Their head of legal, their CEO, their CIO — senior people in the room. We were moments away from signing a multi-million-dollar deal.

I walked into the meeting room carrying a Sprite.

Sprite is a Coca-Cola product. Not PepsiCo.

Their head of legal looked at me and said, 'You better walk out with that drink and don't come back in with it. And never do that again.'

I walked out, put the Sprite in a bin and walked straight back in. The deal was signed the following week.

It was a one-time lesson. From that moment on, I've always thought about competitors — about making sure I'm never seen with competitor products. Details like this matter, especially at the executive level.

For the first time since sport, something powerful was re-awoken inside me: self-efficacy, the belief that I could do something and do it exceptionally well.

Winning the war

The war on shame, which ran throughout my twenties, wasn't over. It wouldn't be over for years.

But for the first time, I was winning battles instead of just surviving them.

The tool I was ashamed of was the tool that helped. The systems that failed me weren't a reflection of my ability. The people who saw disability and assumed weakness were blind to their own limitations.

And the woman who couldn't be intimate with me because I couldn't look her in the eyes? She taught me something more valuable than she'll ever know: that the right person wouldn't need me to see them to feel seen by me.

I use the cane almost every day now: airports, getting around, everywhere. I've got Billabong stickers on one of them — one of my sponsors as a professional surfer. People offer to help, and I let them. I've got no issue with it whatsoever because I've accepted who I am.

I'm proud to be a man with a disability because, despite my disability rather than because of it, I've become a world-beater in multiple areas.

But back then, I was still becoming. Still fighting the shame. Still learning that the things I was most afraid of were often the things that would set me free.

Researcher Brené Brown spent two decades studying shame and vulnerability. Her conclusion upended conventional wisdom: vulnerability isn't weakness—it's the birthplace of courage, creativity and connection. The people who live the most wholehearted lives aren't the ones who hide their flaws—they're the ones who own them. Brown found that shame thrives in secrecy and silence. The moment you speak it, name it and expose it to the light, it loses its power. The cane I was terrified to unfold became the tool that set me free. The blindness I spent decades hiding became the story that connected me to others. The thing I was most ashamed of became the thing that made me most human.

• • •

What are you hiding that's actually holding you back? What would happen if you stopped hiding it?

Chapter 9

Busy Going Nowhere

The Bullshit Audit

> I could walk with a fractured sternum for weeks. I could stand calm in a room full of guns. But I couldn't tell my girlfriend the truth about our future because I was scared of being alone. I had to look at what I was running from, and why. And sometimes, you have to travel to the other side of the world to find out you've been running from yourself.

This chapter steps back to right in the middle of my 10-year war on shame. While I was grinding through corporate roles and starting to find my professional footing, my personal life was heading somewhere else entirely.

I'd been with my long-term girlfriend at the time for about two years. It was long enough that the cracks between us weren't cosmetic anymore — they were structural. It seemed we wanted different futures, that our values didn't align. That our goals didn't align. It seemed like we had different ideas about what a relationship meant.

The thing is, to me, we weren't in the grind together in our relationship—we were in the grind alongside each other. *Together* means you're facing the same direction, pulling the same weight and building something shared. *Alongside* means you're just nearby—you may be occupying the same space while heading in different directions.

We booked a six-month trip to Southeast Asia to bring us closer together. We'd taken time off work, saved every dollar and invested everything into this journey. Optimism that we could make this work, plus a shared history with some good times, led us to go ahead with the trip. But in reality, it was our last chance to save the relationship—though neither of us said that out loud.

Some people travel to find themselves. I travelled to avoid the truth I already knew.

Broken in Vietnam

We started our travels in Vietnam, where the noise of Hanoi hit like sensory violence: motorbikes swarming without traffic lights, horns blaring in continuous conversation. For someone with five per cent peripheral vision operating entirely on sound and spatial memory, it was complete system collapse. Every navigation tool I'd spent two decades building was useless.

It became impossible for me to hide my blindness in the markets. Every price negotiation was played out on calculators in the universal language of haggling. Numbers would appear on a calculator screen; my girlfriend would tell me the price. I'd suggest a counteroffer, which she'd type in to show the seller. An entire negotiation was being conducted in a visual language I couldn't access.

I was part of the conversation, but I also wasn't part of the conversation—I was waiting to be updated, unable to contribute to outcomes that directly affected me. The shame I'd experienced in the corporate world didn't stay in Australia. It got on the plane and followed me.

After Hanoi, we took a sleeper train north to Sapa, near the Chinese border. Hired a guide for a three-day trek. I was carrying both our backpacks — six months of gear, including masks and snorkels for the diving we'd planned later.

About three-quarters through the first day, we came to a stream crossing. Just rocks and water, nothing complicated for someone who could see where to step, but I slipped, the weight of the two backpacks driving me forward. I went down hard on a pointed rock, which hit me straight in the chest. I heard the crack before I felt it.

I'd fractured my sternum.

I managed to get back up, then asked my girlfriend if she could carry her backpack.

She said no. It seemed like the trek wasn't her thing, it was mine, so she wasn't carrying her backpack.

We continued with the trek, and I kept carrying both packs — fractured sternum and all.

The nights were brutal. Every breath felt like the two broken parts were sliding against each other. Bone grinding on bone. I started taking shallow sips of air that wouldn't move my chest as much. I was holding myself together physically but falling apart inside.

I never got it properly treated. It just healed over time. There's still a lump today — you can feel it if you run your hand down my sternum, about a quarter of the way down. And my girlfriend's indifference hurt more than the fracture.

But our trip continued. Three weeks later, in Nha Trang, I completed my advanced dive certification — fractured sternum and all. I didn't tell the instructors because I knew they'd stop me from diving.

The ocean has always been my safe place. Whatever's happening in my life, the noise goes away when I'm underwater. It's just me, the bubbles and the silence. In the water, the pain stopped. I was weightless, free.

I worked out a system to cover up my injury — I got the crew to throw my oxygen tank and diving equipment into the water, then I'd jump in and put my gear on while floating. 'That's how we do it in Australia,' I'd tell them. A complete lie, but it was the only way I could avoid lifting that heavy steel tank with a fractured sternum.

To top it all off, I got a gastro bug. The first time I vomited, I thought the break was going to tear through my spine. Every contraction sent fire through my chest. I was on my knees in a Vietnamese bathroom, sweating and shaking, feeling like my ribcage was being pulled apart from the inside. But I was still covering for my injured chest, so I cleaned myself up, walked back into the bedroom and said I was fine.

Cracked open in Cambodia

Cambodia confronted me with disability in ways Australia never had.

Phnom Penh was the first place I'd seen impairment at scale. The Khmer Rouge era had left visible scars across the population — missing limbs, blindness, damage that couldn't be hidden. For the first time, I felt as if I wasn't the only one navigating a world that wasn't built for me.

But even so, I was the only one with privilege.

These people had grown up in an actual war zone — physical and emotional. I'd grown up in Narrabeen. My war zone was psychological, not literal. No one had macheted my family. No one had planted landmines in my backyard. I'd been offered support, even though I didn't want to accept it. I'd had opportunities, even though I couldn't see them for what they were.

That realisation cracked something open. Despite how hard everything was at work, despite how much nothing was built for me, I had something these people didn't: a chance. And with that chance came a responsibility—to stop hiding; to stop running from what I was capable of.

Liberation in Laos

We crossed the border into Laos. When we reached the Four Thousand Islands, there was a monkey chained outside a café. It was a tiny thing, shorter than my shins. The chain was so short that the animal could barely move. People were throwing scraps just far enough away that he'd run for them and choke against the chain.

I started asking if he was for sale. They started at US$300. I got them down to a hundred. It was a fortune in that economy, and money I couldn't really afford. But I paid it.

He came with us on the next boat. I had long blonde hair at the time, down below my shoulders. The monkey climbed onto my shoulder and just sat there the whole journey, playing with my hair strand by strand. He was treating me like one of his troop—grooming my hair, looking after me.

We released him on a forested island. As he climbed down from my shoulder he hesitated for a moment, as if he wasn't sure what to do with his new-found freedom, and then he disappeared into the trees.

That act—spending money I couldn't afford on an outcome I couldn't control—felt like the first authentic decision I'd made in months. I'd made a choice because it was the right thing to do, not because it served some larger strategy.

Crossing the border

Then my girlfriend got sick. It started as stomach pain. Within hours, she couldn't stand.

The local 'hospital' was a converted French schoolhouse with one surgery room, a metal table and a single pair of latex gloves that the staff washed and hung in the sun between uses. She wasn't getting better; we needed a better hospital. We had to leave Laos and get to Thailand.

The border crossing happened at night. We reached the checkpoint at around 10pm. It was officially closed; after hours of negotiation, Thai soldiers agreed to escort us through mined territory. One carried my girlfriend while another walked point. I followed closely, carrying our backpacks, being guided by the soldier behind me whenever I drifted off course.

I'd been awake for hours. My vision was useless in the darkness, on this treacherous, uneven ground. All I had was the footsteps ahead, the soldier behind me, the sound of our breathing.

We made it. The Thai hospital diagnosed my girlfriend with both types of dysentery simultaneously. She'd been hours from death.

But we still needed our passports stamped, so the next morning I went back to the border.

It was one of the two scariest moments of my life. (The other was while scuba diving the wreckage of the *Adelaide*, which is covered in Chapter 21.)

Something escalated at the border. I couldn't understand the Thai being shouted, but I heard the tone shift from bureaucratic to hostile between the police officer at the border and the soldiers — then I heard weapons being drawn. Screaming; the blur of guns. Other people were being pushed out of the room. I couldn't see the details — just shapes, movement, metallic glints pointed in directions I couldn't track.

I thought the soldiers were going to shoot me.

I don't normally pray. I grew up Catholic, I went to Catholic schools ... my mum was a scripture teacher. But I'm not religious. That model doesn't work for me. But I do believe in something — a higher power, an energy that runs through everything.

Standing in that room, surrounded by armed men screaming in a language I didn't speak, completely blind to what was happening, I prayed silently: *Please look after my parents. My sister. My brother.* Standing right there, I made peace with the possibility that I wasn't walking out of there.

The only thing I could control was my composure. I stood still, kept my face neutral — I didn't look like a victim. I didn't look like a threat. I just existed in the chaos without adding to it.

The standoff felt like it lasted minutes, but it may only have been seconds. Time collapsed. Eventually, they lowered their guns, stamped our passports. I was free to leave; I walked out alive.

An hour later, I was back at the hospital. I walked into my girlfriend's room carrying the passports — proof that I'd navigated bureaucracy, bribery, armed standoffs and 72 hours without sleep to keep her alive.

Her first words: 'Where have you been? Out partying?'

I stood there, sleep-deprived, still shaking from nearly being shot. Holding the documents that represented everything I'd just survived. And even though I was standing there with our stamped passports in my hands, the tension between us was clear.

I didn't argue. Didn't explain what had happened. What was the point? We'd both tried to make the relationship work, but we were incompatible — and we were both past the point of appreciating each other's efforts to find a way forward.

The relationship ended in that hospital room. Not officially, but I knew in that moment it was over. And yet, as she recovered from her illness in that hospital, I realised I would rather have walked through another minefield and faced down another room full of guns than have an honest conversation about our failing relationship. Physical courage was masking my emotional cowardice.

The end

We flew home early. Two weeks later, the Boxing Day tsunami hit exactly where we'd planned to spend Christmas. Missing that wave was luck, not wisdom.

Back in Australia, we kept the delusion alive for six more weeks. We moved into a new apartment together, pretending the trip had fixed something.

But I couldn't do it.

I was so broken by that point that I went to a counsellor — for the first and only time in my life. She was based in Mona Vale, very professional and direct. The kind of person who looked at you and actually *saw* you.

'Am I a bad person for walking away?' I asked. 'Am I being unreasonable?'

She said: 'No. You're not being unreasonable. It's good that you're able to hold your values and not stray from them.'

She also said something else that stuck with me. After I told her what I did for work, she said: 'It sounds like you want to do more. And you could do more.' In a couple of hours of talking, she'd picked up that I was hiding in my corporate role — I wasn't working to my full potential.

The counsellor gave me what I needed: permission to trust my own judgement, and a sense that I could be doing more with my life.

The lesson

That year, midway through what I think of as my 10-year war with shame, taught me things I couldn't have learned any other way.

I learned that physical courage can mask emotional cowardice. I could walk on a fractured sternum for weeks. I could appear calm in a room full of guns. But I couldn't tell my girlfriend the truth about our future because I was scared of being alone.

I learned that the people who don't see your sacrifice aren't villains — they're just not your people. She wasn't cruel. She was a warm, caring girlfriend and we'd had some genuinely good times together — we just wanted different things from our lives. We had different values and goals; we were looking in different directions. And by the end, the structural cracks in our relationship meant we simply couldn't see what we had to give each other.

And I learned where my boundaries actually were. Not the theoretical boundaries I thought I had, but the real ones — the lines I discovered only when someone asked me to cross them.

Choosing to trust my values over my fear of being alone was the first real Bullshit Audit I ran. I was finally being honest with myself.

The trip didn't fail. It succeeded at revealing what was already true.

Seeds don't become trees overnight. They sit in the dark first. This was the seed.

Neuroscience research has shown that the brain treats emotional pain in a similar way to how it treats physical pain and will go to extraordinary lengths to avoid it. Brain imaging studies reveal that when we anticipate confronting an uncomfortable truth, the same regions activate as when we anticipate physical injury. So, we build elaborate avoidance systems: we stay busy, we create distractions, we develop physical courage to mask emotional cowardice.

• • •

What uncomfortable truth is your brain working harder to avoid than to face?

Chapter 10

So What, Loser

The Hard Way Is the Easy Way

> People say you're worthy. We're all worthy. Everyone deserves love just by existing. But that's not how it works. If you haven't done the work to be the best version of yourself, and you're sitting around waiting for some amazing person to show up and save you, you're lying to yourself. Worthiness isn't granted, it's built: through accountability, through standards and through becoming the person who deserves the life you want.

Dave had been my surf buddy for years. He drove me to the beach because I couldn't see well enough to drive myself, and I taught him to surf. We were living together in my apartment in Artarmon on Sydney's North Shore, a nice place I owned with a scary mortgage, so I rented out the other rooms. On paper, I had everything sorted. I was 30 years old with property, a decent corporate job and enough money to keep the lifestyle ticking over.

Then Dave got engaged to Sarah and moved out.

They didn't go far — just downstairs to another apartment in the same building — but the distance felt enormous. Suddenly I was alone, rattling around with tenants I barely knew, watching my best mate build a life with someone while I was still treading water.

One Sunday, a mate called to tell me how good the surf was. Perfect conditions. And I couldn't get there. With no Dave to drive me, I sat in that apartment alone, surrounded by all the superficial markers of success, and felt completely empty.

By that evening, I'd decided to move towards the beach, to Manly. Once I decide something, I don't procrastinate: I just move. Within a week, I'd found a share house 10 minutes from the beach. The ferry into Sydney became my morning meditation — the only part of the day when I wasn't rushing, wasn't performing. It was just me and the harbour and the question that kept coming back.

Where is she? How can I find her?

The pattern

Within a week of moving in, I'd hooked up with the sister of one of the housemates. She'd just finished a law degree and moved up from Adelaide. She wanted to party; I wanted to settle down. For the first time in my life, I was the serious one in a relationship — I was finally ready to settle down.

The relationship revealed the pattern I'd been running for years. Any time a girl showed interest and we had chemistry, I'd immediately want to lock it in — to make it work, even if all the signs suggested this wasn't the right relationship. The dream was always the same — to have what Mum and Dad had. A lifelong partner: someone who stayed.

The problem was, I had no filter. My standards were superficial. As long as my mates gave me the thumbs up and she wasn't a complete psycho, I'd commit and try to make it work for life. I couldn't recognise when a relationship was fun but we weren't compatible. I'd push through every warning sign until the relationship descended into complete failure.

I realised it was over on a Sunday morning. I was putting on my shoes to run the City to Surf. She came home just as I was leaving — her voice breaking and rough, like she'd been out all night. She tried to get me to stay home. Her breath stank of alcohol.

I went to the run anyway. On that ferry into the city, it hit me — this relationship had reached its expiry date. We were at completely different stages of our lives. It wasn't her fault, but it wasn't what I was looking for.

But I was still following the pattern I'd followed for so long, so I didn't end it straight away. I was still scared of being alone. I didn't have the self-worth to just leave. So, I let things get worse until separation was the only option.

When everything finally did fall apart, I had to get out fast. I'd already bought an apartment north of Manly, in Dee Why, but there was a six-week gap before it settled. My sister Jacqui owned an apartment in Killara, so she agreed to let me stay.

I wasn't partying as hard as I used to, but I was still going out maybe once or twice a week after work with colleagues or at the weekend with my mates. I promised I wouldn't do that while staying at her place.

That promise didn't last.

A few weeks after the breakup, I was depressed and dealing with it the only way I knew how: drowning the pain. I went out hard and came home late, waking Jacqui up when I stumbled in.

The next day, she didn't say much — which was worse than if she'd given me a verbal bashing. But I could hear the disappointment and anger in her voice when she did speak to me. It sounded like she'd given up on me, which cut deep.

When we were young, Dad had told me I needed to be Jacqui's protector. That was my role as her older brother. And yet there

I was—crashing in her spare room after another failed relationship, waking her up at 3 am. The role reversal was humiliating. She was protecting me.

No more excuses

Jacqui's apartment was built in the 1950s or earlier. It was right next to the Greengate Hotel on the Pacific Highway, so you could hear the traffic constantly. You could hear people in the pub at night talking and laughing, being social, which made the loneliness worse.

The windows faced the pub side, where trees blocked most of the light, so it was always dark inside. I was living out of a bag, with all my stuff in storage until Dee Why settled, so I had no computer. This was before smartphones and all the accessibility they offer today. I couldn't read; I couldn't access anything.

It was like experiencing sensory deprivation. And it was exactly what I needed.

I'd been reacting, partying, training, repeating for so long that I'd never stopped or given myself the time to think about what I wanted from my life. Now, I had nothing but time. I spent hour after hour in that small lounge, staring at the wall, with nothing to do except confront the state of my life.

I was 30 years old, living in my little sister's apartment. My career was cruising along while I made excuses for why I wasn't getting promoted. It was everyone else's fault. It was my disability's fault. The systems weren't accessible. It was harder for me than everyone else.

I told myself it was all valid, but these were just excuses.

There was another older guy living in one of the other apartments at the time. He was about 60, living there with his mum. He didn't work. Every time I went out to hang washing on the clothesline, he'd appear. He had this soft, passive voice, but he talked like someone who'd achieved great things. He'd tell me about this awesome job he used to have — past tense.

His mum made excuses for him constantly. Whenever you spoke to her, it was the world's fault he was unemployed and living with her.

One afternoon, I came inside after hanging my washing and thought: *What a loser.* And then I caught myself, as I realised: that could be me. If I didn't change something — if I kept drifting, kept making excuses, kept blaming everyone else — I was on track to become that guy. Telling strangers about the awesome things I used to do while accomplishing nothing in the present. And he had less excuses than me.

I was blind. I had a disability. I experienced discrimination. I had inaccessible systems. I had so many real excuses I could fall back on — but they were still excuses. And if this guy — with no real barriers, with the world literally at his feet — could waste his life on excuses, then I had even more reason to stop using mine and start taking accountability.

And then I realised the one thing I had that he didn't: time. He was 60, and he had wasted so much time, but I was 30 — still on the better side of time and age. But at 30, the time bomb was seriously ticking. I needed to sort my shit out fast.

I felt the world crushing in on me — negativity pressing from every direction, trying to make me feel small. Trying to make me nothing.

I could either let it crush me, or I could fight back.

And that's when my inner voice changed. The self-pitying voice that had been whining about how hard everything was became a different voice. Harder. Meaner. More like the kid I used to be.

So what, loser? So what if you're blind? So what if the systems at work aren't accessible? So what if it's harder for you than everyone else? Is this the way the young Matt Formston would have behaved? The kid who tackled boys twice his size? The kid who did triathlons before school? The kid who got selected for rep teams when everyone said it was impossible?

Would that kid be proud of this shell of a person you've become?

It was a harder voice, but it was motivating.

I thought about the bullies at school. The ones who'd hold up fingers and ask how many they were showing. I used to bend their fingers back until they screamed.

That kid wasn't scared of failing. Taking the bullying was scarier than fighting back. So he chose the harder discomfort — the one with a chance of winning — over the easier discomfort of just accepting the abuse.

I needed to start bending back fingers again. Not literally — I'd grown past that, I was more mature. But I did need to seize the superficial things that were holding me back and break them. I did need to face my emotional cowardice in relationships, overcome the repeating pattern of being afraid of being alone, and be clear about what I did and didn't want. By choosing the uncomfortable path, it might actually lead somewhere worthwhile.

The list

It was a Sunday afternoon. I'd been sober the night before — rare for that period — and I was clear-headed.

I was sitting on the floor of Jacqui's living room, an old antique-style coffee table in front of me. And on it sat a notepad with a pen.

I don't write things by hand. Ever. It's pointless: I can't read my own handwriting. But I'd heard something about the power of writing things down, making them real — creating a line in the sand.

So, I started writing.

What did I want in a life partner? Not the superficial stuff my mates would rate. I wanted the real things, the non-negotiables.

My list started to take shape: needs to want children in the next few years; needs to have a desire to get married or have a lifelong partner; needs to be more keen on outdoor activities than sitting around; needs to not be a party animal.

The values came next: honest; kind; feminine and gentle; strong maternal instincts.

I kept writing until I had 12 things on my list. Some were flexible, others weren't, but all 12 together painted a picture of the person I wanted to spend my life with.

Then it hit me.

I didn't tick my own boxes.

I'd just written 12 non-negotiables: standards I would hold any woman to before I'd even consider dating her seriously. But if she had the same list? If she was looking for the same qualities in a man? I wouldn't make the cut.

'Oh fuck.' I said it out loud to the empty room.

I needed to tick these boxes myself. I needed to become the person who would deserve the person I was looking for.

I was a 30-year-old man with standards for others he couldn't meet himself. I wanted a partner who wasn't a party animal, yet I was still partying hard myself. I wanted someone who had got their life together while his own life was falling apart.

I wasn't worthy of this relationship yet. But I was about to start becoming worthy.

The chin-up bar

When the Dee Why apartment finally settled, I moved in with a new mindset, starting with installing a chin-up bar in my bedroom doorway. It was a cheap bit of equipment, but it became the first non-negotiable I'd given myself in years.

Every time I walked through that doorway — in or out — I had to do 10 chin-ups. No exceptions. No excuses. No rationalising why today was different.

I'd been making excuses for years, finding good reasons to change the goalposts and letting my standards slip whenever it was convenient. The chin-ups were my line in the sand. If I let the chin-ups slip, I'd let everything slip.

Sometimes I'd be in my suit, about to head to work, and I'd realise I'd forgotten something in my bedroom. Back through the doorway I went, so I did 10 chin-ups on the way in and 10 on the way out. I learned to take my suit jacket off first after ripping the back out of one.

Sometimes my brain would whisper that I might miss the train, that it didn't really matter — just this once, I could skip the chin-ups. But I did them anyway.

They only took less than a minute. But every time I did them, I was building something more important than biceps: I was building trust with myself, proving I could be relied on. I was proving I was the guy who did hard things, who kept promises, who didn't let himself off the hook.

Standards without consequences are wishes. The chin-up bar was where I stopped wishing and started building.

The nightly review

The physical training was just the beginning. The real work — the work that related to how I lived and behaved — would happen at night.

I started replaying my day each night, at the end of the day while lying in bed. I wasn't analysing my day in a self-pitying way — this was deliberate, surgical.

I'd replay every significant interaction — every meeting, every conversation — and I'd critique myself with brutal honesty. Could

I have treated that person better? Could I have used different words? Could I have done more to help my team?

The hardest skill to learn was leaving space — pauses, silence. Letting people fill the gap instead of rushing to fill it myself. Learning to shut up and let others speak was one of the most valuable lessons of that period.

Nothing was off limits. Everything had to be analysed. Some nights I'd realise I'd completely fucked up a situation. Over time, I learned to see mistakes as tools for development. I would almost enjoy identifying my mistakes, because each one showed me something I could improve.

During this analytical period, I also realised that as a person with a disability, it would be easy to live a life of mediocrity. No matter what happens, people can find a way to make blindness a reason for failure or for not trying hard. People cared too much about any excuse I could make. In fact, people would make excuses for me before I even had the chance to make them myself.

'Oh, he's blind, of course he couldn't do that.' 'Don't be too hard on yourself, you've got enough to deal with.' 'That's pretty good, considering ... '

This is the reason most people with disabilities don't achieve what they're capable of. It's not because of their disability — it's because everybody else makes excuses for them. They set lower ceilings for them, which lowers people's expectations of them.

When I was a kid, the ophthalmology professor at the Sydney Eye Hospital did the same thing: 'Matt needs to go to a special school. Matt needs to do less. Matt can't have a normal life.' He set a ceiling before I'd even had the chance to try.

The honest answer is I needed to fight through that. I needed to create my own standards and not just fight against the problems I experienced along the way. I needed to fight against people's constant desire to create excuses for me. Their kindness was a trap. Their understanding was a ceiling. Their compassion, however well-intentioned, was keeping me small.

My standards needed to be higher than everyone else's.

Becoming worthy

The transformation didn't happen overnight. It took months of lying awake, replaying conversations to better understand myself. Of dating with purpose instead of desperation, and refusing to waste time on anyone who didn't tick the boxes. I was finally being honest about my compatibility with a potential partner instead of forcing broken things to work. I was searching for the right kind of relationship rather than staying because I was scared to be alone.

I was more content being alone than I'd ever been. I had the beach, I had training, I had routine and standards and a version of myself I was starting to respect.

The internal voice that had said, *So what, loser?* became my internal compass. Whenever I caught myself making excuses — blaming my blindness, blaming circumstances, blaming other people — that voice cut through.

It said, *So what? Is that going to stop you?*

The harder you work, the easier things get. That's the secret of hard work. Put in the effort up front — the extra training, the early mornings, the brutal self-analysis — and the actual execution becomes simple.

My goal was still the same: find the woman who could be my best mate. The one who'd call me out when I was being a dickhead. The one who'd be there when shit got hard.

I wasn't there yet. If I'm being honest, I wouldn't fully realise I was ready until I met Bex. She was the final key.

But I was closer than I'd ever been. I was becoming the person who deserved the person I was looking for.

I was becoming worthy.

Psychologist Angela Duckworth spent years studying what separates high achievers from everyone else. Her conclusion wasn't that talent, intelligence or luck made the difference. It was grit: the combination of passion and perseverance for achieving long-term goals. Duckworth found that grit predicts success better than IQ, better than natural ability, better than any other measurable factor. Grit doesn't deliver heroic bursts of effort. Grit is what makes you show up every single day. It's the chin-ups you do when you're running late. It's the nightly review you prioritise when you'd rather sleep. It's the way you build worthiness one small, boring, unglamorous choice at a time. The hard way doesn't just build results. It builds the person capable of achieving them.

• • •

If you wrote down the standards you hold others to, would you make your own cut?

Chapter 11

Time Well Invested

Two Gears, One Engine

> The Sydney to Melbourne bike ride taught me to be completely present — every second a decision, no autopilot allowed. Finding Bex taught me that when you take the time to analyse whether you're making the right decision, the right investment doesn't feel like a cost. Both situations required knowing exactly when to commit fully and when to let the moment unfold.

My colleague Scott and I were on the corporate bus, which took 15 minutes from the city to our office campus. It was just another Tuesday morning — the kind where you're half-awake, staring out the window, not really expecting anything to happen.

'Do you have any holidays coming up?' I asked.

'Yeah,' Scott said. 'I'm going to ride a pushbike from Sydney to Melbourne.'

'Why would you want to do that?'

'It's a bucket list thing. Something I've always wanted to do, and I'm just going to commit this year and do it.'

'I'll come with you,' I said. The words came out before I had thought them through.

Scott looked at me like I'd lost my mind. He knew what I was like at work — screen magnifier blowing up text to about four inches high, software reading my emails aloud, constantly running into walls and struggling to find the doors to meeting rooms. My whole setup screamed 'This guy can barely function.' And yet here I was, volunteering to ride a 1200 kilometres-long coastal route down Australia's highways, with trucks screaming past at 100 kilometres an hour.

He started backpedalling immediately. 'Well, I'm not sure I'm actually going to do it ... '

But something in me had already decided. I didn't own a bike. I hadn't ridden seriously since I was a kid messing around with my mates. But I was desperate for a new challenge — to do something hard.

I remembered what it felt like to be a teenager, doing triathlons before school every morning, and hundreds of push-ups to make myself stronger than everyone else on the rugby field. I had to be fitter than the sighted kids because I was going to make mistakes they wouldn't — miss a pass, run the wrong line, react a half-second too slow because I couldn't register the ball until it was almost on top of me. My fitness was my insurance policy. Hard things made me feel validated. Hard things made me feel alive. Somewhere in my twenties, I had lost that amidst the drinking, the drifting, the years of not really trying at anything. Now I was 31 years old, clawing my way back, and I needed something that would break me open.

If you think about anything you've done in your life — the hardest thing you've ever accomplished versus the easiest thing you did today — which one gave you more satisfaction? I can guarantee it was the hard thing. Because when you succeed at something difficult, you feel like you've actually achieved something. Easy things don't create fulfilment. Easy things don't build character. I was starving for that feeling again.

A blind man riding 1200 kilometres on a single bike seemed like a good place to start.

Jump first, figure it out later

The training was as reckless as the decision.

I didn't own a road bike, so I borrowed Jacqui's. Scott and I got on a train and went 300 kilometres north of Sydney. The plan, if you could call it that, was to ride 150 kilometres back the first day, sleep somewhere, then do another 150 the next day. No build-up. No progressive training block. No base miles or recovery weeks or any of the sensible things that coaches recommend. Just jump in and find out if it was possible.

My logic was simple: if I could survive two days of cycling 150 kilometres each day, back to back, on a borrowed bike with no preparation, then with a bit of training I could probably manage 120 kilometres a day for 10 days. It was the kind of reasoning that makes sports coaches want to cry. But I didn't have coaches. I had a borrowed bike, a mate who was equally crazy and the kind of stubborn determination that refuses to accept logical limitations.

We made it. Barely. Our bodies were wrecked, our legs were screaming, our bums were torn to pieces from saddle rash…we weren't used to sitting in the saddle for that long. But we rolled back into Sydney having covered 300 kilometres in two days. Proof of concept achieved.

Then we rode up the Blue Mountains on some of the steepest climbs in Australia. The relentless switchbacks rose out of the Sydney basin, while the road tilted upwards and never seemed to stop. My brother Stu came, along with my flatmate Keith and Scott. By the time we reached the top, only Stu and I were still riding. Keith had the wrong bike and didn't have the fitness for it, and Scott had mechanical issues. So it was just the two brothers, standing at the summit of one of Australia's most famous climbs — lungs burning, legs destroyed, staring at each other like we couldn't quite believe we'd made it.

And then we descended.

Picture this: a blind guy flying down one of the steepest mountain roads in Australia, eyes locked on the white line right next to his front wheel, hoping — praying — not to smash into something. The road unwinding beneath me at speeds I couldn't safely process. Corners appearing and disappearing before I could properly register them. The sound and feel and the blur of the line were the only things keeping me alive. The wind roared in my ears; the bike shook as it passed over imperfections in the road; my hands gripped the bars so tight my knuckles went white. I was veering on and off the road the whole way down.

I know it was completely reckless. It should never have been done. But that was the whole point. I wasn't trying to be sensible; I was trying to prove something to myself.

Feeling my way

We started the ride at the Sydney Opera House. We chose that location deliberately, and not just because it was iconic. The Opera House was designed by Jørn Utzon, a Danish architect who went blind from macular degeneration in his old age — the same disease that had taken my sight. We were riding to raise money for the Macular Degeneration Foundation (now the Macular Disease Foundation Australia), trying to fund research into the condition that had shaped my entire life. Starting at Utzon's masterpiece felt right. Poetic, even.

The harbour was like glass that morning; the city was still asleep at dawn as we prepared to depart. We took photos, did a couple of quick interviews and then pointed our bikes south.

The plan was to travel 120 kilometres a day for 10 days, with no support crew following behind us carrying spare parts and energy gels. We were just two stubborn and determined blokes on bikes, with pannier bags strapped to the back carrying nine litres of water each, all our clothes for the journey, cameras to document the trip and Scott's laptop so we could update our fundraising page from our motel rooms each night. Everything we needed to survive was loaded onto bike frames that weighed a fraction of what we were asking them to carry.

I kept my front wheel two or three inches to the left of the blurred white line on the edge of the road. That was my entire navigable world — a strip about a foot wide. Any further left and I'd hit potholes, debris, the uneven edge where the road crumbled into gravel. Any further right and cars would clip me. The world beyond the blurred white line was a smear of colours and shapes — cars appearing as dark masses that grew and shrank, trees and buildings merging into an impressionist painting that offered no useful information.

I hit every single cat's eye from Sydney to Melbourne. The reflectors were embedded in the road every few metres — little raised bumps designed to catch headlights and guide drivers at night. For a sighted cyclist, they're easy to avoid. For me, they were invisible. I couldn't detect them at all — all I could do was follow the line. And because I was riding a couple of inches from the edge, I ran into every single one: bump, bump, bump. Each bump jarred through my handlebars, into my wrists, up my arms, rattling my teeth.

By the end of each day, my wrists were bruised black. Not figuratively — literally black, the blood pooling under my skin from thousands of impacts. It was the most painful part of the whole ride.

My legs adapted to the distance after a few days; my lungs found their rhythm. But my hands and my wrists suffered constantly from the relentless pounding of those cat's eyes.

I'd never learned to read braille—never had the patience for it, always preferring to find workarounds that let me avoid admitting I needed help. But I rode to Melbourne using a form of braille as my guide. Each reflector was a dot under my wheels, telling me where the road was going and confirming I was still in my safe zone, still alive.

Scott rode behind me most of the way, calling out what was coming. Car. Pothole. Gravel. Truck! His voice became my early warning system. But I couldn't rely on him alone. Sometimes the wind was too loud, a truck drowned him out or he was too focused on his own riding to notice something in time. So, I developed other systems.

I used echolocation to listen to the sound bouncing off the trees on the side of the road, the curb of the gutter, the walls of buildings as we passed through towns. Trucks created pressure waves I could feel before I heard them—a change in the air, a sense of something massive approaching. Cars had different pitches depending on their speed and distance.

It was a combination of everything: the tiny bit of vision I had, Scott's voice, the echoes, the feel of the road through my handlebars. My entire nervous system was engaged every second, processing information constantly, making micro-adjustments to my line, my speed, my position. There was no cruise control: I was always 'on'.

It fried my nervous system. The constant vigilance, the never being able to relax, the knowledge that one wrong move could end everything—it added up. By the end of each day, I was physically cooked from the riding, but I was mentally exhausted because of my blindness. Having to use my whole nervous system just to stay alive on the side of a highway takes something out of you that sleep doesn't fully restore.

The line between adventure and disaster

There were moments that could have ended it all.

Coming into Ulladulla, halfway down the coast from Sydney to Victoria, there was a rise where the road climbed a hill with little to no shoulder on my left. The bitumen fell away to a drain and a ditch. The safe zone I'd been riding in all day had disappeared.

Scott called something out but I didn't quite catch it, and suddenly I was off the road. My front wheel dropped into the drain, my bike tilted, but then somehow, instinctively, I wrenched the handlebars and came out of it again, back up onto the bitumen, heart pounding as I narrowly avoided a collision with a car that had been coming up behind me.

Another time, we were crossing a T-intersection when a median strip in the middle appeared right in front of my wheel at the last second—a raised concrete island that would have sent me over the handlebars if I'd hit it straight on. Without thinking, I lifted my front wheel and bunny-hopped the whole thing on a bike loaded with nine litres of water and all my gear, pannier bags swinging. Somehow I cleared the median, landing cleanly on the other side, but then I nearly smashed into the gutter because the road veered right through the intersection.

They were close calls: the kind that make you realise how thin the line is between adventure and disaster. The kind that make your hands shake for an hour afterwards, replaying the moment in your head, thinking about all the ways it could have gone wrong. But we kept going.

The crash happened in Foster, on day eight, when we were so close to the finish line. It was raining: not heavily, but it was the persistent kind of rain that makes roads slick and reduces visibility, even for people who can see properly. It reduced my visibility from almost nothing to absolutely nothing. The white line that had been my guide for a thousand kilometres was now just a wet smear I could barely make out.

Scott hit his brakes for something I couldn't detect. A pothole, debris, maybe an animal on the road — I never found out. I was following too close, relying on him to be my eyes, and when he stopped suddenly I had no time to react. My front tyre clipped his back wheel; I slid on the wet road, and I went down hard.

The handlebars bent on impact. My knee smashed into the bitumen. When I got up off the ground, Scott was gagging. He told me he could see bone. The skin at the bottom of my kneecap had split open, a gash maybe two inches long, and my kneecap (the patella) was pushing out from the impact.

We went to the hospital in Foster and they patched me up. I needed 12 stitches, then we were back on the road the same day. We stayed in Foster that night, then had two more days to get to Melbourne.

Every pedal stroke after that, I could feel the stitches pulling. The circular motion of cycling meant my knee was constantly bending and straightening, and each time it bent, the stitches strained against the wound. It felt as if they were going to rip out with each rotation. But we were so close now. We had come too far to stop. Pain was just information. It wasn't a reason to quit.

Finally, 10 days after leaving the Sydney Opera House, we rolled into Federation Square in Melbourne.

No one was there to meet us. Literally no one. We had ridden 1200 kilometres, raising money for charity for our efforts. I had 12 stitches in my knee that felt like they were about to tear open with every pedal stroke, and the only people waiting were a news crew from Channel 10. They filmed us for a segment that aired on national news that evening, just before the weather — prime time television, the kind of slot advertisers pay millions for. They put up the link to our fundraising page.

One person donated. Eight dollars.

It was one of my first lessons in philanthropy — something I would later apply when I ran sustainability and community programs in my corporate career. People need a heart connection to a cause. Without that emotional link, without feeling personally invested in the outcome, they won't put their hand in their pocket. A 15-second clip on television, no matter how inspiring, isn't enough. The donations we'd received along the way — almost $20 000 — came from people we'd met face to face: people who understood why it mattered because they'd been in the room with us and felt something.

But while we were standing there in Federation Square, on our own, none of that mattered. We had done it: 10 days, 1200 kilometres, 12 stitches. My wrists were bruised black from bumping over a thousand cat's eyes. At that point in my life, it was probably the greatest achievement I had ever accomplished. It was time well invested. And it was the foundation for everything that came next.

Finding Bex

A year after the bike ride, I found something else worth investing in. Her name was Bex.

I'd been on RSVP for a while — one of those online dating sites that charges you credits to send messages. Fifty dollars for 10 credits. Each message cost one credit. By late 2010, I was down to my last credit.

I'd put 15 years of market research into finding a life partner — that's how I thought about it. Fifteen years of getting it consistently wrong. Before Bex, I'd always rushed in — as soon as I was attracted to someone, I committed too fast, ignoring the warning signs because I was more interested in not being alone than in finding the right person. But by 2010, I was finally taking my time and being deliberate about who I invested in.

Late one night, my flatmate Keith was sitting with me. Three women had reached out to me through the site's free messaging system. He was scrolling through their profiles on my laptop — I couldn't make out the photos, so he was describing them to me.

'Most of the photos on these sites look staged,' he said. 'Forced smiles, too much makeup.' But one profile was different.

'She's pretty cute,' Keith said. 'Looks genuinely happy. Looks down to earth. Doesn't look fake.'

After 15 years of getting it wrong, those three qualities sounded like everything I'd been looking for. I spent my last credit on her.

Our first date was on Manly Beach in September 2010. She told me she'd be sitting near the stairs in a blue hoodie. I walked around that area hoping I knew where I was going. But, of course, I couldn't make out a blue hoodie. I was wandering, hoping she'd spot me before I ended up somewhere embarrassing.

'Matt?'

It seemed like I'd found her. But really, she'd found me.

We walked to Shelly Beach, talking the whole way, then headed back to the Manly Wharf Bar for a beer. That's when she handed me the menu.

I held it. Had the familiar experience of making out nothing but a blur. I put it down.

'I can't read the menu,' I said.

She knew I couldn't see well — I'd mentioned it in our messages. But I hadn't told her I was legally blind. This was the full disclosure. The moment of truth where I found out if she was going to treat me differently, feel sorry for me, make it weird.

'Okay, cool,' she said. And she read me the menu.

No hesitation. No pity. No big deal. Just 'Okay, cool.' And then she helped, like it was the most normal thing in the world — like reading a menu to a blind guy was no different from passing the salt.

Alignment shows up in the quiet moments

On the October long weekend, we went to Booti Booti National Park.

We hired a little hatchback, and Bex drove us up on Friday night after work, navigating the dark, winding roads of the Great Lakes region — bush pressing in on both sides, no streetlights, just headlights carving through the black in the middle of the night. This English girl, who had barely been in Australia for a few months, went on a road trip with a guy she'd known for only a couple of weeks. And then my family called ahead to say they were planning to drop by to meet her at some point over the weekend.

I was giving her directions: a blind man navigating her through unfamiliar bush roads in the dark. I'd learned to map journeys through other senses — the way the car tilted on corners, the rhythm of the turns, the duration of the straights. She trusted me. We found the caravan park without incident.

It rained for the entire weekend.

We sat in that tent for hours, rain drumming on the canvas, talking about our families, what we wanted from life — not our future together, it was too early for that, but our individual futures. Somewhere in those hours, it became clear we wanted the same things. You could feel that our energy and values were compatible. The same resonance. The same frequency.

Then my entire family showed up early. Mum, Dad, my brother Stu, his wife, their kids — suddenly they were all there. Bex just came out and met them, with no fuss about putting on makeup — she just walked out and handled it. She was warm and natural and completely herself.

That was a big tick. She was authentic, down to earth and willing to meet new people with no drama. We had a great weekend.

When we were driving home from Booti Booti, we hit traffic at Bulahdelah.

We were stuck for hours, barely moving. It was the kind of situation that reveals the worst in people — impatience, frustration, the childish anger of being delayed.

Bex didn't complain once. We just sat there chatting and laughing. There was no frustration. No impatience.

That sealed it. Sitting in that traffic, barely moving, I realised she was the one. I thought, *I'm going to marry this girl.*

The right person doesn't feel like a cost. Every hour with Bex felt like compound interest — all the time invested was building toward something greater than what I was putting in. That's how you know.

Two stories, one lesson

The ride to Melbourne and finding Bex might seem like unrelated stories. One was about physical endurance — 10 days of suffering, navigating by sound and feel, riding blind down highways that could have killed me. The other was about emotional connection — opening up, being honest about who I was, trusting another person with the parts of myself I usually kept hidden.

But they taught me the same thing.

The ride required a fast gear — intense and focused, where every second counted. I needed complete presence because the alternative was crashing and potentially a serious injury.

Finding Bex required a slow gear — patient, deliberate presence. I needed to take the time to analyse whether this was the right decision, instead of rushing in like I'd always done before. It required me to recognise authenticity when I encountered it, and to be honest about my blindness instead of hiding it. I had to trust my instincts about energy and alignment.

Both were investments, but neither felt like a cost. That's how you know you're investing in the right things: when the price doesn't feel like a price. When every hour feels like it's building towards something.

That's time well invested.

Daniel Kahneman and Amos Tversky's decades of research on human decision-making revealed that the real cost isn't using the wrong thinking system—it's failing to switch when the situation changes. Their work showed that people who defaulted to a single mode, whether fast and intuitive or slow and deliberate, consistently underperformed those who could read the situation and shift accordingly. The problem isn't the gear: it's the rigidity. Being locked in slow gear when the moment demands fast action costs opportunity. Being locked in fast gear when a situation demands patience costs accuracy. The skill—the one most people never develop—is the switch itself.

• • •

Where in your business are you still planning when you should be executing? Or executing without a plan? The leaders who win know when to slow down, lock in the strategy, and then shift gears and execute furiously without second-guessing. Which gear are you stuck in—and what would change if you shifted?

Chapter 12

Many Hats

Own Every Hat

> Most people give 50 per cent to everything and 100 per cent to nothing. They're physically in the room but mentally elsewhere — in the meeting but thinking about lunch; out for dinner but checking their phone. I learned to wear many hats — athlete, executive, husband — but never at the same time. Each hat gets everything; each moment gets my full presence. The constraint isn't time. The constraint is focus.

Tom Skulander met me at Stella Blu Italian restaurant in Dee Why a few months after the Sydney to Melbourne ride.

He was a coach from Cycling Australia. People had been telling me for months that I should talk to him. Ever since the Sydney to Melbourne ride, word had spread that there was a blind guy on the Northern Beaches who could actually ride. Tom wanted to see for himself what kind of athlete was hiding behind those stories.

But this meeting was about something more than training advice. Tom wanted to discuss tandem cycling — riding on the back of a bike with a sighted pilot at the front. Para cycling.

When I was younger, people used to say to me: 'You should go to the Paralympics. You should be a para athlete and compete against other athletes with disabilities.' I used to get offended by that. I hadn't owned my disability yet. Except for a brief stint playing blind cricket, I'd spent my whole life competing against able-bodied people — in rugby union, rugby league, ice hockey. The idea of being on the back of a tandem, letting someone else steer, felt like surrender.

But the Sydney to Melbourne ride had cracked something open. I was starting to own every part of myself, including the blindness I'd spent decades trying to hide. Riding a tandem meant accepting help — it meant trusting someone else with my life. It required me to finally say: 'I am blind, and that's not a weakness. That's just who I am.'

We sat down with coffees, and Tom studied me. I was still carrying my rugby player's build — broad shoulders, thick arms, the kind of upper body that had served me well in scrums and tackles — and the occasional pub fight — but was dead weight on a bike.

'Those muscles,' Tom said. 'Those arms. They look nice. But they are not going to do anything for you on a bike. You will need to make big changes.'

The way he said it — 'big changes' — made it sound like a test, as if he thought those changes would be too big for me to make.

'Stop telling me it is going to be hard,' I replied. 'Tell me exactly what I need to do, and I will do the work. I am a robot. Program me with the right code and you will get the right output.'

Tom smiled at that. Then he mentioned Phil Thuaux.

Phil had just retired from riding for Team Drapac in Europe. He was one of the fastest four-kilometre pursuiters in the world — he'd won world cups, raced at the highest level and was an absolute weapon on a bike. And Cycling Australia was considering putting him on the front of a tandem with me. A retired professional cyclist piloting a blind guy who'd never raced in his life. It sounded like a massive opportunity. It sounded terrifying. The conversation went for two hours. By the end, I had a plan.

Diving in at the deep end

My first race was a criterium in the Central Coast region. We weren't racing against other tandems. It was just a normal club race, and Phil and I were on the tandem racing against single bikes.

A criterium is a short, fast race — multiple laps of a closed circuit, all riders starting together, first across the line wins. The pack rides tight, drafting off each other to save energy, moving as a single organism. When a rider attacks — accelerating hard to break away from the group — the pack either chases them down or lets them go. If the breakaway holds, the front rider wins. If not, the whole bunch sprints for the finish.

Positioning and tactics matter as much as raw power in a criterium. The bunch moves as one, attacks launching and being reeled back in. But I couldn't see any of it. For a blind stoker on the back, it requires complete trust in your pilot — Phil had to tell me everything. Attack coming. Sitting back. Gap opening.

Normally, someone who'd never raced before would start in D grade with the beginners. However, because Phil was a professional cyclist, we started in A grade. We were racing against the best riders in the area.

Bex came to watch. We'd only been together for a couple of months. I told her: I'd better win. It's going to be embarrassing — I'm on the back of a bike with a professional rider.

We didn't even finish.

I was so cooked by the end that I couldn't even help Phil. He was doing all the work, dragging my useless legs around the circuit while I gasped for air. We pulled out before the finish. The other riders — just club level, A-grade locals — were chatting to each other while we were dying.

But I remember being excited. If you want to feel achievement, you need to do something hard. These guys were so much better than me, and they were only at A-grade club level, not even world class. My goal was to become world champion, which was going to require real work. The tandem riders at the world championships would be much faster than these club riders.

To ride effectively on a tandem, I had to work on three core elements: steering, gears and balance.

If you don't follow the pilot's steering direction, you crash. If you lean the wrong way and try to guide the bike, it will actually steer that way. The hardest part is surrendering control and letting the pilot be the pilot. Many people struggle with this and end up fighting each other the entire time, which costs enormous energy and makes it unsafe.

The stoker (me — the rear rider) can't select gears, as the pilot controls the gears and the brakes. I was often spinning faster than I wanted to. I would have preferred a bigger gear and a slower cadence, but the pilot chooses the gears based on what works for them.

The final element, balance, is extremely difficult on a tandem. It takes a long time to master getting out of the saddle, standing up and being efficient as a pairing.

For all these elements to work well, trust is essential.

Phil was an engineer as well as a cyclist, and he became the best first pilot I could have asked for. I trusted him completely. He was an absolute weapon on the bike, but he was also brilliant at communicating. I learned so much from him — the mechanics of bicycles, aerodynamics, all the technical pieces that would later give me an edge.

We won criteriums at club level in our third week together. Six months later, the Australian National Road Championships gave us third in both events — the time trial and the road race. Enough to earn selection for the 2011 UCI Para-cycling Road World Championships in Denmark.

Denmark was a wake-up call. It was my first time representing Australia on the international stage. The race was 118 kilometres. We were preparing for a training ride one morning, and Cycling Australia's head performance director, Peter Day, was standing at the back of a truck.

'Can someone pick that trainer up, please?' he called out.

I was standing right next to it. I could sort of see where it was, so I bent over to pick it up.

'Matt Formston, don't you fucking touch it.'

I froze.

'You're not here to touch anything,' Peter said. 'You're not here to do anything. You're here to ride bikes and win medals. If you want a coffee, you ask someone else. You want your bag carried, you ask staff. That's what they're here for.'

Growing up, I'd always chipped in, done whatever was required. But this was a different environment. I wasn't able to chip in. I just needed to sit back, train, recover and race. It was a whole different world.

The other athletes had been doing this for years — decades, some of them. They had coaches and sponsors and support staff. We had enthusiasm and not much else.

We finished eighteenth.

Crossing that line, I knew I had given everything. I had pushed through the moments when my lungs were burning and my legs were screaming. I had dug as deep as I knew how to dig. And it was not good enough. Not even close.

But instead of being discouraged, I was excited. Because now I knew the price. I knew exactly what it would take. The riders ahead of us weren't super-human: they were athletes who had invested the time. They had respected the years required to become world-class.

I needed to do the same.

Finding my competitive match

Phil and I trained as hard as we could to qualify for the London 2012 Paralympics, but we didn't make selection. We were the third qualifier, and Australia only had two spots. First reserve was so close, but it wasn't close enough.

Phil decided to retire. His wife had fallen pregnant, and he had achieved what he needed to achieve in cycling. He had other priorities now — a family to build, a new stage of life. I understood. Phil was an amazing guy who had done so much for me. But it meant I needed a new pilot.

Mick Curran was a racer who had been competing in Europe for years. He was also the one cyclist on the Central Coast that Phil and I had never beaten. He read races like a chess master reads a board. If you can't beat them, join them.

When I called him to ask if he would pilot for me, I could hear two things in his voice: reluctance and hunger.

The reluctance I understood. Mick had never ridden a tandem before — just like Phil, who hadn't had any tandem experience until he rode with me. But beyond that, Mick didn't know what would be required to help a blind guy. How much extra work would it be? How awkward? There's a perception in the community around people with disabilities — stigmas that attach themselves, whether they're deserved or not. I thought I could hear that concern in his voice.

Maybe it wasn't there — maybe I'd imagined it. But I'd felt that hesitation from people my whole life.

Underneath that hesitation, though, I could hear something else: the competitive fire that had driven him through years of European racing. The racing bug was so deep in his blood that even retirement couldn't kill it. He had told his wife he was done. He'd hung up the bike. But that hunger never really goes away.

'Only for this race,' he said. 'I have told my wife I am done with racing. One race, and then I am finished.'

We won our first two races together at the 2012 Australian National Road Championships: the tandem road race and the tandem time trial. My first two gold medals. Convincingly.

Whatever Mick had told his wife about being done with racing evaporated the moment he remembered what winning felt like. He went all in.

Switching hats, changing uniforms

Bex and I had moved up to the Central Coast. My brother Stu had been living there for over a decade and loved it. We settled in Wamberal and, by coincidence, Mick lived in the same suburb.

Six days a week, on the dot, Mick arrived at my house at 4.30 am — never late. He'd get up early enough to ride his bike from his place to mine, and I'd be kitted up and ready to go when he rolled into the driveway.

The world was dark and quiet, the only sound the click of cleats on concrete and the whir of chains as we rolled out. Bex was still asleep. My day job was hours away. The sun would barely crack the horizon before we were done.

Sometimes we cycled 120 kilometres in just over three hours, doing hill repeats until my lungs burned and my legs went numb.

We didn't eat before we trained — I'd only have a protein shake with no calories afterwards. I was still trying to get my weight down, and I didn't have fat to lose, so I had to let the muscles I'd taken years to build evaporate away. My body ate itself to reach the weight the coaching staff were asking for.

We talked during the tempo sections and the recovery periods of each ride — when you're training for hours, you get moments when you can have a chat before getting back into the zone. We'd talk about our families, our fears, what we were chasing and why it mattered. You learn a lot about someone when you suffer alongside them in the dark.

You also learn a lot about yourself.

Every time we rolled out at 4.30 am, I had this feeling I'd left something behind. It took me weeks to figure out what it was.

A mouth guard. For every sport I'd played — rugby league, rugby union, ice hockey — I'd worn a mouth guard when I went into battle. That piece of plastic between my teeth was the signal: now you're competing. Now it's time to hurt and be hurt. Cycling was a sport where I didn't need to wear one, and it felt like something was missing.

That feeling taught me something about uniforms. The uniform determines the hat. When I was in my cycling kit at 4.30 am, I was an athlete. When I got home at 7.30 am, showered and changed into a suit, I was an executive. The athlete hat came off, and the businessman hat went on: it was a complete switch. And the same applied to my home life too: when I got home and put on my boardies and thongs, I was 100 per cent family — 100 per cent husband. Completely present in every role.

The clothes weren't a costume — they were commitment. They signalled to my brain that this is who you are — right now. This role gets everything.

The price of excellence

The weight that was slowing me down came off in kilos. I went from 94 down towards 73 — 21 kilos of muscle.

Mum said I looked like I had cancer. I understood why — when your son loses 20 kilos, his cheekbones start showing and his clothes hang off him, it's hard not to be concerned. But the power was still there. The speed was there. I wasn't sick: I was becoming what I needed to become.

I didn't consciously set out to become a world leader at time management. I was forced to learn it because I wanted to fit multiple lives into one life. A blind guy on a bike can't afford autopilot. A guy trying to become world champion while holding down an executive job and building a relationship can't afford distraction. Every second had to count: I had to give 100 per cent to everything.

If I wasn't doing the hours on the bike, there was someone in Colombia doing the hours — and they would beat me. So, I had to do everything I could, which meant I had to learn to say no to almost everything else beyond my training, my job and my relationship with Bex.

I said no to nights out. No to birthday parties. No to beers at work events — and I love a beer. For my entire cycling career, I'd have a couple of beers between track season and road season, and between road season and track season. That was it. A few beers twice a year.

I sold both apartments in Sydney. I could have kept them — I'd be financially further ahead now. But the mental energy of being a landlord would have distracted me, so I exchanged wealth for focus.

At work, I started telling people where they sat on my priority list. That's a hard conversation — no one wants to hear, 'You're currently number four on the list.' Most people smile and nod and say yes to everything, even if they have no hope of making it happen, and then they deliver nothing well. At least I was being honest.

The bedrock of my success

In May 2012, I took Bex to Lady Elliot Island on the Great Barrier Reef. It's one of my family's favourite places — I'd first gone there as a teenager, and I have a deep connection to the island that's hard to explain. We went scuba diving together, watched huge manta rays glide past us in the blue ... and I proposed.

A year later, we went back to the island to get married.

We basically had the whole place to ourselves for a three-day wedding: 40 of our best friends and family flew in on light planes, and everything was brought to the island by barge. I'll never forget it.

On my wedding day, I went diving in the morning. Most people wouldn't understand that, but I try to fit as much into every day as I can — that's the whole point. While we were down there, a large tiger shark appeared and hung in the distance for most of the dive. I only found out she'd been watching us when I got back on the boat and the dive group started talking about it. I see that as a wedding blessing from Mother Nature.

After the wedding, we spent two weeks in Fiji on honeymoon. It culminated in a dive with three massive bull sharks. They came within almost a metre of my head. For once, I could actually see their outline — the bulk of them, their shapes moving through the water towards me. It was a beautiful moment: one of those experiences where the world becomes very simple and very clear.

Four months after marrying Bex, I won my first international gold medal. That lady is such a beautiful human being — and she's the bedrock of all my success. With her in my corner, I feel unbeatable.

Going for gold

We travelled to Matane, Quebec — a small town on the south shore of the Saint Lawrence River, in French-speaking northeast Canada — for a world cup race. It was a 120-kilometre road race. Team management gave us clear instructions: 'Stay under the radar. Save yourselves for the world championships the following week.'

Mick is a racer. Trying to tell a racer not to race is like telling a dog not to chase a ball.

Within the first five kilometres, a local Canadian rider — one of the favourites — launched an attack. Mick didn't hesitate. He followed the wheel, and suddenly we were in a breakaway with about four other tandems. A Canadian bike, an Irish bike, a Dutch bike: the whole peloton of 30-plus tandems chasing right behind us.

We'd been in that breakaway for over 100 kilometres — not really doing our turns, sitting in, conserving our energy. No one had ever heard of us. We were just these blokes who'd turned up out of nowhere. I hadn't raced overseas for two years. Mick and I had been working at home, building our capacity, and we were ready to make our challenge.

At the 105-kilometre mark, there were only two bikes left with us: an Irish and a Dutch team. We were sitting on the back of our little three-bike breakaway as we hit a small rise. Mick couldn't tell me we were going to attack — they would hear it — so we used hand signals. A touch on my hands, a bounce in the saddle — signals we'd developed so I'd know what was coming.

We attacked over that rise and got away clean.

The final lap was 15 kilometres, and we did it solo. I was 73 kilos; Mick had got down to 69. Our power-to-weight ratio meant we were driving the bike at almost 50 kilometres an hour. There's some epic footage from the highlights reel, with a camera motorbike beside us and, on the bridge, a red Ferrari pacing us in normal traffic. Just keeping up with a tandem.

By the time we reached the finish, we'd put three minutes into the breakaway. The Irish and Dutch riders got swamped by the peloton, and there was a sprint finish for second place. But it didn't matter. We'd already won.

Thousands of people lined the barriers. Cowbells were ringing. We were so far ahead that Mick said: 'Let's enjoy it.' We backed off a bit, still going hard but able to chat.

'Let's go over the line with our hands off,' he said. 'I'll count it down.'

Taking your hands off the handlebars on a tandem requires skill and coordination. One wrong move and both riders hit the deck.

Three. Two. One.

We sat up together, hands out wide, and flew through the finishing tape as world cup gold medallists.

What had started as a conversation on a corporate bus about a bucket-list bike ride had ended with a world cup gold medal. And along the way, I'd met and married Bex, the love of my life.

The journey wasn't measured in kilometres: it was measured in time. I found this time in the hours before dawn, and in the discipline of being fully present in each part of my life.

Husband. Corporate leader. Athlete. These are the three main hats I wear, and each hat requires a different version of me. But every version gets 100 per cent of my attention and commitment when I'm wearing each hat.

It doesn't matter how many hats you wear. What matters is that when one hat is on, the others are off. Each hat deserves your full presence, not the scraps left over from the ones you're still mentally wearing.

I don't have more time than anyone else — there are only 24 hours in a day — but I've learned to respect the time I have. I use it deliberately — I never waste a moment by being mentally elsewhere.

Cal Newport's research on 'deep work' at Georgetown University, Washington, D.C., found that the ability to focus without distraction is becoming increasingly rare and increasingly valuable. Elite performers don't manage their time; they manage their attention. They create hard boundaries between roles and give each role their complete presence. The difference between good and great isn't the hours worked: it's the presence applied.

• • •

Which hat are you wearing right now? Is it getting everything or just the scraps left over from the other hats you're still mentally wearing?

Chapter 13

The Weight of Access

Empathy Is a Superpower

> To lead others, you need to understand their whole life, not just their KPIs. The physical stuff is easy: you train; you push; you lock out the pain and get it done. But the daily grind of inaccessibility is something else entirely. It's relentless. It's everywhere. And, most of the time, no one even notices it's happening to you. Without access, you appreciate first-hand what happens when the world forgets you exist — and what it means when someone remembers.

When I went to vote for the first time, I realised that democracy isn't for everyone.

I was 18 years old, standing in a community hall in Warriewood, holding two pieces of paper I couldn't read.

Andy Kannard had driven me there. We'd walked in together, excited in the way you get when you're about to do something for the first time as an adult. We were going to vote, have our say — be citizens.

A volunteer handed me the papers. I looked at them. Shapes. Blurs. Nothing I could make sense of.

'Can someone help me fill these out?' I asked. 'I can't see them.'

The woman behind the table shook her head. 'That's illegal. No one can help you with your voting papers.'

I stood there for a moment, not quite believing it.

'Can my mate help me?'

'No,' she replied. 'That's illegal. You have to do it yourself. If your mate helps you and we catch you, you'll both be fined.'

She and the other volunteers just looked at me. I was holding democracy in my hands, and I couldn't participate in it. No alternative was offered, no suggestion of a way to work within the system. That was the rule — simple as that.

I walked towards the ballot box. Kannard grabbed the papers off me on the way, folded them up, and dropped them in. There was nothing on them. I hadn't voted for anyone. I'd just performed the ritual of voting without actually doing it.

That was in 1996 — 30 years ago. And what still gets to me isn't the anger I felt walking out of that hall — though there was plenty of that — but that I didn't feel surprised. I was used to pushing back about my bus pass, fighting for half-price taxi fares and navigating a world that wasn't built for me. This was just another day of not being included; another door that looked open but turned out to be locked.

I didn't bother going to the next election. Why would I? I knew I couldn't vote. And then the fine arrived.

Two or three hundred dollars. Compulsory voting — one of the pillars of Australian democracy — meant that everyone had to participate. Except, apparently, blind people like me.

It took multiple phone calls, letters and explanations for the fines to be revoked. I had to go through the stress and anxiety of proving, once again, that I was blind. That I hadn't just chosen not to vote. That I physically couldn't participate in the system they'd built. Something no sighted person would ever have to deal with.

This went on for years — election after election. The same calls; the same explanations; the same stress. Eventually, someone at the Electoral Commission must have heard the frustration in my voice. They did something I didn't even know was possible: they took me off the electoral roll. Rather than fix the system, they just removed me from it entirely.

And yet, the solution is simple. Digital voting through myGov — the app that every Australian already uses for tax, Medicare, everything. My smartphone is accessible. I use the myGov app all the time. If I could vote through that app, I could participate in democracy like everyone else.

Digital voting wouldn't just help blind people. It would help the mum juggling multiple sport drop-offs on a Saturday who can't get to the polling booth. It would help the elderly person who doesn't want to drive down to the local scout hall. It would help anyone who'd rather cast their vote from their phone in 30 seconds than stand in a queue for an hour. When you fix accessibility for one group, you usually fix it for many.

When people talk about accessibility, they always use the example of the ramp at the front of a building. You build the ramp for people in wheelchairs, but it also helps the elderly man with the walking frame, the pregnant woman, the guy on crutches, the parent pushing a pram. When you build for people on the margins, you build for everyone.

The invisible labour of existing

Most people don't understand the amount of extra work it takes to exist when the world isn't built for you.

Before I got a smartphone, I had an old Nokia. To dial a number, I'd feel for the bump on the five — there's always a little dot on the five key — and work out how to dial it from there. I'd memorised about eight numbers: my parents' number, a few friends, a few colleagues. That was it. If I needed to call a customer, I'd have to ring someone else first, ask them for the number, try to memorise it while I was still on the phone, hang up and dial it quickly before I forgot it.

Going to client meetings was its own production. The night before, I'd sit down and memorise the address on Google Maps. I'd work out the nearest cross street, figure out how many doors down from the corner the building was and plan my route from the train station. I'd use the position of the sun to work out which way was north, south, east and west. I'd leave ridiculously early because finding places was hard and I couldn't afford to be late.

And then I'd arrive, and sometimes the receptionist might say: 'Oh, sorry, that meeting was cancelled a couple of hours ago, Mr Formston.'

I didn't have email on my phone. I didn't have a calendar that could ping me with updates. My colleagues and clients all had BlackBerry devices, with the latest information at their fingertips. I had a Nokia with eight memorised numbers and a bump on the five.

The feeling in those moments wasn't just frustration at the wasted time. It was shame. I felt the embarrassment of being different — of not having access to tools that a child could use.

When I was in meetings, I'd bluff my way through. If documents were handed around the table, I'd watch out for shifts in body language, listen for any hesitation in people's voices, ask clarifying questions to extract the information I couldn't read.

One time, a customer was pushing back on a point in a contract. I had no idea if their claim was accurate, but something didn't feel right. I kept probing: what page? What clause? I could hear the uncertainty in their voice.

'That's not in the contract,' I said. 'I've read it.'

They backed down.

Later, I went back to our legal team and got them to clarify. Turns out the clause *was* in the contract. I called the customer back and apologised. I'd been caught out by my best strategy at that time, which was to get good enough at reading people and calling bluffs to overcome the information I was missing. The alternative was being caught out, being exposed, being the blind guy who didn't know what he was talking about.

At work, I had a piece of software called ZoomText on my computer. It cost $1400 — an additional expense just to do my job — and it would enlarge the screen and read things out to me. But because it wasn't part of the business's operating system, sometimes it would clash with our work systems. My computer was forever crashing. Every day was a battle just to get the basic tools to function.

When the world opened

In June 2009, Apple released the iPhone 3GS with a feature called VoiceOver — a screen reader built into the phone that could speak whatever was on the display. For the first time, a blind person could walk into a store, buy the same phone as everyone else, and use it out of the box. No extra software, no $1400 add-on. It was just a phone that talked.

I got mine in 2010. Within a couple of days, something shifted.

I was sitting on a train in Sydney, going between meetings, and I started listening to articles about surf breaks around the world — places I'd heard about but never been able to research. I was going from one website to the next, the phone reading to me through my headphones. I couldn't stop listening.

I became ravenous. Ocean trenches. Space. Engineering research. Chain rings and cycling technology. I could lie in bed with my eyes closed, move my finger across the touchscreen of my phone and the device would read each article to me. I went down rabbit hole after rabbit hole, just because I could.

I'd been starved of information for 30 years. I'd never learned braille. I'd never seen text big enough to enable me to read more than a paragraph with my eyes. And for the first time in my life, I had access to what everyone else had always had. I could access the entire internet through my ears.

That one innovation — VoiceOver on a touchscreen — changed my entire life. Everything before 2010 had been hard. Everything after 2010 got easier. Not easy, but definitely easier.

Privacy is a form of dignity

All my life, if I wanted to know something, I had to ask someone to read it for me. Which meant I only asked about things I was comfortable sharing. If I wanted to research something boring — like how to maintain a lawn — I'd hesitate, because who wants to ask someone to read that out loud? But now I could look up whatever I wanted privately, without having to justify my curiosity.

Bex came into my life at around the same time. She changed my life — and then the phone came, and digital accessibility changed my life again. That time was a perfect storm of love and technology that unlocked a version of me I didn't know was possible.

Think about all the devices that have numbers on them. Scales. Heart rate monitors. Blood pressure machines. None of them were ever accessible to me. Every single one required another person to read the display.

When you're an elite athlete, weight in particular is critical data. I weighed myself every day when I was cycling to keep a close check on my weight. But I'd never weighed myself without help in my entire life. Every single time, I had to get Bex to come into the bathroom, stand there with me and tell me the number. Every single day.

Then Bluetooth scales were invented. Suddenly, I could step on the scales and the number would appear on my phone for VoiceOver to read to me. I could weigh myself when I wanted, without interrupting someone else's day—without needing another human being present for something so private. That might sound like a small step forward, but when you've spent your whole life dependent on others for the most basic information about your own body, independence feels like freedom.

Simple solutions that scale

When I was in Year 10, we went on a school excursion to see the Steven Spielberg film *Schindler's List*. It's a long movie, and about halfway through I was busting to go to the toilet.

I went out by myself. More than a hundred Year 9 kids from my school were all standing in the foyer, waiting to go into their session. And I walked into the wrong toilet.

I didn't realise at first. I heard them laughing, but I didn't know they were laughing at me. I thought if I turned around, I'd make myself a target, so I kept going. Walked all the way in. And then I realised there were no urinals—just cubicles. Different shapes to what I was expecting.

I was in the girls' toilet.

I turned around and walked out. They laughed at me again. And then I couldn't find the men's toilet. I had to stand there, awkwardly, trying to spot another rectangular shape that looked like a door, while they kept laughing. Eventually, someone walked out of one of the doors, and I went in.

When I came out, they laughed at me again. And then they told everyone.

It went on for weeks. Matt goes into the girls' toilets. The joke was that I was gay, which made no sense, but that's what they said. Every time I left class to use the bathroom, they'd all be laughing — which was ridiculous, because it was an all-boys school. There were no girls' toilets. But the joke just kept going.

I never told my parents. Never told a teacher. I couldn't deal with anyone in particular because it was a whole group — I couldn't hear any specific voices. So, I just absorbed the humiliation.

To this day, if I'm in an airport or a shopping centre by myself, I still can't tell which toilet is the men's and which is the women's. I have to watch for shapes that look like men and follow one of them in. That's how I find the bathroom. Every single time.

Some small, helpful shifts have become noticeable, however. In 2024, I was at Haneda Airport in Tokyo. Outside one of the bathrooms, there was an audio speaker. Just a simple announcement on a loop, in English and Japanese: 'This is the bathroom. The women's toilet is the first door on the left. The men's toilet is the second door on the right.'

Nothing high-tech or expensive — just a simple solution arising from someone thinking, *What if a person can't see the signs?*

I've never seen this in place anywhere else, but it's a perfect example of what 'good' looks like. A simple solution that costs almost nothing. The only requirement being that someone, somewhere, gives a shit.

That same year, I went surfing in South Sumatra in Indonesia. A place called Amy's Place — two flights from Australia, then a six-hour drive. It was remote as hell. When I arrived, Amy, who runs the camp, was nervous. She'd never had a blind person stay there before.

She said: 'Matt, I give everyone a stainless steel bottle when they arrive. I put a name tag on them so people know whose is whose. But I know you can't read the name tag. So I was walking on the beach, and I found this piece of sea glass — just a little pebble of glass that's been smoothed by the ocean — and I stuck it on the front of one of the bottles. That's yours. Everyone will know it's your bottle because it's got the piece of glass on it. And you can feel it when you pick it up.'

I didn't understand her at first. My brain didn't compute her gesture because no one does those kinds of things for me. It took her explaining it twice for me to get it.

She hadn't just thought about accessibility — she'd thought about me. She'd thought about it before I'd even arrived. She'd found a solution that cost nothing and took almost no effort. And it made me feel welcome in a way that nothing else could.

You can have the multi-billion-dollar VoiceOver software from Apple that changes your entire life, or you can have a piece of sea glass on a water bottle from a woman in Indonesia who gives a shit. Both work. Both matter. Both require someone to stop and think: *What does this person actually need?*

People ask me about my worst moments of exclusion. But I don't think it's about single moments — it's about the way they accumulate over time. The ex-girlfriend who couldn't be intimate with me because I couldn't make eye contact with her. The guy at work who said, 'No wonder we can't resolve customer issues, we've got a blind guy running things.' A hundred kids laughing outside the toilet. They all blur together into this constant low-level hum of exclusion that becomes white noise after a while. You stop noticing individual incidents because there are just too many of them.

Knowing changes things

When I talk about accessibility, the one thing I want people to walk away thinking is: *I had no idea.*

I had no idea that blind Australians can't really vote independently. I had no idea what it takes to navigate a world without being able to read signs, emails, contracts. I had no idea how much invisible labour goes into just existing. I had no idea that something as simple as an iPhone could change a person's entire life. I had no idea that a piece of sea glass on a water bottle could make someone feel seen.

Somewhere, right now, there's a kid counting bus stops. Memorising routes. Pretending they can see more than they can. Working three times as hard as everyone else just to stay in the game.

I was that kid.

I've surfed the biggest waves on earth. I've won world championships. I've broken world records. And the hardest thing I've ever done is try to participate in the basic functions of society — voting, working, going to the bathroom — in a world that wasn't designed with me in mind.

The physical stuff is easy. You train. You push. You lock out the pain and get it done.

The daily grind of inaccessibility is something else entirely. It's relentless. It's everywhere. And most of the time, no one even notices it's happening.

Until now.

Now you know.

And knowing changes things. Maybe you'll think twice about accessibility the next time you design a website, build an app, run a meeting, set up a voting booth. Maybe you'll be the person who sticks a piece of sea glass on a water bottle and makes someone feel like they belong. It doesn't take much. It just takes giving a shit.

Google's Project Aristotle studied hundreds of teams to identify what makes them effective. The single most important factor wasn't talent, resources or strategy. It was psychological safety—the belief that you won't be punished or humiliated for speaking up, asking questions or making mistakes. When people feel seen and included, they perform better. When they feel invisible or excluded, they withdraw. Accessibility isn't charity. It's the foundation of human performance.

• • •

Who in your life might be doing invisible labour just to exist? What would it cost you to ask them what they actually need?

Chapter 14

Own the Delusion

The Future Is Already Real

> Declare your goal before you've earned it. Live in the reality of already being that person. Manifestation is not closing your eyes and wishing — it's identifying every barrier, owning each one, doing the work to resolve them and then, crucially, continuing to live in the space knowing that you are already the best in the world. You visualise this future already being real. When I was living it, I felt as if I was owning the delusion — but it's supposed to feel completely delusional. That's how you know the goal is big enough.

At the end of 2013, Mick and I won the world cup road race in Canada. Our win had been so convincing that the race organisers drug-tested us. That felt like a nod of acknowledgement to us: they thought we were good enough that we may even have cheated.

We were on a high. Our partnership was clicking — the kind of synchronisation between pilot and stoker that takes years to develop. We'd found our rhythm, and we were winning. We'd already mapped out our plan for 2014: the tandem Tour of Belgium, races across France and Italy.

Road racing was our focus; the track was just an obligation. But as part of being on the Australian endurance cycling team, we were required to compete at the Australian Track National Championships in Melbourne. It wasn't our priority: we went because we had to.

A few minutes before we started at the Melbourne Nationals, my shoulder dislocated.

I was putting on my speed suit — those skin-tight Lycra things that look like children's clothing before you stretch them on. As I pulled my arms through, my shoulder popped out. The suit was so tight it actually locked the shoulder into the dislocated position rather than allowing it to pop back into place.

My shoulder had been problematic since I was 18. I'd had hundreds of dislocations over the years. As I'd let my upper body atrophy for cycling, stripping away every gram of unnecessary muscle, the joint had become increasingly unstable. By this point, even getting dressed was a risk. So, when my shoulder popped out, it wasn't a shock. What I felt in that moment was almost resignation.

Someone helped me get the suit off. We popped the shoulder back into place, and I put the suit back on. Five minutes later, I was in the starting gate, ready to begin the race, while the pain continued to radiate through my arm.

And then we went out and posted the fastest four-kilometre tandem pursuit time in the world for 2013.

I reckon half the reason we went so fast was that I had endorphins flooding my body from the dislocation. Pain became my fuel. It always had been.

The coaches sat us down the next day. 'Look,' they said, 'if you guys are this good at the pursuit, you should focus on this. There are fewer variables than in road racing. On the road, you're dealing with hills that might not suit your body type, teams ganging up on you, weather, tactics. On the track, it's just you against the clock.

Every velodrome is basically the same. If you can be the fastest, you can dominate.'

They were right. The four-kilometre pursuit stripped away everything except raw power, strategy and the willingness to hurt yourself more than anyone else. Two tandems start on opposite sides of the track and race the clock, and the fastest time wins — no teammates to hide behind, no tactics to mask weakness.

The world championships had been announced for April 2014 in Aguascalientes, Mexico.

Track racing had started as an obligation but had become a revelation. We had about five months to transform ourselves from road racers who happened to be fast on the track into genuine pursuit specialists capable of winning a world title.

A new obsession

The world record stood at four minutes and 16 seconds.

We weren't focused on breaking it. Our goal was a world title, nothing else. But to win gold, you have to qualify fastest. The fastest qualifier earns the right to race in the final. And we knew that if we could get close to 4:16, we should have done enough to qualify first. Once we were in that final, we had the mongrel — that raw, ugly toughness that refuses to quit when the pain is at its worst — and the ability to suffer to beat anyone. But we had to get into the final first.

We built our entire training block around reaching 4:16. We lived it. We breathed it. We talked about it constantly — to our wives, to our colleagues at work.

I'd mention it in meetings, trying to explain to people who'd never watched cycling why this number consumed me. Bex heard it so often she could probably recite our split times in her sleep. The number followed me everywhere. When I closed my eyes at night, I'd visualise crossing the line at 4:16. When I woke up, my first thought was about the next training session that would get me closer to 4:16.

The 4:16 world record had stood for years. If we could match it or come close, we'd earn our ticket to the gold medal final. That was the goal.

The training block was the most intense of my life. Three sessions a day, while still working full-time in a corporate job. Mornings would begin with a long ride together — 120 kilometres, sometimes more, where we would build the endurance that would carry us through four minutes of agony. Then I'd shower, change and head into the office for meetings, calls and client work. At midday I'd slip out for weights. I was leg-pressing 440 kilos at a bodyweight of 75 kilos, doing box jumps to chest height for explosive power out of the gate and focusing on hip flexor work because the pursuit start requires you to pull the pedals as much as push them. Then I'd head back to the office for the afternoon.

Evenings would include a Wattbike session in my garage. Power intervals on an indoor bike, with one-minute efforts and four-minute efforts — zoning in on the specific demands of the pursuit, over and over, until my legs screamed. The Wattbike doesn't lie. It measures exactly how much power you're producing, and you either hit your numbers or you don't.

As we got closer to Mexico, we tapered back the long morning rides — but the weight and Wattbike sessions continued right up until we flew out. We were building a machine — two bodies that could produce more sustained power than any other tandem team on the planet.

To train effectively, you never actually do a full four kilometres in your training sessions. It hurts too much. Your body learns to fear that level of pain, and if you go there too often, it starts protecting itself—you can't access the same depth on race day. So, you train all the components separately and put it all together exactly once: when it counts.

The only time you truly know what you're capable of is on race day.

Remembering who you're fighting for

Halfway through the training block, my first son, Max, was born.

His birth took over 24 hours. Bex was in a lot of pain. The longer the labour went on, the more worried I became—not about training or racing, but about her. That was real. Everything else was just bikes.

When I first held him, I was terrified. I've always been scared of little babies—they're like little blobs of blur to me. I can't see which end is the head and which end is the feet. I'm terrified of dropping them or mishandling them. Holding Max for the first time was one of the most exciting, wonderful and terrifying moments of my life.

Six weeks later, I would be in Mexico.

Bex never complained. She understood what we were building. But I carried the weight of her sacrifice with me. If I was going to leave my wife at home alone with a newborn baby, if I was going to fly to the other side of the world to ride a bike in circles, it had to mean something.

Speak the future into existence

Alongside the physical preparation, we brought in a mindset coach named Louise Laffey. I'd met Lou at an event and felt her energy—there was a resonance about her that I wanted to tap into. So, we asked her to work with us on the goal of becoming world champions on the track. Mick and I weren't leaving any stone unturned. We had the training dialled in. We had the equipment sorted. But I knew from experience that the gap between good and great isn't just fitness: it's what happens in your head and your heart when everything hurts and the finish line is still two minutes away.

The first time Lou made us declare it aloud, I wanted to run.

'Say it,' she said. 'Say "I am world champion." '

I wasn't a world champion — not even close. Yes, Mick and I had won the world cup road race in Canada, but that's a single event — it doesn't make you a world champion. The world championship title was what we were chasing. And Lou was asking me to claim it before I'd earned it.

My stomach lurched. I actually stepped back from her, like she was something dangerous. My whole body was screaming that this was wrong. Australians don't talk about things before we do them. We act first, talk later. We have massive tall poppy syndrome — don't stick your head above the crowd or it will get cut down. What Lou was asking us to say felt fake, like we were tempting fate.

I remember thinking: *I don't know if I want to work with this woman. This is too much.* But I said the words anyway.

'I am world champion.'

It felt like someone else was saying it — like I was watching myself from outside my body, listening to a stranger claim something he hadn't earned. The dissonance was almost unbearable. And then, it started working.

Lou's sessions weren't just about words. We would visualise problems we might encounter — mechanical failures; tactical scenarios; the pain cave at three minutes (a place you enter where the pain pushes you further and further into the dark, deeper and deeper, until your body and mind are begging you to stop) — and we'd resolve them in our heads and hearts before they ever happened. If those things came up on race day, we'd already dealt with them.

She got remarkably technical. We'd talk about gearing and aerodynamics, and Lou actually learned our cycling lingo even though she'd never ridden at any level that would make her understand that language naturally. She took it all on because she understood that manifestation isn't abstract — it's specific.

Lou would always correct us: not 'you will be' but 'you are'. Present tense, not future tense. She made us talk about our future dreams as if they were our current reality. And when you do that — when you declare something to already be true — you make yourself do the work to ensure that future version of yourself doesn't disappear. You can't let that version of yourself down.

Mick and I had sessions with Lou both together and separately. And then, in our hotel rooms before races, we'd sit in silence doing the visualisations and energy work in our heads. Saying it out loud to each other — two Aussie blokes declaring we were world champions — was a step too far. It felt way too wanky.

But in our heads and hearts, we both knew. We had already won.

One night, after we'd had a session with Lou during the day, I was lying in bed going through the exercises she'd asked us to do. It's not just about the sessions — there's energy and presence training you have to do every day, multiple times a day. Most people think manifestation is a one-time declaration, but it's not. It's constant work.

As I lay there, I remembered how fast we were in Melbourne at Nationals. I remembered how good we were in Canada. I knew how much more powerful and dialled in Mick and I had become. I knew how much we wanted it, and how much mongrel we were both willing to put in to make it happen. If anyone stood in our way on the track, we wouldn't back down. We would destroy ourselves in pain and suffering to ensure we got the result.

That was the moment I started living as a world champion before I even was one. The declaration stopped feeling fake. Those thoughts were the evidence I needed. In my head, in my heart, it felt true.

Into uncharted territory

The velodrome in Aguascalientes sits in the mountains of Mexico, at 1887 metres above sea level — roughly 6200 feet. We knew we were racing at altitude, but we didn't know what that would mean for us.

The physics cut both ways. Less air means less resistance — you travel faster for the same power output, with better aerodynamic efficiency. But less air also means less oxygen. And for an endurance event like the four-kilometre pursuit, oxygen is everything. Your muscles are screaming for it. Your lungs are burning for it. And there's just … less of it.

I was fully prepared for racing at altitude. I'd been using the 'live high, train low' method, including training while sleeping in an altitude tent at home (to simulate altitude).

There was no world-championship-level data available for endurance tandems racing at altitude. We were stepping into completely unknown territory. Would the reduced resistance outweigh the oxygen deficit? Would our bodies adapt? Would the times be faster or slower than sea level?

Nobody knew. We were about to find out.

Because we'd posted the fastest time in the world for 2013, we were the highest seed. That meant we qualified last. We got to see everyone else's times before we raced. That 4:16 was in our sights.

About 20 tandems were competing. We were sitting in the Team Australia area in the pits, hours before our heat. Mick was following the early qualifiers, feeding me updates. We hadn't even started warming up yet.

One of the Spanish teams went out in the very first heat of the day.

They clocked 4:12.

They didn't just break the world record. They obliterated it. Four seconds faster than the time that had stood for years. Four seconds faster than the number we had lived and breathed for months. In elite sport, world records fall by hundredths of a second — by tenths if you're lucky. This was unprecedented.

The entire velodrome deflated. I could hear it around me — helmets being thrown, bike gear being dropped, the collective exhale of defeat. Teams that had trained for years to challenge 4:16 suddenly realised they weren't even close. The goal had moved four seconds further away in an instant.

Within two minutes of the 4:12 being announced, before the second heat had even started, Mick and I turned to each other.

At exactly the same moment, we both said: '4:11.'

And then we giggled.

It wasn't something we thought about. It wasn't a discussion. We both just said it at the same time — a reaction, not a decision. Without using words, we had told each other: 'We've got this.'

It was a moment of absolute alignment when two people who have trained together, suffered together and believed together recognise the same thing at the same time. Everyone else had given up. The 4:12 had broken them. But we had spent months with Lou, owning a reality that didn't exist yet. We had declared ourselves world champions before we'd earned it. And now, when the moment demanded something absurd, we were ready to be absurd.

Why not? If they could go four seconds under the old record, we could go five.

Heat after heat went by as we waited. Nobody came close to the 4:12. The Spanish time stood alone, untouchable. But we had already made our decision.

Our heat was last. We were up against another Spanish tandem team — strong competitors who would push us. To qualify for the gold medal final, we needed the fastest time of the day. We needed to beat a world record that had only existed for a few hours.

We went to our coach. 'We're going to do 4:11.' He shook his head. 'Boys, I don't think so. That's unrealistic. You've never trained for that.'

'We didn't come here to come second,' we said. 'Full gas win, or don't worry about it.'

However, to do 4:11, we needed a bigger gear than anyone had ever ridden at a world championship.

Track bikes have fixed gears — you pick one gear and that's it for the entire race. We had a 58-tooth chainring that we'd had custom-made in titanium by an engineer in Melbourne. It was massive, like a dinner plate on the front of the bike. No one had ever raced a gear that big at this level. And the thing was, we had never actually ridden with it either. We'd never put it on a bike or tested it in training. Even our coach didn't think we could race with it. It was insurance — a gear we'd made just in case we ever needed to go faster than we thought possible.

Now we needed it.

We bolted the 58-tooth ring to our tandem, prepared to race.

The longest wait

The bike is held in a starting gate by a hydraulic claw gripping the rear wheel. You can't roll forward until it releases. Twenty seconds before the start, a beep sounds. Your heart rate wants to spike, adrenaline flooding your system, but you can't let that happen. If your heart rate climbs too high before you've even started, you'll blow up before the finish. So, you breathe. You control. You find that space where everything goes quiet.

At 10 seconds, another beep. Another spike of adrenaline. You absorb it. Keep breathing.

Then the final five: beep, beep, beep, beep, beep. And the gate releases.

Those five seconds are the longest of your life. Your head is fighting a battle of a thousand thoughts. You're trying to think of nothing but the timer, trying to block out the sounds of the crowd, but little thoughts keep flashing through. Flash: my son at home. Flash: my parents sacrificing to bring me up. Flash: my wife alone with the baby. Flash: don't go back to work without a gold medal, that will be embarrassing. Flash, flash, flash, flash. But you're trying to just focus on the timer and get your timing right. You're thinking, *Don't fuck this up.*

If you don't have split-second timing coming out of the gate, it's all over. Literally all over. The tandem adds another layer — you have to be in absolute sync with your pilot. Then balance on top of that; thoughts of staying calm. Adrenaline is pumping through your body and you're trying to stop it.

People think it's stressful waiting outside a meeting room before a big pitch. You get to go in, do small talk, repeat yourself if you get something wrong. There's no repeating anything in the racing environment. Every single thing has to be perfect, and you need to be putting out more physical power than any other human on the planet while getting all the technical excellence correct. That's a lot. But that's those five seconds.

Finding my deeper why

When we finally came out of the gate, the gear felt enormous. The resistance was unlike anything I had felt before — that much force required just to get the pedals turning. We couldn't hold the bike on the line. We started dropping down towards the centre of the velodrome.

For anyone who doesn't know cycling: that's not supposed to happen. You're meant to stay on the race line. Dropping below it means you're struggling. It means the gear is too big to push.

It felt like we were showing up to a Formula 1 race with an engine nobody had ever tested at race speed and bolting it on five minutes before lights out.

But we got on top of it. The bike started moving. We rolled through the first corner, finally got in the saddle and settled into our pace.

After about a minute, the altitude started kicking in. With less oxygen, breathing was getting harder. I focused on rhythm, on a song I'd been singing in my head during training — The Wiggles asking who's in the house, with me answering that I was. The simple call-and-response rhythm matched my pedal cadence perfectly. Max was six weeks old, and that song had wormed its way into my brain during all those nights helping Bex with the baby.

At two and a half minutes in, everything started hurting. It was the kind of pain that makes your thoughts fragment. But I had to keep going: keep my form. Stay aerodynamic. Keep pumping the power out.

At the three-minute mark, the pain went beyond anything I could describe. And that's when something shifted.

I started thinking about my parents. All the sacrifices they had made. The years of driving me to training. The times Dad defended me at school. They had been told their blind son would never play sport, never get a real job, never amount to much. And here I was, on the other side of the world, racing for a world title. I couldn't let them down.

Then I thought about Bex. At home with our six-week-old baby. Alone. Exhausted. Handling everything while I chased a dream that most people would call selfish. She had never once made me feel guilty. I couldn't let her down.

And then I thought about Max. My baby boy. I wanted to give him something to be proud of. I wanted to show him and his future siblings, from the very beginning, that their dad didn't give up when it got hard.

Something unlocked in my body. The pain was still there, but it stopped mattering. The emotional fuel of the people I loved — the desire not to let them down, the desire to make them proud — became my secret weapon. I had tapped into my deeper why.

The last 30 seconds of a four-kilometre pursuit is a place most humans will never visit. Your lungs feel like they've been turned inside out — like they're drying out. I can't explain how much your lungs hurt. Your legs feel like they have lava running through them, but it's lava that's turning into solid rock while staying hot.

Everything wants to fail. Your core, your calves, your quads — they all just want to stop. The only thing making them continue to turn is the thousands of hours of pain you've put them through. You go into turbo pain mode. Suffering mode. It's race day stuff. You could never access this in training. The crowd, the gold medal and the pride drive you on. And if you've done the training, if you've built enough power in your legs and your mind, the suffering turns into a gold medal.

Even within this suffering, you actually start putting even more effort in during the last few laps. Well, you think you are. You increase your effort, but your power is draining away as your muscles run out of the ability to generate any force. If you wobble the bike at all, you slow down. If you change your pedal technique, you slow down. If you lift your head slightly, you create drag and slow down. If you do anything different, you slow down.

So you stay in that exact position and continue to suffer.

With about a lap and a half to go, we caught the other tandem. They were in our way — we had to swing wide to go around them, which meant we had to travel further, which cost us time. Tom was yelling out our splits, and although I couldn't hear them all through the crowd noise, I heard enough to know we were flying. We later found out we were averaging nearly 70 kilometres per hour.

We crossed the finish line and the place went absolutely mental. Thousands of people were screaming. But I was blind: I didn't know what had happened. I couldn't see the numbers. And Mick couldn't talk—he was so cooked he could barely breathe.

We just rolled around the track as the bike slowly lost momentum. The crowd was going crazy, and I assumed that meant something good, but I wouldn't let myself celebrate until I was sure. I knew we could break the world record, but years of bluffing shame had taught me not to claim something I wasn't certain of. I didn't have the visual data I needed to know it for a fact.

It was almost a minute before one of the physios who had helped us come to a stop said the words: 'You did it. 4:11.'

4:11.213. We had broken the world record we'd been aiming for by over five seconds in our qualifying race. On a gear no one had ever ridden at a world championship, at altitude. With a newborn baby at home and a shoulder that could dislocate at any moment. All the work with Lou had been about becoming world champions, not breaking a world record. The record was a shock—a product of us chasing the title, not the goal itself.

At that point, only two humans had ever ridden a four-kilometre pursuit faster than Mick and I just had, and they were riding single bikes, not tandems. The individual world record was held by another Aussie, Jack Bobridge, with a time of 4:10.534 set in 2011. Before him, it was Chris Boardman's 4:11.114 from 1996. On a tandem, you have more weight, so more coordination is required and you have a slower start. And we had come within 0.6 seconds of the current individual world record. This wasn't a para world record. This was the fastest two humans had ever travelled together on a tandem, and almost the fastest any bike had ever completed four kilometres from a standing start in competition.

But that was only the qualifier. We still had to race the final.

It would have been easy to lose ourselves in that moment. We'd just broken a world record. The crowd was screaming. The adrenaline was still coursing through our bodies. We could have celebrated, let the emotion take over, gotten ahead of ourselves.

We didn't. We knew the job wasn't done.

As professionals, we got back into our recovery immediately. The velodrome that morning had been 38 degrees. By the afternoon, it would be 48 degrees inside that wooden bowl. We needed to be ready. We found a cool spot under the stadium to recover and get everything sorted: hydration, nutrition, rest. We treated the afternoon final like a completely separate race, because it was.

The world record was a trophy we'd earned on the journey to the title. But we'd come for gold.

Finish what you started

A four-kilometre pursuit takes a year off your life. It's not literally true but it's something we say in cycling, and it captures something real — the stress it places on your heart, the depth of suffering required. And we had to do it twice in one day.

As we warmed up for the final, Mick made eye contact with the other team's pilot across the room. He turned to me afterwards. 'We've already beaten them,' he said. 'I could see it in their eyes. They're already defeated.'

We had already broken the world record in qualifying, and we'd already broken them mentally. Then we went out and smashed them physically. We were world champions. World record holders.

Standing on that podium, the medal was heavy around my neck — and hot in that high heat. I could feel it burning against my skin while the Australian anthem played.

That gold medal was for my boy. For Bex and my parents. And for everyone who'd told me I couldn't do it.

Lou was one of the first people we called with the result. We called her from the velodrome, still covered in sweat, with our medals around our necks.

'Oh, that's great,' she said, with absolute confidence in her voice. 'You backed yourselves and believed it, and it turned up. I knew from the moment we started working together it would.'

She wasn't shocked; she wasn't surprised. She had owned our victory before we ever did. She had lived in the reality of us being world champions from the very first session, even when we were stepping back from her, sick to our stomachs, unable to say the words. She had believed it enough for all of us until we could believe it for ourselves.

Alignment, not magic

In the years since Mexico, I've used manifestation in every arena of my life.

The thing that separates manifestation from delusion is that you have to do the work. Lou never told us we could visualise our way to a world title. She made us identify every obstacle and address them. The mental work amplified the physical work.

Manifestation is not magic: it's alignment. It's getting your conscious mind, your subconscious mind and your physical preparation all pointed towards the same target. It's owning the delusion until it stops being delusional.

On that day in Mexico, when one of the Spanish teams smashed the world record and everyone else gave up, Mick and I turned to each other and saw two men who had already become world champions in their minds. We giggled because we knew 4:11 was possible. And then we went out and made it real.

That same year, in 2014, I smashed my sales target at work. I earned a place on our company's Pace Setter trip for top achievers. I'd done it all: had my first baby, won a world title, broken a world record and delivered corporate success. But as I was about to find out, burning the candle at both ends like that would come at a cost.

Neuroscience research has demonstrated that the brain cannot fully distinguish between vividly imagined experiences and real ones. When athletes mentally rehearse a movement, the same neural pathways activate as when they physically perform it. Studies at Harvard Medical School found that participants who merely imagined practising piano exercises showed nearly the same brain changes as those who physically practised. The mind shapes the body's capacity. Own the delusion long enough, and your neural architecture rewires itself to make it possible.

• • •

What would you attempt if you already knew you were capable of it? What's the goal you haven't declared because it feels too big to say out loud?

Chapter 15

From Wheels to Waves

Two Gears, One Engine

> I had spent my whole cycling career learning to push — to override the signals, to mongrel through pain, to find another gear when the tank felt empty. But there was a gear I had never learned to use: the one where you stop; where you let your body rebuild instead of tearing it down. I had to learn what happens when you refuse to shift down. And para surfing taught me what becomes possible when you truly learn to use both gears — to know when to go fast and when to go slow.

'You are never going to believe it. They are going to let you blind fuckers compete against each other.'

That was the text message. It was July 2016. I was lying in a nice hotel room at Lake Garda in Italy, curtains open, wind billowing in over the balcony, tired after a big day of speed training on the track. My phone buzzed, and VoiceOver read the message aloud. It was from a mate from Sydney, who'd also shared a hyperlink.

I clicked on the link, which took me to the International Surfing Association website. A press release announced the first-ever world championships with a blind category, to be held in La Jolla, California, in December 2016.

The boys and I had joked about this for years. Out in the surf at Narrabeen, sitting in the lineup waiting for sets with salt water dripping from our faces, someone would always bring it up. Usually after I had done a good turn or caught a wave where everything connected.

'Imagine if they let you blind fuckers compete against each other,' they would say. 'You would destroy them. Surely there is no blind guy out there who can beat you surfing.'

And we would all laugh and say it would never happen. There would be absolute carnage — guys running each other over, boards flying everywhere, fins slicing through the chaos.

It was a joke. A fantasy. Something we talked about to pass the time between sets. And now it was real.

The Rio Paralympics were just weeks away, and I was super excited. I was still focused on winning, still doing everything I could to get it right. But while reading that press release, I felt a spark of excitement for something other than cycling.

The whole time I had been cycling, I had not been surfing — too much risk of a fin chop or injury that would stop me from training or racing. Now, there was a chance to go back to my first love. Not just to surf, but to compete.

It was a distraction while I was trying to prepare for the Paralympic Games. But it was also a reason to be excited about what came next.

Withdrawing without depositing

My body had started breaking down a year earlier, in the Netherlands.

The moment we landed at the Apeldoorn Velodrome for the 2015 Para-cycling Track World Championships, I got sick. A virus hit me like a truck — the kind of illness that doesn't announce itself gradually but arrives all at once, overwhelming your body before you have time to react. I had a high fever and pounding headaches that made light feel like pain. My lungs were rattling like a diesel engine.

I spent the entire week in bed, lying in a dark room, getting up only to eat a little and then falling back asleep. The coaches were sort of neutral — telling me to look after myself while hoping I would race. They didn't want one of their top athletes to pull out. The medical staff told me to be careful about elevating my heart rate while I was sick.

But we were in the qualifying window for Rio. Mick and I were the reigning world champions and world record holders. We had built something special together. This was not the time to quit. Or so I told myself.

On race day, literally the morning of the world championships, I dragged myself out of bed and went to warm up. I was sitting in the Team Australia area, feeling absolutely terrible. I had taken some Panadol, which had helped, but the headache was still there, the fever was still burning, my lungs were still aching with every breath. And then I heard a bang echo through the velodrome — a tyre blowout, then the thud. You always listen for the thud that follows the bang. If you hear the bang without the thud, the rider has stayed upright; if you hear the thud, someone has gone down hard.

The thud came. Someone had gone down at speed.

The coaches told everyone not to look as the rider was stretchered out. I didn't need to look away — I couldn't see anyway — but I heard later what had happened. The crash had lifted a piece of timber from the track, and at 60-plus kilometres per hour, that splinter had gone straight through the rider's abdomen. A piece of wood as thick as a middle finger, piercing all the way through. The rider was rushed to hospital in a critical condition.

We raced. We qualified second fastest out of the whole field, which meant we were in the gold medal ride that afternoon. But I had given the qualifier everything my sick body could muster — pushed my heart rate into the 180s while my immune system was already failing, then held it there for four brutal kilometres. When it came to the final, I had nothing left. The tank was empty. We got silver, which felt like a loss when we were there to win another gold.

Afterwards, I shook hands with the Dutch stoker who had beaten us. Just a normal post-race moment — two competitors showing respect. But as we stood there, he started to tear up. His voice broke.

'I was never going to lose today,' he said. 'I was racing for my brother.'

And then it clicked. The crash. The splinter through the abdomen. The rider stretchered out in critical condition. That was his brother — a pilot on a sprint tandem in the Dutch team, racing in a different discipline. This was their home world championships, with their family and friends in the crowd. Now his brother was in a hospital bed instead of on the track, and this stoker had lined up for the pursuit final carrying something I never knew I was competing against.

I understood that fire. I had felt it myself the year before, racing for my family. He had that same burning inside him, and I'm not sure I could have matched it even if I was healthy. Not that day. Not against that.

From that world championship event on, my body never really recovered.

There was a world cup road race in New Zealand a few weeks later. We raced it. We won. But I wasn't well. I could feel something fundamental had shifted inside me, some reserve that had been depleted and wasn't refilling. And Cycling Australia kept asking us to race. We were in the qualifying window, winning points for Australia's Paralympic allocation, and the pressure was on.

We kept saying yes. We kept racing. We kept winning. And I kept getting sicker.

At home between races, I could barely train. I would spend weeks in bed, completely exhausted, then drag myself back onto the bike, fly to another country, race again. I was tapping into reserves I had built over years of 4.30 am sessions, but I wasn't depositing anything new to recharge myself. I was withdrawing from the bank account without making any deposits.

Eventually, inevitably, the account ran dry. A sports medicine doctor tested my blood and gave me the diagnosis: post-viral fatigue. He said it was something that only athletes and business executives get, and I had been doing both at the same time, burning the candle way too hard at both ends. I hadn't given my body the time to recover from that first virus; I'd pushed my heart rate into the 180s while my immune system was already compromised; I'd stripped away my body's ability to defend itself. My immunity was gone. Completely gone.

The doctors told me to rest. Bex told me to rest. Everyone who cared about me could see what I was doing to myself. But I ignored them all, terrified that if I stopped, I would lose my spot in Rio.

The lesson I should have learned — the lesson I did eventually learn — was simple: when your body says no, you have to listen. I didn't listen. And I paid for it.

Partnerships cannot be manufactured

Then Mick decided he wasn't going to Rio.

He is one of the only people in Australia — maybe the world — to qualify for a spot at the Paralympics or Olympics and say, 'No thanks.' But Mick had been racing for years. He had given everything to the sport, sacrificed time with his family and pushed his body through the same suffering I had. Now he was looking to move into the next part of his life.

He didn't think he could give Rio what it deserved — the total commitment, the obsessive focus — so he retired.

I understood, but understanding didn't mean it hurt less. This was the man I had giggled with before we broke the world record. The man I had spent thousands of hours training beside, suffering beside, winning beside. We had built something together that felt almost supernatural — the ability to make a tandem feel like one body instead of two. And now he was moving on.

They paired me with a younger pilot. On paper, he had a higher power profile — more raw watts, more physical potential — but we hadn't done the time together: we hadn't built the trust that lets you descend at speed or attack at exactly the right moment. It didn't feel the same as when I was with Mick — we didn't have that certainty, that unshakeable confidence that we had already won before we even lined up. Partnerships like that cannot be manufactured in a few months.

As a result, Rio wasn't what I'd hoped for. We finished fifth in the pursuit, just outside qualifying for the bronze final. I had a similar result in the kilo — a one-kilometre time trial where everyone gets one effort and the fastest time wins. The road race and road time trial were much worse. I was excited to be there, but I felt nervous — I didn't have the confidence I'd had with Mick. It wasn't the Louise Laffey version: *We have already won this.* It was a more superficial version: *I hope we win this.*

The fire was still there. I was trying my hardest. But the circumstances didn't help, and the results were not what I had hoped for.

Starting from zero

As soon as I got home from Rio, I started hammering Surfing Australia. Within a couple of weeks, I was on the phone asking what I needed to do to get on the team for 2017. I didn't think 2016 was even a possibility.

The lady on the phone said: 'Well, we have got a qualifier on the Gold Coast next weekend.'

Ten days from that phone call. I rang Bex, and we organised a family holiday to the Gold Coast.

She said I probably wouldn't win because I hadn't been doing much surfing while I was cycling, but we went anyway.

I had never had a spotter before. I had always been too independent to let anyone help me in the ocean — I would just surf by myself, reading the waves through feel. Now I had some random person in the water with me, telling me what waves to catch. I don't even remember who it was.

Neither of us knew what we were doing; it was all very clunky. But I won. I won that competition and qualified for the 2016 ISA Para Surfing world championships as part of Team Australia.

At that qualifier, I connected with a coach named Samba Mann from Surfing Australia's high performance centre. He saw something in my surfing, and we started talking about what was possible. I was starting again, but everything was starting to come together.

My brother Stu came with me to the world championships in La Jolla. This time he was my spotter. Neither of us had ever done a surf comp before. We didn't even know about the wave count. Each competitor has a maximum number of waves they can catch in a heat — exceed it and you're done, regardless of the time remaining. I nearly exceeded mine in one of the heats. We had no idea what was going on.

Everything about competitive surfing was different from competitive cycling. In cycling, there were physios, nutritionists, bike mechanics and coaches tracking every metric. In surfing, we had one guy who doubled as a team coach and team manager, and he wasn't doing a lot of either. Everyone was drinking beers. The atmosphere was relaxed in a way elite sport rarely is. It felt like coming home.

We came third: a bronze medal at the first-ever ISA World Para Surfing Championships. Standing on that podium with my brother, with both of us getting medals together, was pretty cool. But I was super hungry to get gold. Bronze was not enough.

Building new systems

After La Jolla, I reached out to Samba about coaching me properly. He agreed, and we started working together towards the 2017 World Championships.

The gold standard of surf coaching is video comparison — you watch yourself on an iPad next to footage of the best surfers in the world, frame by frame, seeing exactly where your body position differs from theirs. It is the most effective way to identify bad technique because surfing happens so fast and is so visual. You cannot feel what you are doing wrong, but you can see it instantly when your technique is playing beside Hawaiian surfer John John Florence's technique.

But I cannot see video. I cannot see the iPad. I cannot see John John Florence.

So, Samba had to invent a completely different method. He would film my surfing, then watch the footage himself so he could bring it back to his memory. After a surf, we would stand on the beach, and he would say: 'Remember that turn you did on this wave?' I would have to memorise the wave, the turn. Then he would talk through the corrections — where I should have had my hands, how I should have had my weight over my front foot or back foot.

Then he would physically move my body into the positions he was trying to describe. His hands were on my arms, adjusting the angle. His foot was nudging mine into the right stance. He would rotate my hands in or out, open my shoulders or close them, depending on what was needed. He would place my hands exactly where they needed to be at the top of a turn, shift my weight between front foot and back foot, and say: 'This. Feel this. This is what it should feel like.'

I would memorise the position in my muscles — the angle of my shoulders, the bend in my knees, the distribution of weight through my feet. Then I would paddle back out and try to recreate that feeling on a moving wave.

He was reprogramming 30 years of bad habits through touch alone.

The other thing we built was the spotting system for competition. No manual existed. We tried clock directions at first — paddle to 10 o'clock, paddle to 2 o'clock. But it didn't really help much, and there were too many words, so we stripped it back to basics. Six words: in. Out. North. South. Yes. No.

'In' meant closer to shore. 'Out' meant closer to the horizon. 'Yes' meant paddle for the wave. We learned never to say 'go' — it sounds too much like 'no' in the water. 'No' was important, too — it could mean someone else was on the wave and I was about to drop in on them, or it was the wrong wave. I had to stop as soon as I heard anything that sounded like 'no'.

Once I was on the wave, it was all feel — 30 years of instinct and reading the water through my feet.

Quality over quantity

The 2017 World Championships were back in La Jolla.

I came prepared this time. I had six boards instead of two. I was sponsored by Firewire now and had spent the year testing their equipment. Samba and I had trained together for 12 months.

The six-word system was second nature. We had won every heat to get here.

And then came the final.

We sat out the back, waiting for sets. I got one good score early, a 7.6, and then the ocean went quiet where we were sitting. The other three competitors were all sitting on a different bank a bit further south. They were catching waves. They were scoring. We were not. My backup score was only a 4. In surfing, your final score is your top two waves added together. A 7.6 and a 4 was not going to win a world championship.

I had three minutes left. The ocean was flat out the back. No sets were coming.

Samba and I discussed paddling in a bit — not all the way to shore, but closer to where the mid-sized waves were breaking. We would have more options there. But they were lower-quality waves. They were unlikely to get us the score we needed.

We decided to stay out the back and hope a set rolled through. Quality over quantity. It was a gamble

After sitting in a start gate and hearing the clock tick down on a velodrome, nothing in surfing was ever going to stress me out.

I had 45 seconds left, and then a set came.

'Matty, get ready. Get ready.' His voice transformed — urgent, focused. We paddled south, positioning. 'Yes, yes, yes, yes, yes.'

I caught the wave. I could feel it was good — the power under my board, the face opening up in front of me. I hit four turns, each one connecting, each one flowing into the next, feeling the rail dig in and release. And then the wave was done.

As I finished, I could hear Team Australia screaming from the beach: 'Aussie, Aussie, Aussie!' I knew they were all frothing. Within half a minute, the finish horn sounded.

Samba and I sat on our boards, bobbing in the ocean next to each other. The Pacific was quiet around us. The crowd on the beach was distant. Neither of us said a word. We were too scared to speak in case we missed the beach broadcast announcer.

Then I heard the blur of the far-off loudspeaker. Fragments of words carrying across the water: 'Australia ... Formston ... World Champ ...'

Samba turned to me. 'I fucking knew it. There were buckets coming off the back of that thing.'

He was talking about the spray — the water my board had been throwing off the back of the wave with every turn. When you are surfing well, when your rail is digging in and releasing properly, it throws buckets of spray off the lip. He had seen it from the back of the wave. He knew before the score dropped.

Then the number came through clearly: 9.2.

We both jumped off our boards and wrestle-hugged in the water, almost drowning each other, laughing and yelling, salt water in our mouths. And the sound from the beach was amazing — the whole crowd screaming and cheering, their voices carrying across the water to where we were thrashing around in celebration.

I was a world champion in two sports.

We caught the same wave in together, shoulder to shoulder, while lying on our boards — riding the whitewater all the way to shore.

When we arrived on the sand, Team Australia was waiting. They had formed a tunnel — Australian flags, boxing kangaroo flags, blow-up kangaroos, the whole bit.

In surfing, there is a tradition: the world champion doesn't walk up the beach. The world champion doesn't touch the sand. You get chaired — hoisted onto the shoulders of your teammates and carried like royalty through the crowd to the stage.

Samba and one of the other boys grabbed me and lifted me up. Suddenly I was sitting high on their shoulders, looking out over the beach I couldn't see but I could feel it — the energy, the noise, the cameras clicking, the crowd clapping.

Someone had my board behind me, holding it up so all the footage and photos would include the sponsor stickers. Firewire. Optus. Billabong. All the brands that had backed a blind surfer when no one knew if this was even possible.

Red Dog Wheatley led the chant. Red Dog was a giant redhead from Newcastle with no legs and one of the most respected para surfers in the country. His voice boomed across the beach: 'Aussie, Aussie, Aussie!'

And the whole team responded: 'Oi, oi oi!'

The chant echoed as we moved through the tunnel. Cameras surrounded us. The whole beach clapped as we went up towards the athletes' area. I sat up there on their shoulders, salt water still dripping from my wetsuit, sand I was not allowed to touch passing beneath me, and I thought about everything it had taken to get there.

The illness in the Netherlands. The silver that felt like a loss. The post-viral fatigue. Mick retiring. Rio. The phone call six weeks later. The qualifier I almost didn't enter. The spotter system we built from nothing. The wave that came with 30 seconds left.

And now this: carried up the beach as a world champion, in the sport I had loved since I was 11 years old.

Using both gears

The first person I called was Bex and the kids.

The second person I called was my boss at work — Stu Pritchard — because without my workplace giving me the flexibility to live dual lives, none of this would have been possible.

Then I called my parents. And after those calls, we celebrated.

Winning world titles in cycling had been incredible — years of 4.30 am sessions and altitude camps. The surfing title came faster, just over a year from that first Gold Coast qualifier to standing on top of the podium.

Surfing was where my heart had always been. It was my first love. To win a world title in the sport I truly loved was an absolute privilege.

A year and a half earlier, I had been lying in a dark room in the Netherlands, my body broken. Then came a text message about a joke that became real. A recovery. A phone call that led to a qualifier 10 days later. A spotter system we invented from nothing. A wave that arrived with 30 seconds left.

'You are never going to believe it. They are going to let you blind fuckers compete against each other.'

Turns out, we could. And I did. Why not?

Sports scientists at the Australian Institute of Sport have studied overtraining syndrome and its relationship to immune function. Their research confirms what my body taught me the hard way: when athletes push through illness without adequate recovery, they don't just delay healing, they can cause lasting damage to their immune system. The body keeps score. Elite performance requires knowing when to push and when to stop. The athletes who last longest are not the ones who train hardest—they are the ones who recover smartest. Two gears, one engine. You need both.

• • •

What signal has your business, your team, or your own energy been sending you that you've been refusing to hear? The declining numbers you've explained away. The role that no longer fits. The strategy you know isn't working but haven't had the courage to kill. What would change if you stopped ignoring the signal and acted on it?

Chapter 16

No Worries, I'll Take Him Out

The Hard Way Is the Easy Way

> Most people wait until they feel ready, but the work you do now makes your future self's life easier. Champions build capacity before they need it. They do the hard work before the hard work, so when the moment comes, they have already done it a hundred times in their body and their mind.

I was surfing at Hollow Trees in Indonesia, working the lineup alone, and I was terrified.

This was one of the most famous right-hand waves in the world—meaning the surfer rides to the right from the take-off point. The guys from my boat were out there somewhere but, without a dedicated spotter, I was fending for myself. And somewhere down the line from where I was sitting, hidden in water I couldn't see through, was a section the locals called the surgeon's table. A flat plate of coral with fingers sticking up like little hands. If you fell there, those fingers would rip holes in you. Big holes. The kind that needed serious stitches.

The nearest decent hospital was in Singapore. Twelve hours by boat to Padang, then a flight across the strait. If something went wrong out there, you were a long way from help.

I had been in the water for three hours. Made maybe two waves. Got absolutely pumped on every other attempt. I kept being in the wrong spot, too far in front of the waves, too far behind. I couldn't get into the right position to make it down the line. I would get smashed on the take-off, washed over the reef and then have to paddle in over shallow coral, skimming my hands over the top so I could find my way around the back of the surgeon's table, and then paddle all the way back out again. The paddle of shame, over and over.

Every time I surfaced, I kept my body as flat and rigid as possible, staying shallow on the surface so I wouldn't get ripped on the coral beneath me. The waves weren't huge — four to six foot — but you aren't worried about drowning out there. You're worried about getting shredded on the reef.

This was supposed to be the trip of a lifetime. The Mentawai Islands, a chain off the coast of Sumatra, accessible only after two flights from Australia and a 12-hour overnight boat crossing. Eight surfers, two cameramen, 10 of us on a boat chasing perfect waves.

And I had come without a dedicated spotter. That was my mistake.

Before we even paddled out that morning, a guy from another boat was brought back from the lineup with blood streaming down his face. He needed 16 stitches to put his head back together. He had fallen on the surgeon's table on day one of this trip of a lifetime. And now he was sitting on a boat with his head sewn shut, watching everyone else surf through the window.

I paddled out anyway. Because that is what I do.

Most of the other guys weren't having the session of their lives either. The conditions weren't perfect that day — bumpy, inconsistent, hard to read. Half the guys on the boat actually went back in because it was too difficult, even though they could see. Only a young semi-pro with us was landing airs over the surgeon's table while everyone else struggled.

But that isn't how I roll. I stayed out there and kept trying. Trying and trying and trying. Because that is what I do.

Sitting in that lineup, more uncomfortable and nerve-wracked than I had ever been in the ocean, I thought about the question everyone asks me: 'How did you get here — alone at a world-class wave on the other side of the planet without a spotter?'

The answer starts with a text message.

Two words that changed everything

I had just retired from cycling. It was February 2017, just after my daughter, Elsie, was born. I was back home, back in the ocean, and I was excited. This was what I had dreamed about as a kid — chasing waves like the pro surfers I grew up hearing about from my mates. Now I was a sponsored surfer, travelling the world and competing in the sport I loved.

There was a big swell coming: six to eight foot. And there was a wave near my house, near Wamberal on the Central coast, that I had always wanted to surf but never had — a right-hand point break that peeled off a headland and broke over rocks. I had lived in the area for five years while I was a professional cyclist, and the whole time I had heard about this wave. I had been desperate to surf it once I retired.

As a blind person, I was the ultimate outsider. I had never surfed this wave. I had no mental map of where the rocks were, where the deep water channels ran, where to paddle out to and where to sit. Starting from zero at a dangerous break is hard enough when you can see. When you cannot, it borders on reckless.

Bex put out a message on the mothers' group WhatsApp: 'There's a big swell coming on Monday. Can anyone's husband take Matt out?'

I found out later that every other dad in that group said no: too sketchy, too big. That wave is scary. He is blind, what if something happens? All the perfectly reasonable excuses that keep most people safely on the shore.

But one guy said yes.

Phil Shaw. I had never met him. Never surfed with him. Never even had a conversation with him. His wife Helen messaged back: 'Yeah, Phil said no worries. He'll take him out.'

No worries. Two words that changed everything.

Most people treat a blind surfer like a liability. They hover. They over-explain. Their anxiety becomes my anxiety.

Phil did none of that. Phil picked me up the next morning and treated me like another surfer. Paddled out, orientated me to where the rocks were in relation to the breaking waves. Called me into a couple of good ones when he saw them coming. The rest of the time, he let me do my own thing. Trusted me to read the water, feel the waves, make my own decisions.

The wave was everything I had hoped. A long right-hander with enough power to really drive down the line. The rocks at the beginning kept most people away, though there were still a fair few out. I caught some of the best waves of my life that day. Waves I had been dreaming about for years, finally ridden.

When we paddled in, Phil said, 'I think there's more waves tomorrow. Want to go again?'

Build capacity before you need it

What began as a one-off favour became a partnership. Phil and I started surfing together every chance we got. We never made excuses. Whatever the conditions were, we just went out. He would paddle out and I would paddle next to him.

Eight foot became comfortable, so we looked for 10. Ten foot became manageable, so we started chasing 12, then 16. We bought gun boards together, seven-foot-eight and eight-foot-six boards we could share, designed for serious waves. The kinds of boards that sit in the corner of your garage most of the year, waiting for the days when everything else feels too small.

A few years after that first session, we paddled out at the same spot in conditions that made our first day together look like a warm-up: 15- to 20-foot faces. One of the biggest swells in 30 years.

Up the coast, houses were nearly washing into the ocean. The beach eroded so badly in a single day that staircases collapsed, backyards disappeared, debris was strewn across the sand. Emergency services were evacuating dozens of residents. News helicopters were filming the destruction from above.

We were the only two people who paddled out.

A few of the other boys who normally surf bigger waves with us had driven up to watch from the headland. They saw us out there, two dots on a churning ocean, and later told us they had been wondering who those two idiots were. When they realised it was us, they just shook their heads. Of course it was us. Who else would it be?

The paddle took 40 minutes. We had to go wide, way out through open water, because the waves were breaking so far out that the normal channel was impossible. We made it about halfway when a freak set came through and completely rolled us both. The whitewater dragged us back across the reef, all the way into the bay. Forty minutes of paddling erased in 30 seconds. We had to start the entire paddle again.

There is something funny about Phil and me in the water together. When he gets water in his ears, he basically goes deaf — cannot hear a thing until he clears his ears out. So, you have the deaf guy and the blind guy, paddling out in 15-foot surf, trying to communicate through a wall of noise and chaos. He would be yelling stuff at me, which I could hear. Then I would yell back, but he couldn't hear me.

I didn't catch a single wave that day. I couldn't find my way into position. But I was out there. I was comfortable enough to function in conditions that would terrify most surfers. That was the point.

The real danger lives on land

While I was building capacity locally with Phil, I was also travelling internationally with different spotters. After winning the world title in 2017, I went to events across the globe. Sometimes I would use local surfers who knew the lineup better than anyone I could bring from Australia. Their understanding of that particular wave would get me more waves than someone who knew how to spot but didn't know the break.

People always ask about the waves: the barrels, the wipeouts, the coral. They assume the ocean is where the danger lives.

It isn't. For me, the real danger lives on land.

Uluwatu, one of the most famous waves in Bali, sits at the bottom of a cliff. Hundreds of steps are carved into the rock face, winding down through caves and overhangs to a paddle-out point at the base. Each step is a different height and depth. Some are shin-height. Others barely cover your toes. The rock is worn smooth from decades of foot traffic. When it is wet, it becomes treacherous.

And to the left of the staircase is a sheer drop. No railing. No barrier. Just a cliff face falling away into nothing. It would mean death if you fell.

I couldn't see any of those steps. I had to feel each one with my feet, testing the depth before committing my weight. My toes would search for the edge, find it, then my whole foot would follow. One wrong step, one moment of impatience, one tourist bumping into me at the wrong time, and I would tumble.

My spotter would carry both our boards so I could use my hands for balance and to feel the rock wall on my right. We moved slowly. Methodically. What took other surfers five minutes took us 20, sometimes longer if the staircase was crowded.

Tourists would push past me, frustrated at how slowly I was moving. I could feel them pressing against my back, hear their annoyed sighs, sense their impatience building. Some would try to squeeze past on the narrow sections, jostling me towards the edge where the cliff dropped away.

My spotter would get angry with them: 'He can't see. Give him room.'

They had no idea what they were looking at. To them I was just a slow guy holding up the line. They didn't know I was a world champion; they didn't care. They just saw an obstacle between them and their Instagram.

Once I made it to the water, everything changed. The lineup was predictable. The take-off was consistent. The waves did the same thing every time. And the locals at nearly all those waves really looked after me. Once I was in, I could surf those waves as well as anyone.

The land was the obstacle. The ocean was the reward.

The skill lives in you

The spotter relationship in surfing is fundamentally different from the pilot relationship in cycling.

In cycling, the partnership was absolute. Mick and I had trained together for years. We could anticipate each other's movements without speaking. A shift in his body weight told me a corner was coming. A change in his cadence told me the gradient was about to steepen. Winning required complete synchronicity — two bodies operating as one machine on a bike built for two.

Without Mick, I was a different athlete entirely. And on a tandem with a different stoker, Mick would be completely different as well. It wasn't just about me. The partnership was everything.

Surfing doesn't work that way. A spotter's job is to be my eyes in the water. To tell me where to paddle, when to turn, when a wave is coming, when to kick out. As long as they were a decent surfer themselves who understood how waves worked, as long as we had a couple of days to calibrate together, we could make it work. I would teach them how to call waves my way, what worked for me, what worked for us as a partnership.

This meant I could work with different spotters all over the world. I wasn't locked into one partnership. The skill had to live in me, not in the partnership.

Between 2017 and 2021, I was basically undefeated. I won competitions in Hawaii, Japan — across the globe. The only event I didn't win was a second-place finish in Indonesia. Four years of dominance in a sport I had committed to professionally after cycling, built on 30 years of surfing experience. I had been in the water since I was a kid. There were at least 10 000 hours of surfing in my body before I ever competed at the elite level.

And the thing that always surprises people is that every world title I won was with a different spotter.

Four world championships. Four different spotters. Four different partnerships formed in the days or weeks before competition. Each time, I had to build trust quickly, teach them how to call waves my way and figure out what worked for us.

The first Hawaiian Adaptive Surfing Championship I won was with Phil as my spotter. The guy who answered 'no worries' to a text message from a stranger's wife. I went on to win that event four times.

The skill lived in me — but it was only built because Phil had said yes to that WhatsApp message. Without his willingness to take me out, I could never have built the capacity that eventually took me to Nazaré. The thousands of hours in the water. The willingness to paddle out in conditions that scared everyone else.

Back on that boat in the Mentawai Islands, after the most uncomfortable and nerve-wracking day I had ever experienced in the ocean, I made a decision. I would never travel overseas again without a dedicated spotter. The risk was too high; the reward wasn't worth it. Not like that.

That trip taught me something important about the difference between courage and recklessness. Courage is paddling out in 15-foot surf with Phil beside me, building capacity systematically, pushing limits in a controlled way. Recklessness is paddling out at Hollow Trees when you can't see where the surgeon's table is and no one's watching out for you.

Both feel like bravery in the moment. Only one of them builds something sustainable.

Phil still surfs with me regularly. He has become one of my best mates — not because of our shared history or childhood connections, but because of what we have been through in the water together. There is something about trusting someone with your safety in an environment that doesn't forgive mistakes that creates a bond you can't manufacture any other way.

What he gave me that first day was permission: permission to believe that my blindness didn't have to limit where I could go. Permission to push into conditions that other people thought were off-limits for someone like me. Permission to fail, get scared, get humbled by the ocean, and come back and try again.

The easy path would have been to stay in my comfort zone. Surf the waves I already knew. Accept the limitations that everyone assumed came with being blind.

The hard path was to build capacity. To push limits locally until the fear became workable. To travel to places that terrified me and figure out how to navigate them. To fail at Hollow Trees and then learn from it. To keep showing up even when the ocean humbled me.

Because once you have surfed 15-foot waves, six foot feels like a playground. Once you have worked a lineup alone with coral beneath you, ordinary reef breaks feel routine. Once you have descended hundreds of steps on a cliff face using nothing but your feet to guide you, the paddle out becomes the easy part. Once you have been that scared and survived, you know you can survive anything.

The hard way is the easy way. It just doesn't feel like it at the time.

Research on expert performance from psychologist K. Anders Ericsson, whose work on deliberate practice shaped our understanding of mastery, found that elite performers don't just practise more, they practise differently. They systematically push beyond their current abilities, operating at the edge of their competence where failure is likely. This 'desirable difficulty' is what builds genuine capacity. The discomfort of working at the edge, of failing repeatedly in controlled conditions, is what creates the neural pathways and muscle memory that allow experts to perform under pressure. Ericsson's research suggests that comfort is the enemy of growth. The athletes, musicians and professionals who reach the highest levels are those who consistently choose the hard path, who build capacity before they need it, who do the work when no one is watching so they can perform when everyone is.

• • •

What capacity are you building now that your future self will need?

Chapter 17

Diversity as Value

Empathy Is a Superpower

> Empathy without clarity creates confusion. When we lump different people with different needs into the same category, when we treat capable professionals like charity cases and people with genuine inclusion needs like diversity hires, we insult everyone. Real empathy means seeing people clearly — understanding what they actually need, not what makes us feel good about helping.

My oldest son has been playing rugby league for seven years. He has never won a game. That's not because his team is bad. It's because the National Rugby League decided that junior players, anyone under 13, cannot keep score. Therefore, you get no winners. No losers. No premierships. Everyone gets a participation ribbon and goes home feeling equally average.

The logic, apparently, is inclusion. We do not want any child to feel bad about losing.

Here is what that actually means: my son will play his entire junior career without ever learning how to lose. Without ever feeling the sting of coming up short and having to get back up. And then, at 13, right when everything else in his life is already challenging, he will suddenly be thrown into a world where results count: where someone wins and someone loses.

We are not protecting these kids. We are setting them up for a harder fall later.

I think about this every time someone talks about 'diversity and inclusion' in the workplace. Because there is a version of that same mushy thinking creeping into corporate Australia, and it is doing more harm than good. Not because diversity doesn't matter — it matters enormously. And not because inclusion is wrong, as real inclusion is essential for people who genuinely need it.

The problem is that we have married 'diversity and inclusion' together like they are the same thing. One phrase. One department. One budget line. One conversation.

But they are not the same thing: they are two completely different concepts. And bundling them together is causing confusion, resentment and harm.

Diversity and inclusion need to get a divorce. They can stay mates, but they need separate lives.

Diversity is about value. It is the recognition that teams perform better when they include people with different perspectives: different genders, different cultures, different professional backgrounds, different lived experiences. When everyone in the room comes from the same background, went to the same universities and thinks the same way, you get groupthink. You get blind spots. You get a room full of people who all miss the same problems because they all see the world the same way.

But when your team includes genuine difference — a woman who has navigated male-dominated industries, an immigrant who has built a career in a new country, someone from a working-class background, a person with a disability who has spent their life solving problems others never face — suddenly you've got multiple angles on every challenge. Someone sees what the others have missed.

That is diversity. It is a competitive weapon, and it creates better outcomes.

Inclusion is something else entirely. Inclusion is about creating space for people who genuinely need the community to step up and make room for them. People who may never 'compete' in traditional terms but deserve to belong, to experience joy, to be part of something bigger than themselves.

These are two different things. They require different approaches. And when you conflate them, when you treat them as one concept, everything gets confused.

The protective perimeter

Jacob had Down syndrome and lived next door to us in Lennox Head.

He was maybe seven or eight years old — this awesome little boy who would run into our house all the time wearing his Parramatta Eels jersey. He had speech difficulties but endless energy, and he was in my oldest son's class at school. My son would look after him. They were mates in that simple, uncomplicated way kids can be before the world teaches them to sort people into categories.

Jacob loved football. You could see it in the way he moved, the way he would light up when the boys were playing. But he couldn't understand the rules properly. He couldn't process the game the way other kids could. He was never going to make a team through normal channels.

His mum was a single parent doing everything on her own. I asked her one day: 'What if we made Jacob part of the team?' Not just turning up on game day to watch — actually part of it. Training with the boys. Registered as a player. Taking the field.

We set it up properly. Our neighbour on the other side had teenage sons, so we got one of them to come to training as Jacob's minder. Jacob would do the drills he could do — the simple ones, the fun ones — and sit out the technical stuff. He was there. He belonged.

On game day, I would talk to the opposing coach before kick-off: 'Mate, this is the situation. We have got a player with Down syndrome who is going to take the field. He will run with the ball. He is wearing his Parramatta jersey, not our Red Devils strip, so you will know who he is.'

Every single coach was awesome about it. They would brief their players. Everyone understood.

Here is how it worked: the other team would kick off, one of our boys would catch it, and then Jacob would get the ball. He would start running down the field with three or four of our players forming a protective perimeter around him. The opposition kids would charge in like they were supposed to and then peel away at the last second. Bodies would fly everywhere like a scene from Rambo, but no one would touch him.

Jacob would just run. Straight down the field, me jogging beside him, his teammates around him, the whole crowd watching this kid with Down syndrome score a try.

One time, a boy from the other team actually tried to grab him. One of our players just picked the kid up and threw him out of the way. They made it work.

As soon as Jacob scored, he would leave the field, then the kids would play the game properly. But every week, before the real competition started, this boy got to experience something he never would have otherwise: he got to score. He got to celebrate. He got to be part of something.

This is what real inclusion looks like. It requires effort from the whole community. The other coaches, the other teams, the parents on the sideline, the boys who formed that protective wall around their mate — everyone had to buy in.

And it wasn't just good for Jacob: it was good for the other boys, too. They learned something that year that no coaching manual could teach them. They learned how to protect someone who couldn't protect himself. How to make space for someone different. How to use their strength for something bigger than winning.

That is inclusion done right. It is about belonging. It is the right thing to do *because* it is the right thing to do.

Accessibility plus accountability

Diversity is different.

Diversity is not about creating protective perimeters — it's about recognising that different perspectives make teams stronger. It is about hiring to diversify your team — hiring the woman, the immigrant, the person from a non-traditional background, the individual with a disability — because each person brings something the rest of the team does not have.

When you hire for diversity value, you're not doing anyone a favour — it's not charity, or a box-ticking exercise. You're making a smart business decision.

People from diverse backgrounds don't need inclusion in the Jacob sense. They don't need protective perimeters. What they need is accessibility — the removal of barriers that prevent them from competing on a level playing field.

If someone has a workplace injury, you adjust their workspace. You get them the equipment they need. You make the workspace more accessible to them so they can do their job. That isn't charity, it's just sensible management.

Accessibility for people with disabilities is the same thing. Screen magnification software. Accessible documents. Flexible arrangements for someone with a chronic condition. It's the equivalent of providing a chair for someone to sit on. You're not giving special treatment; you're giving capable people the tools that allow them to do capable work.

Once their barriers to accessibility have been removed, you hold these people to the same standards as everyone else — the same expectations, the same accountability, the same consequences if they don't deliver.

That is diversity value, not inclusion as charity. You have accessibility plus accountability.

The problem is that corporate Australia has bundled 'diversity' and 'inclusion' together to create one initiative. And because the words have become entwined, the approaches become confused.

Companies hire capable professionals from diverse backgrounds and then treat them like Jacob — as if they need a protective perimeter. They treat them like charity cases who should be grateful for the opportunity, rather than competitive assets who have earned their place. This is an insult to these professionals, plus it breeds resentment among colleagues who see 'inclusion hires' as a sign that standards have been lowered.

Meanwhile, the people who genuinely need inclusion — people like Jacob, people with significant disabilities who require real community support — get lumped into the same category as high-performing professionals who just need their laptop screen to be adjusted.

The whole conversation becomes muddy. No one knows what they're actually trying to achieve. Are we hiring for value or hiring for charity? Are we removing barriers or lowering standards?

When you have clarity about a problem, you can solve it properly. When there is no clarity, everything falls apart.

Your disability built something

If you are someone who brings diversity value, whatever form that takes, you need to be able to articulate it.

When you buy a television, the manufacturer doesn't sit back and wait for you to figure out why their product is better than the competition. They tell you. They market their differentiator.

Employment works the same way.

If you are a woman who has navigated male-dominated industries, the experience will have built something within you — resilience, the ability to read rooms, pattern recognition for bias that others miss. That is a differentiator.

If you are an immigrant who has built a career in a new country, you have developed adaptability, cross-cultural communication skills, the ability to operate in unfamiliar systems.

That is a differentiator.

If you are a person with a disability, you have spent your entire life solving problems that others don't even know exist. That is a differentiator.

Let me give you my version.

I am blind. Because I am blind, I have developed world-class problem-solving skills. Every day of my life has required creative solutions to obstacles most people never face. I am also an exceptional verbal communicator. I cannot rely on visual cues, body language, facial expressions — the things sighted people read automatically. I have learned to communicate with precision — to listen for tone, for hesitation, for the things people do not say out loud. And I am a world-class listener. All through school, I couldn't read the board or follow along using textbooks. My only option was to listen: to absorb information through my ears, to process it in real time, to remember it because I couldn't go back and review it later.

Those skills are directly transferable to business. They make me better at my job — not in spite of my blindness but because of it.

That is my pitch. Everyone from a diverse background has their own version. The question is whether they have done the work to identify it and sell it.

I coached a woman once who had cerebral palsy. She was going for an IT job, a role primarily about written communication and documentation. She was worried about her verbal communication, which was affected by her condition. She had been hiding her disability, hoping employers wouldn't notice.

I told her to flip it. Lead with it. Explain what her disability had built in her: the precision, the attention to detail, the ability to communicate complex information in writing. The job didn't require perfect speech. It required excellent written work.

She got the job.

That is what happens when you stop hiding and start selling.

I need to say something controversial here. There is a movement to rebrand disability as 'all abilities' or even as a 'superpower'. I understand the intention behind this movement, but I think this kind of language is making things worse.

A disability is a disability. It is something in your body that does not work the way it is supposed to. My eyes do not function properly. That is a fact. Using phrases like 'all abilities' does not change the reality that I cannot see.

What is true is this: because of my disability, I have developed other capacities. Skills I wouldn't have built if everything worked perfectly. Workarounds that became strengths.

Here is what I think we should say instead:

> *I have a disability. There are things my body cannot do. But because of that disability, I have built capabilities in other areas that most people have not had to develop. And those capabilities are my differentiator.*

That is honest. That is clear. That is something people can work with.

Excuses poison the well

There is another side to this that people do not like to talk about — the fact that some people use their diversity category as an excuse.

I sat on a panel once where I had to review an accessibility request. A long-term employee, who had been with the company for more than 10 years, wanted to work from home permanently. The reason given was their disability.

I asked a simple question: has their disability changed?

No.

So how were they able to come into the office five days a week for 10 years before COVID, but now they cannot come in at all? It was the same person, the same disability, the same office.

They had gotten used to working from home and didn't want to go back to the office. Their disability wasn't the reason they wanted to work from home — it was the excuse.

That behaviour hurts everyone. When people see someone using their diversity category as leverage to get what they want rather than what they need, it poisons the well. It makes organisations suspicious of the next person who genuinely does need their workplace to be more accessible.

Diversity value requires accountability. You get the accessibility you need to compete on a level playing field, and then you are held to the same standards as everyone else.

When I started winning gold medals in cycling, comments appeared almost immediately, even from other blind people: 'Of course Matt wins, he knows all the pro cyclists.'

I didn't know a single professional cyclist until I became a world champion. I met them because of my achievements, not the other way around.

And then there is the accusation that cuts deepest: 'He must not be that blind.'

The logic seems to be that if I can do these things, my disability must not be as severe as I claim it is.

What they are really saying is 'his achievements make us uncomfortable'. It is easier to believe I'm not actually disabled than to accept that someone with a disability could achieve the things I've achieved.

I run into things constantly. I cannot see objects a foot in front of my face. I use VoiceOver on my phone because I cannot read the screen. I have got less than three per cent peripheral vision. But because I have achieved things that others have not, some people think I must be faking my disability.

Creating real diversity and real inclusion

Diversity is valuable. Different perspectives create better outcomes. People from underrepresented backgrounds, whatever form that takes, bring capabilities that homogeneous teams lack.

Inclusion is essential. People who genuinely need community support deserve to belong, to experience joy, to be part of something bigger.

But these are different things, so I urge people to stop conflating them.

If you're an employer, understand what you are actually trying to achieve. Are you hiring for diversity value? Then provide accessibility and hold people accountable. Are you creating genuine inclusion? Then build the protective perimeter and create space for belonging.

If you're from a diverse background, articulate your value and identify your differentiator. Stop waiting to be discovered and start selling what you bring.

Real diversity value means being held to the same standard as everyone else — being given the tools to deliver on a level playing field.

Real inclusion means creating space for people who genuinely need the community to step up.

Both matter. They are just not the same thing.

Research from McKinsey's 'Diversity Wins' report, analysing over a thousand companies across 15 countries, found that organisations in the top quartile for ethnic and cultural diversity were 36 per cent more likely to achieve above-average profitability than those in the bottom quartile. But the research also revealed something critical: diversity without inclusion led to higher turnover and lower engagement. The companies that succeeded were those that understood the difference — that provided the accessibility and support diverse talent needed while holding them to high performance standards. Tokenism and lowered expectations produced resentment. Genuine investment in removing barriers, combined with accountability, produced results. The data is clear: diversity creates value when it is treated as a competitive advantage, not as a charity exercise.

• • •

Are you treating the capable people around you as competitive assets who need accessibility, or as charity cases who need protection?

Chapter 18

Reports, Not Commands

Two Gears, One Engine

> The same engine that powers explosive action also powers patient preparation. Champions do not just have one speed. They know when to push and when to hold; when to attack and when to build. The gear you choose determines whether you win or whether you burn out before the finish line.

In August 2022, I was at home in Lennox Head, filming an interview for a Netflix documentary called *The Blind Sea*, when my phone kept ringing. It was Dylan Longbottom, a big wave surfer I'd been mentored by since 2020. I ignored it three times.

Daniel Fenech, the director, who I'd worked with before and trusted with the documentary, stopped me. 'Just answer it.'

What I didn't know was that they had a camera on Dylan at his end. They were hunting for a moment.

Dylan said, 'Matty, I've been thinking about this wave for the end of the movie. Just be open-minded, okay? I'm thinking Nazaré could be the wave.'

He expected me to resist. He had arguments prepared.

I said, 'Oh yeah. That sounds good. Let's do it.'

My face lit up like a kid at his birthday party, and I hung up the phone.

The room was silent. Daniel was staring at me. The camera was still rolling.

'You just said yes to Nazaré,' he said.

I had. Without hesitation. Without asking for time to think. The word had come out of my mouth before my brain could intervene. I'd been big wave surfing for a while, training hard and doing plenty of breath hold training. Despite this, I had previously considered Nazaré to be unachievable — saying as much in an early interview for the documentary — but somewhere, deep down, I had already made the decision to go. I had just needed someone to ask the question.

The number

Five minutes and 48 seconds. That is how long I held my breath in a pool in Kingscliff, one week before I boarded a plane to Portugal to surf at Nazaré, home to the biggest waves in the world. Nearly six minutes underwater, with my diaphragm convulsing and every cell in my body asking me to surface.

I stayed down anyway.

When I finally came up, I asked my breath coach, Dwaino (Dwain Fitzsimmons), a question I had been avoiding for months of breath hold training.

'What can the other boys do?'

I was referring to Dylan and the best big wave surfers on the planet. The names you see when Nazaré is pumping.

Dwaino smiled. 'Dylan's probably less than two minutes. Most of the best guys are somewhere between that and four.'

I sat in the shallow end of the pool, water dripping down my face, and let that sink in. I had just held my breath for five minutes and 48 seconds. The best big wave surfers in the world were mostly between two and four minutes.

I hadn't just met the benchmark. I had obliterated it.

And the reason I'd obliterated it was simple: I never knew what the benchmark was.

If I had known at the start that Dylan could hold for less than two minutes and the best guys pushed four, I would have trained until I hit four. I would have felt satisfied. I would have stopped.

I never would have discovered that I could hold for 5:48.

Dwaino knew this. That is why he refused to answer when I asked early in our training what the pros could do. He just said, 'Let's not set a glass ceiling. Let's find out what you can do.'

So I trained blind. No benchmark. I had no target except yesterday's version of myself.

But that 5:48 didn't come from talent. It came from a single insight that rewired everything I thought I knew about pain, fear and the lies my body tells me.

Rethinking discomfort

When my father used to go to Rotary on Monday nights, I would lie in bed alone, staring at the cupboard in the corner of my room, absolutely certain that something was hiding inside it. Every sound was a threat. Every shadow was a monster. I would pull the covers over my head and wait for morning, terrified of something that didn't exist.

The boogeyman was not real. But my fear was.

I carried that lesson into adulthood without realising it. Fear feels real even when the threat is not. Your body doesn't know the difference. It sends the same signals either way.

Breath holding works in exactly the same way.

Before I started training seriously, I did a session with Lucas Handley, a breath coach who had trained the Australian spearfishing team. We started with a baseline test. I lay on the floor, took a breath and held it for as long as I could.

Two minutes and 50 seconds.

Then I let my breath go. A gasp, then slow exhales as I tried to return to calm. I lay there on the floor of his training room, satisfied with myself. Two minutes and 50 seconds. That seemed like a solid number.

I had no idea how wrong I was.

Lucas asked me a question that changed my life.

'Why did you breathe?'

'Because I needed air,' I replied.

'How do you know you needed air?'

I listed the symptoms. The burning. The spasming. The feeling that I was dying.

He nodded slowly. 'Is that what was happening? Or is that what you *thought* was happening?'

He didn't give me an answer. He just let the question sit there, doing its work.

We trained all day. Different exercises, different techniques, building my lung capacity and working on breathing mechanics. By the afternoon, we went to a pool. Lucas told me I was going to hold my breath for three minutes underwater.

I just nodded. I had done three minutes a couple of times in the right conditions. I thought I could do it.

I slipped into the water, took a breath, put my face under and held it.

Because of all the work we had done that day, it was actually quite relaxing. The time seemed to slip away. The discomfort was there, but manageable. My body was sending me reports, and I was filing them away without acting on them.

At approaching three minutes, Lucas tapped my shoulder. I kept my face underwater and put my hand out on the side of the pool. He dried it with a towel, then clipped a pulse oximeter onto my finger. He was taking the reading in the last 20 seconds of the hold so he could tell me how much oxygen was left.

'Okay, three minutes,' he said. 'You can come up.'

I lifted my head out of the water.

'Ninety-seven per cent blood oxygen saturation.'

I thought about that number for a long time.

During that first baseline test, I had felt all the symptoms of oxygen deprivation. The burning. The panic. The absolute certainty that I was about to die. I had experienced what I believed was my body running out of air.

And my blood oxygen was still at 97 per cent.

Lucas explained it simply: humans pass out at around 50 per cent saturation. Everything I had felt during that first test — the burning, the diaphragm contractions, the doubt — was just my body sending me information. Warning signals. Discomfort reports. It was telling me it was uncomfortable.

It was *not* telling me I was in danger.

The boogeyman in the cupboard. The monster that was not there.

I had been breathing because I was scared, because I was confused about what the data actually meant — not because I needed to breathe.

That single insight rewired everything.

My body's distress signals were not commands; they were reports.

I could acknowledge them. I could file them. And I could keep going.

The work that costs you dignity

Most people think preparation looks like training montages. Sweat and determination and inspirational music.

Real preparation looks like humiliation.

Dwaino became my main breath coach after that session with Lucas. He had grown up with Dylan Longbottom, and he specialised in training big wave surfers. His methods were brutal in ways that do not photograph well.

I would swim full laps in the pool, underwater, with no fins — sometimes on full lungs, sometimes on empty. I would surface, take a single breath and go straight into another lap. Sometimes I would swim multiple laps in sequence, the oxygen debt building with each stroke, while my body screamed its discomfort reports at me.

I would work with battle ropes while wearing a hypoxic mask that restricted my oxygen intake. I could only breathe through my nose while whipping those heavy ropes up and down; my heart rate was spiking into the red zone, while my lungs were desperate for air that the mask wouldn't be able to provide.

The worst was the CO_2 tolerance work. Dwaino had me doing squats and burpees while holding my breath: heavy, high heart rate breath holds. I'd start at one rep, then two, then build up until I couldn't complete the set. One breath hold per set. Only one exhale and one inhale between them.

The skill was not the exercise. The skill was the recovery.

Your body wants to breathe fast after exertion. It is screaming for oxygen. But fast breathing won't let you recover in time for the next breath hold. So, while my heart was pounding out of my chest, I had to breathe out slowly. Then in slower. Then go again with another set of burpees while holding my breath.

It was horrible. These training exercises simulated being held underwater after a wipeout — heart pounding, muscles burning, body demanding oxygen then having to make decisions with a brain that is starving for air — because that is what happens at Nazaré. The ocean doesn't care that you can't think straight; it holds you down anyway, and you have to know which way is up and when to pull your inflation vest.

Through all my breath hold training, I learned to slow my breath when everything in me wanted to gasp. I learned to stay calm when calm felt impossible. I learned that panic is just another report, and I could file it like all the others.

But the real work happened on my daily walks.

Breath capacity is like any other fitness quality: you have to build it every single day. I would walk around my neighbourhood holding my breath, using my phone to track the time through my AirPods. I started with a one-minute, 15-second breath hold while walking, then a one-minute, 30-second recovery standing still — then another hold. I'd make every recovery shorter by 15 seconds, until the last recovery was only 15 seconds.

The neighbours thought I was insane.

People would say good morning, and I wouldn't be able to respond because I was mid-hold. I would just nod and keep walking, my face turning purple, looking like a complete idiot. They probably thought I was rude. They probably thought I was having some kind of medical episode. I couldn't explain, and I didn't try.

One morning, a woman I had never spoken to before stopped me on the footpath. She put her hand on my arm, genuinely concerned, and asked if I was having a stroke. I was 40 seconds into a hold. My face must have looked purple. My eyes were watering. I couldn't speak without losing the breath.

I just shook my head and kept walking.

She called after me: 'Should I phone someone?'

I waved her off without turning around. I could feel her watching me walk away, certain she had just witnessed a man in crisis. She wasn't wrong; I was in crisis. I was choosing crisis, every single day, because the alternative was showing up at Nazaré unprepared.

And then there was the other thing.

When you push breath holds to the extreme, your body does something called a blood shift. The pressure builds. Your spleen releases blood. It pushes on your bladder.

You wet yourself.

Early in my training, it was barely noticeable. By the end, when I was doing one-minute, 30-second holds with 15-second recoveries, I was walking around my community with a wet patch the size of a 50-cent piece — visible, undeniable, humiliating.

It didn't stop me. It *couldn't* stop me.

This isn't the inspiring part of the story — it's the real part. The part where you look stupid in front of your neighbours. The part where you sacrifice dignity for capability. The part where the work is so unglamorous that no one would ever do it unless they were truly committed to something bigger than their ego.

I did it every day for months: not because I enjoyed it, but because I needed to survive what was coming. Because I had learned that my body's complaints were just reports, and I was done with letting reports run my life.

The lesson written in blood

Fiji taught me that not all warning signals were just reports.

Dylan and I went there with a small crew just after COVID restrictions lifted. We were filming for *The Blind Sea*, and we found a wave that no one had ever surfed before: a right-hand barrel breaking over shallow reef. Perfect. Untouched. They let me name it. I called it 'The Blind Spot'.

We surfed it for days. I was getting barrelled consistently. Everything was working. I was in the best shape of my surfing career.

Then came the last day.

The last surf of the last day is when you let your guard down. I had been disciplined about safety the entire trip — always using a spotter, always knowing where I was in the lineup. But this one time, I went out with Dylan's daughter, Summa. Everyone else was still packing up, so we jumped on the same jet ski together. We both jumped off. Summa caught a wave, and I was just sitting there by myself.

I decided to paddle into one.

It was a left-hand wave, where the surfer rides left from take-off. All the waves on that side were on my backhand, so my back was to the wave face. I caught it, sort of made it, kicked out too far inside. Then I felt another wave jacking up beneath me. I paddled, felt it sucking up steep, pulled into the barrel.

The wave pushed me forward over the falls, so I was thrown off the top as the lip crashed down — like a waterfall — and then I landed head first on the reef.

The first thing I heard was my neck crunch, then the coral crunch — and then nothing but the roar of whitewater pushing me across the reef. I could taste blood filling my mouth, warm and metallic, mixing with salt water.

My first thought was, *Oh fuck, you idiot. You might have broken your neck.*

I didn't panic. I let my body go still, relaxed everything. Waited for the air in my lungs to start pulling me towards the surface. That is how you know which way is up — you don't thrash around guessing. You let go and let your buoyancy tell you.

I floated up slowly, trying not to move my neck. When my head broke the surface, I touched my forehead. Felt the flap of skin hanging loose, blood streaming down my face, stinging my eyes. The impact had sliced off a 50-cent-sized piece of skin.

I swam carefully out to deeper water, keeping my neck as still as possible, then I went straight in. I didn't catch another wave that trip.

By pure luck, I escaped with the lost skin and a stiff neck. No spinal injury. No permanent damage. But that moment rewrote my understanding of what those warning signs and discomfort reports actually mean.

Learning to override your body's fear signals is powerful. It lets you hold your breath for nearly six minutes. It lets you walk through the kind of discomfort that would stop most people. But your body also sends reports about real danger — reports you ignore at your peril.

The skill is not ignoring all reports. The skill is knowing which ones are the boogeyman in the cupboard and which ones are the actual threat to your safety.

I don't surf left-hand barrels anymore, not unless the water is deep. That report was real.

Perspective and preparedness

I had built capacity that exceeded many of the best surfers in the world. I had learned that the signals telling me to stop were just reports. I had walked through my neighbourhood with piss on my shorts, day after day, building something no one could see.

I had hit the number — five minutes and 48 seconds — in a pool in Kingscliff, and I had done it without knowing what the benchmark was. But when I thought about that number after Dwaino confirmed it, I considered what it actually meant.

Dylan might only have a breath hold of two minutes or less, but he has more experience in heavy water than pretty much anyone else on the planet. I had maybe 300 per cent more breath capacity than him. But he had 1000 per cent more experience than me in the heaviest conditions on earth.

That put everything into perspective. I had trained my lungs. I had trained my CO_2 tolerance. But I hadn't trained my mind for what it would feel like to be held under by a 60-foot wall of whitewater. That was a different kind of preparation entirely.

I started working on my mental game for this wave. I'd been training for years, but this was different. The training required wasn't just physical, or about how long I could hold my breath. It was the part that no pool session could simulate that would be important at Nazaré. Staying calm meant the training would save me; panic meant it wouldn't.

When he told me the number, Dwaino watched me process it—then he said something I have never forgotten.

'Don't get overconfident. That's just a number. The ocean knows how to deal with numbers. It will teach you a lesson real fast.'

The boogeyman wasn't real. But the ocean was. My preparation was real. And so was the humility I would need to survive what was coming.

The flight to Portugal was booked. The boards were shaped. The breath was trained. The body was ready.

All that remained was the wave.

In Formula 1 racing, the difference between winning and losing often comes down to pit strategy. Teams must decide when to stay out and push pace, and when to pit for fresh tyres and play the long game. The 2021 Abu Dhabi Grand Prix came down to a single strategic call in the final laps. Raw speed matters, but knowing when to deploy it matters more. Research from motorsport analytics shows that teams who master gear-shifting strategy—knowing when to conserve and when to attack—win more championships than teams with simply the fastest car. The same principle applies to breath training, big wave surfing and any high-stakes pursuit: success requires both explosive capacity and the wisdom to know which reports to override and which ones to obey.

•••

What pressure in your business have you mistaken for a crisis when it's actually just discomfort? The difficult conversation you've been avoiding. The decision you keep delaying because it feels too hard. Not everything that feels urgent is dangerous—but some warnings are real. Which ones are you ignoring because it's easier to stay busy than to face them?

Chapter 19

The Generational Gift

Somewhere over the Indian Ocean, I closed my eyes and let the questions come.

Not the questions the media had been asking. Not the headlines about whether a blind man would survive the biggest wave in the world. Those questions belonged to people who didn't understand what we had built.

The question I was thinking about was simpler. And harder.

Where did all of this come from?

Somewhere back in Australia, Bex and our three children were sleeping in their beds. Max, Elsie, Jake. Before they closed their eyes, they would have said the words — the same words they say every night.

'I am brave. I am inquisitive. I am grateful. I am kind. I am happy.'

I thought about those words as the plane pushed west into the darkness — not the words themselves, but the philosophy underneath them. The belief that you can shape who you are by what you repeat to yourself. The understanding that identity is not fixed but built — night after night, choice after choice.

It started with a different word. A word that was banned in the house where I grew up.

The forbidden word

Can't.

My father, Don Formston, was not a philosopher or a psychologist or anyone you would expect to have strong opinions about human potential. He was a sales and marketing manager for an alcohol company. A grog salesman from the Northern Beaches of Sydney.

But somewhere along the way, he'd decided that the word 'can't' was poison. That every time a child said it, they were laying a brick in a wall between themselves and their potential. That the wall got higher with every repetition until eventually you couldn't see over it anymore.

So he banned it. For all three of us: me, my brother Stuart, my sister Jacqui. The word simply didn't exist in our house.

This was not a gentle suggestion. If you said 'can't', there were consequences. It wasn't a *punishment* exactly; actually, it was something worse. You had to prove it. You had to demonstrate, in detail, why this particular thing was impossible — show your working, explain the obstacle.

We learned quickly. If you didn't want to do something, you found other ways to avoid it. You said you didn't feel like it. You said you were busy. You said you would do it later. You would do anything except say the forbidden word — because if you said 'can't', Dad would make you try to do the thing anyway.

The obstacle that was real

Homework was the battleground where this played out most often.

One day, I was sitting at the kitchen table. I was maybe 10 or 11 years old. A maths worksheet was spread in front of me, with multiplication tables arranged in a grid — columns and rows I am supposed to read across and down to find the answers.

I cannot see the grid.

I don't have central vision. I have peripheral vision only, which means I see the world through the edges of my eyes while the middle is dark. The school had given me enlarged worksheets, but even with the bigger print, tracking across a row while keeping my place in a column was beyond what my eyes could do. My peripheral vision could catch movement and shapes, but it couldn't hold a steady enough grip on the grid to do maths.

'I can't see the tables, Dad.'

The forbidden word slipped out before I could stop it. I braced myself for the interrogation. The demand to prove it. The inevitable requirement to try anyway.

But this time, Dad didn't make me prove it. He already knew it was a genuine obstacle. He had watched me struggle for months. He had seen me hold the page two inches from my face just to make out the letters. He knew this wasn't laziness or avoidance.

'Okay. Let's fix that.'

He had heard about something called a CCTV. Not closed-circuit television like the security cameras in shops, but a camera-based magnification system designed for people with vision impairment. You put a document under the camera, and it displays an enlarged version on a screen. Schools had them. Vision Australia had them.

They cost six thousand dollars.

This was the 1990s. There was no government funding for assistive technology. Six thousand dollars on a salesman's commission might as well have been six million.

Most parents would have accepted that reality. They would have written a note to the school, requested special accommodations and done their best to work around the limitation.

My father was not most parents.

He went and looked at a CCTV unit. Studied it carefully. Asked questions. Then he came home and did the maths. A CCTV was really just three things: a camera, a lens with magnification capability and a screen. The expensive part was the proprietary integration. But if you stripped all that away and looked at what it actually did, you could build something similar for a fraction of the price.

He bought a television. Found a video camera with a macro lens. Then he drove to nearby Brookvale and found an engineer who could build a mounting rig that would hold the camera steady over a document while displaying the magnified image on the TV screen.

Total cost: under a thousand dollars.

He set it up in my room. Showed me how to use it — how to slide the paper under the camera. How to adjust the focus. How to zoom in on the parts I needed to see.

Then he delivered the verdict.

'Now you can see the tables. Do the maths.'

That was the deal. He would move heaven and earth to remove the obstacle. Spend money we didn't have. Learn skills he didn't possess. Drive to industrial estates and negotiate with engineers. Solve problems that seemed unsolvable.

But once the obstacle had been removed, there were no excuses. You couldn't hide behind 'can't' anymore — the wall had been taken down. Now you had to walk through the space where it used to be.

That home-built CCTV taught me something I have carried ever since: limitations are often just unsolved problems. The right combination of empathy, creativity and effort can remove barriers that seem permanent. But once those barriers have been removed, you are accountable for what you do next.

Empathy without accountability is just enabling. Accountability without empathy is just cruelty. My father understood the magic possible from combining the two.

The longest walk

When I was 12, I ran a car-washing business in my neighbourhood.

I would knock on doors, offer to wash cars for a few dollars, and spend my weekends with a bucket and sponge. It wasn't glamorous, but it was mine. I had built it myself.

One afternoon, I washed a car for a man down the street. We had agreed on $10. I did the job to the best of my ability, dried off the car and knocked on his door to collect.

He handed me $5.

'The wheels weren't clean enough,' he said. 'Five is fair.'

I took the money and went home. I was upset, but I was also relieved. There was nothing I could do about it. An adult had made a decision. The matter was closed.

Dad listened to my story. Then he said something that made my stomach drop.

'Go back down there and make him pay you what he agreed to pay you.'

I just stood there. He couldn't be serious. This was an adult. A grown man. I was 12 years old.

'I can't do that, Dad. He's an adult.'

The forbidden word was out before I could stop it.

'You had a deal. He's trying to rip you off. Go down there and tell him.'

He wasn't going to call the neighbour and sort this out between adults. He wasn't going to smooth things over while I watched from the sidelines. He was going to make me, a 12-year-old boy, walk back down that street and confront a grown man who was trying to cheat me.

So I walked.

With every step, I felt like I was walking toward my own execution. My heart was pounding so hard I could feel it in my throat. My hands were shaking. My mouth was dry. Every instinct in my body was screaming at me to turn around and accept the loss. To go home and forget this ever happened.

But I kept walking, because Dad wasn't going to let me come home until I had tried.

I knocked on the door. The man answered. He looked down at me.

I told him, my voice probably cracking, that we had agreed on $10. That I had washed the car to the best of my ability. That the wheels excuse was not fair.

I don't remember exactly what he said. I don't remember if he was annoyed or embarrassed to be called out by a child. What I remember is that it worked. He went inside and came back with another $5.

I walked home with the full $10, feeling 10-feet tall.

This happened more than once over the years: different customers, different situations, different uncomfortable conversations I was forced to have. Dad kept sending me back down the street because he knew that every time I did it, I was building something. Not just business skills — something deeper.

The understanding that I could handle things that terrified me. That fear was not the same as inability. That the walk towards the scary thing was always worse than the scary thing itself.

In their landmark study of visionary companies, researchers Jim Collins and Jerry Porras found that organisations which endure across generations share one defining characteristic: a set of core values so deeply held that they never change, even as strategies and practices constantly evolve. Their research, published in their book *Built to Last*, showed that these values are not created by mission statements or corporate retreats—they are discovered through behaviour. They are passed down through action, not words. The companies that have lasted—like 3M, Disney, Sony, Hewlett-Packard—didn't just talk about their values. They built mechanisms to reinforce them. They made the values unavoidable. What Collins and Porras found in corporations, I was learning in a house on the Northern Beaches: values that are lived become values that last. Values that are merely spoken become wallpaper.

What we say before sleep

Max was seven when we started the ritual.

Every night, after stories and teeth brushing and all the delaying tactics children deploy when they don't want the day to end, my kids say five things before they close their eyes.

'I am brave. I am inquisitive. I am grateful. I am kind. I am happy.'

Then they say their names. Their full names. So the values are linked to their identity, not just floating words disconnected from who they are.

This is my iteration: the next generation version of what Mum and Dad gave me. They banned a word and built an engine. I took that engine and added new components.

The 'I am' statements came from studying the philosophy of Wayne Dyer and the ideas in his book *Wishes Fulfilled*. The words 'I am' are the two most powerful words in any language. Whatever follows them shapes your reality. 'I am tired. I am stressed. I am incapable.' Say those things enough and they become true. But try saying, 'I am brave. I am inquisitive. I am grateful.' If you say those things every night as the last act before sleep, they seep into your subconscious. They become the foundation of how you see yourself.

We have done this every night, without fail, since my children were old enough to talk. Jake started around four, just because he heard his older siblings doing it and wanted to join in.

But ritual without reflection is just noise. You can say 'I am kind' every night for years and still be cruel to your siblings during the day. The words become meaningless if they are just sounds.

So, a few times a week, I talk to one of my children and we go deeper.

I ask questions like, 'How were you brave today? What did brave look like?' I ask them to tell me about a time they saw someone else be brave.

I ask, 'What does inquisitive mean to you? Were you inquisitive today? Did you ask questions, or were you just waiting for your turn to talk?'

I ask them to tell me about a time they experienced kindness: 'How did it feel? How could you create that feeling for someone else tomorrow?'

They tell me stories. Moments from the playground. Times they were scared but did the thing anyway. We talk about questions they asked or felt they should have asked but didn't. The conversations are real, with examples from their real lives becoming connected to the abstract values they say aloud each night.

These values are the last thing their minds process before they go to sleep. They're not looking at a screen or watching a cartoon. They're engaging in a focused reflection on the person they are trying to become.

Elsie recently asked to add a sixth word: honest. She had thought about the values enough that she felt something was missing. She identified what it was. And she asked to change the formula.

That's when I knew it was working — when the values became hers, not just something Dad made her say.

The gap in the system

Here is what bothers me.

Our education system focuses relentlessly on maths and English. On tactical skills. On knowledge that can be tested and measured and ranked. And those things matter. But they are the gears, not the engine.

Values and behaviours? They are left to the family unit.

But what if your family unit doesn't have a deep connection to exploring values and behaviours? What if you didn't get the generational gift that was passed down in the Formston house? What if no one ever banned the word 'can't' in your home? What if no one ever sent you back down the street to face something that terrified you?

Ask any leader what they look for when they recruit. They will tell you the same thing: values and behaviours. Anyone can learn skills. You can teach someone how to use a spreadsheet, but you cannot teach them integrity. You can train someone on a sales process, but you cannot train them to be brave.

So why are we not talking more about values and behaviours in schools?

We need to build this engine for the entire community, not just the lucky ones who inherited it. The bedtime ritual I do with my kids should not be a competitive advantage — it should be a baseline. Every child should have someone helping them articulate who they want to become.

Every child should get the chance to build an identity based on values, not just skills.

Until we fix that gap, we are leaving the most important part of human development to chance.

The challenge

Max was 10 when he decided I was wrong.

He had been working on a Rubik's cube for days. Twisting, turning, following tutorials online — getting close, but never quite solving it. The frustration was building. He has my tendency to get hyper-fixated on things. Bex calls it full Matt Formston Fixation Mode. When something captures his attention, it consumes him entirely until he either masters it or it defeats him.

One night he came to me, cube in hand, defeat written across his face.

'Dad, there is such a thing as can't.'

He said it like he was delivering a verdict — like he had thought about this carefully and reached a conclusion. He was challenging the philosophy he had grown up with, testing it against his lived experience.

'I can't fly to the Moon with my arms. That's physically impossible. Some things are actually "can't".'

I smiled. This was exactly the kind of conversation I wanted to have with my kids. Not blind obedience to a family rule but genuine engagement with the idea.

'Mate,' I said, 'I think you can fly to the Moon with your arms. If you made that your whole life's purpose.'

He looked at me like I had lost my mind.

'You'd spend your whole life trying. You'd study physics, engineering, biology. You'd form partnerships with scientists and inventors. You'd push boundaries nobody thought could move. And by the end of your life, maybe you'd have invented some new technology that gets you closer. Or maybe you'd find a completely different way. Or maybe you'd discover something even more interesting along the journey and change your goal entirely.'

I paused to let that sink in.

'But even if you never actually flew to the Moon with your arms, think about everything you'd create along the way. The partnerships. The innovations. The problems you'd solve. It would be a life worth living. The goal is not the point. The pursuit is the point.'

He didn't look entirely convinced. But he went back to the Rubik's cube.

A few weeks later, he was solving it in under 20 seconds.

A task that had seemed impossible had become routine. The wall had come down.

I reminded him of our conversation. 'Remember when you said you couldn't do this?'

He just grinned.

The engine

The plane began its descent into Lisbon.

Somewhere to the north, the Atlantic was stirring. A swell was building. Nazaré was waiting.

Every person who accomplishes something extraordinary is standing on a foundation they didn't build themselves. Parents who refused to accept limitations. Teachers who saw potential before performance. Partners who believed when belief seemed foolish.

My father never let me say the word 'can't'. My mother sat beside me night after night, helping me navigate a world that wasn't built for my eyes. Together, they created something that would power everything I have ever done. Together, they gave me the generational gift that is the foundation for all the Hard Standards in this book: the knowledge that there is no such thing as 'can't'.

Now I was trying to pass that same thing to my own children. The bedtime ritual. The deep dives into values. The understanding that identity is built, not inherited. That who you become is shaped by what you repeat to yourself in the quiet moments before sleep.

The wheels touched down.

I was ready. Not because of the breath training or the custom boards or the thousands of hours of preparation. Those were important. But they were the gears. The engine came first.

It was built 40 years ago by a grog salesman from the Northern Beaches who decided his children would never say a four-letter word.

And it was being rebuilt every night in Lennox Head, where three children closed their eyes and said the words that would shape who they become.

I am brave. I am inquisitive. I am grateful. I am kind. I am happy.

The engine before the gears. It always starts there.

What values are you passing on to the people who matter most—not in the words you say, but in the standards you hold and the obstacles you help them overcome?

Chapter 20

No Gates

The Future Is Already Real

> Declare your goal before you've earned it. Live in the reality of already being what you want to become. It's supposed to feel uncomfortable — that's how you know the dream is big enough. The voices telling you it's impossible are the same voices that have always been wrong. The delusion is never a delusion. It's just a goal that other people can't understand yet.

Sighted surfers have gates.

Many of the world's best waves break near rocky headlands, and the danger is real if you fall. To surf Nazaré, you arrive at the first gate before you even leave home. You watch the footage on YouTube. You see what 50-foot waves look like when they detonate against the cliff face. You can decide right there, sitting on your couch: 'No. That's not for me.'

The second gate is the headland. You stand up there with thousands of other people and watch the waves roll in. You see them build on the horizon, watch them stack up as they hit the underwater canyon, watch them detonate below. The Nazaré Canyon is the largest submarine canyon in Europe, 230 kilometres long and five kilometres deep, terminating just metres from the beach. Waves travel through the canyon and merge with surface waves, amplifying their size up to three times. You can stand there for hours, studying the sets, feeling the power from a safe distance. And at any point, you can decide: 'No. Not today.'

The third gate is the channel. You ride a jet ski into position, and then you are on the water. You can see the waves coming towards you. You can watch them rear up, see how they break, judge their size against the cliff face behind them. And again, you can decide: 'No. It's too big. I'm sitting this one out.'

The fourth gate is the top of the wave itself. You are being towed into position, the rope tight, the jet ski accelerating. You look down the face. You see what you are about to drop into. Five storeys. Six storeys. A moving wall of water that could crush you like an insect. And even now, even at this final moment, you can hold on to the rope and wave your driver away. You get towed back to safety. You never have to let go.

Four gates. Four chances to say no. Four opportunities to assess the risk and decide whether you are willing to take it.

I have none of them.

I cannot see the footage on YouTube. I cannot see the waves from the headland. I cannot watch them from the channel. I cannot look down the face as I drop in. The first time I know whether a wave is too big, too steep, too dangerous, is when I reach the bottom and feel its power under my feet.

By then, it is too late to back out.

This is what it means to surf blind at Nazaré. No gates. No escape routes. Total commitment from the moment the whistle blows.

But that has always been true. That has been true my whole life. I have never had the option to see the thing coming and decide not to face it. I have always just faced it.

Build your own gates

The harbour at Nazaré was like a row of Formula 1 team warehouses. It's an old fishing port where they used to store boats in winter, but it had been taken over by the biggest names in big wave surfing. Red Bull had a warehouse. BMW had one. Different crews were lined up along the waterfront, with jet skis in rows, tow boards stacked against walls and rescue sleds ready to deploy.

Dylan walked me through and introduced me to the local crews. Rodrigo Koxa. Garrett McNamara. Alemão de Maresias. Names I had been hearing for years, now standing in front of me, shaking my hand, welcoming me to their arena.

It was all a big blur to me. As usual, I was tripping over potholes, tripping up steps, trying not to run my face into boards and bits and pieces hanging out from walls. But I could feel the energy of the place. The smooth fibreglass of the boards under my hands. The rubber grip of the jet ski handles.

That first night, the whole crew came together for dinner — my safety team, the camera crew, the production team for *The Blind Sea* documentary. Edu (Eduardo Garcia), Dylan's business partner who ran his surfboard manufacturing factory in Portugal, was our local fixer. His job was to source whatever we needed.

Dan, the director of *The Blind Sea*, had sent Edu a list of equipment. At dinner, Edu went through it item by item. He had found everything except one thing, which he assumed was a joke.

Condoms. Non lubricated.

Dan told him it was not a joke. We needed them to waterproof the microphones. You slip the mic inside, tie off the end, and the condom protects it from the salt water. The non-lubricated part was important because lubricant damages the electronics.

Edu was a good Catholic boy. He did not want to walk into a pharmacy and ask for non-lubricated condoms. We all laughed, but he was serious. This was the funny side of the trip. We were planning something that could kill me, but we were also a bunch of mates taking the piss out of each other.

But underneath the jokes, there was a serious operation being built. Because I had no gates, we had to build something else. We had to build a system so robust that gates became unnecessary.

Most surfers at Nazaré have one jet ski for safety — maybe two on the really big days. Because I was blind, we started at four from day one. No compromises.

Lucas 'Chumbo' Chianca was my tow driver. I had never met him before arriving in Portugal, but Dylan spoke so highly of him that trust came quickly. And after spending a few days with Lucas, watching the way he approached the risks we were about to take on — not with recklessness, not with bravado, but with that careful preparation followed by full commitment once we hit the water — I recognised something familiar. Two gears: the same two gears I had learned from Mum and Dad. He had both.

My crew on the water were all big wave surfers. Dylan was my primary safety support on the second jet ski. Evo Cacao was on the third jet ski. Edu was on the fourth, with a swimmer, Vini Dos Santos — one of the only men who actually swims at Nazaré on big days. He was ready to jump off and grab me if I ended up unconscious in the water. And Stroggy Cordeiro was up on the headland as my spotter, watching everything from above, calling positions over the radio.

There's one more person I need to mention: Kyle Richardson, a mate I had met years earlier in Hawaii. Kyle is a fellow para surfer. He's wheelchair-bound on land, but in the water he is as capable as anyone. He lived at Nazaré, and he drove one of the jet skis for our camera crew.

Having Kyle there meant something—it meant I was not the only person with a disability in that water. It meant the para surfing community we had built extended even to Nazaré, to the biggest waves in the world.

The whistle system came from a near-death experience back in Australia. When I was learning to tow surf, we had used voice commands. The driver would yell 'Yep, yep, yep!' when it was time to let go. Except one day, with a new driver, he yelled what I thought was 'Go, go, go.' I let go of the rope, pulled into the wave and got absolutely destroyed. I ended up near the rocks that day. Afterwards, he told me he'd actually yelled, 'No, no, no.' At 60 kilometres an hour, with wind and spray in your face, those two words sound identical.

At Nazaré, that kind of miscommunication could kill me.

So we went to a sporting goods store and tested a bunch of whistles, including some referee whistles. Dylan picked an orienteering whistle that nearly deafened us all. We bought five. Every member of my safety team wore one around their neck. The first blow meant let go. The second blow meant start your bottom turn. The third blow meant kick out.

My board was Lucas's board, one Dylan had shaped for him. It was designed for 80-foot-plus waves, but it was perfect for the 50-foot day we were chasing. It had 10 kilos of lead built into it, with five one-kilo blocks running down each side of the stringer (the thin strip of timber running down the middle of the board). The whole thing was wrapped in Kevlar and carbon fibre. It was a bullet with fins.

My inflation vest had four carbon dioxide canisters on the back, with four tabs on the front. Pull a tab and the cylinder releases, then the wave lets you go faster. That is all it does. It doesn't pop you to the surface like people think. It just helps the wave release you, and then you slowly come back up.

Dylan and Lucas had drilled this into me until it was automatic. If anything goes wrong, just pull. Don't be a hero. Don't try to prove anything. Just pull.

Sighted surfers have gates built into the environment. I had to build my gates out of people, systems and trust.

Removing the boogeyman

Day seven in Nazaré was day one of surfing. The conditions had finally come together. The waves had 25- to 30-foot faces.

Lucas drove the ski out past the break. I was floating on my back, holding the handle of the tow rope, looking up at the sky. Waiting. The ocean lifted and dropped beneath us as we went over swells that had not yet broken. I could hear waves detonating somewhere behind us, the sound rolling across the surface like distant thunder.

And I discovered something. There was one gate I did have. The only gate that existed inside me rather than outside me.

Fear.

For the first time in my life, I felt it: real fear. The kind other people talk about. The kind I had spent 44 years not understanding.

My whole life, I had been more afraid of being seen as different than of being hurt. More afraid of being seen as disabled than of dying. I know that is hard to believe. But it is the truth that built everything you have just read. That fear had driven me to tackle boys twice my size in rugby. To punch guys whose fists I couldn't see coming. To play ice hockey when I could hardly see the puck at my feet. I would rather have died proving I was no less than anyone else than live having accepted my limitations.

But lying out the back of Nazaré, holding that rope, I felt something new.

I wasn't scared of dying. I was scared of my children losing their father.

Max. Elsie. Jake. Back home in Australia. Sleeping in their beds, saying their words every night before they closed their eyes. I am brave. I am inquisitive. I am grateful. I am kind. I am happy.

The fear was not for me — it was for them. My death was about my three children losing their father. And that actually scared me.

The media had been asking for weeks whether I was going to die. All those voices saying I didn't belong. The same voices I had heard my whole life. Mothers whispering near my mum at junior footy, saying she was irresponsible for letting her blind son play.

The boogeyman in the closet. The fear of something I couldn't see.

This was my one internal gate — the only checkpoint that existed entirely inside my own mind. I could have told Lucas to take me back to shore. No one would have blamed me. But then I looked at the data.

All those doubters. The media. The friends who didn't understand. None of them were experts.

None of them knew the work that Dylan, the team and I had put in to make this as safe as it could possibly be. I was the main person who had worked on our risk profile. I knew the data better than anyone. The doubters weren't inside our systems. They didn't have what we had.

The data told me the fear was unreasonable. My team trusted me to be in this environment. That trust was built on evidence, not emotion.

When I looked at the real data, the boogeyman disappeared. The fear was removed. I used the data to make a decision. And, once I had made that decision, I committed to it.

Lucas revved the ski. Are you ready, Matt? Are you ready? Are you ready? I could hear the energy and excitement in his voice.

The rope tightened. One blow of the whistle. I pulled the rope for that final acceleration, then I let go.

The moment I finished riding that first wave, the fear was gone.

We surfed for three days. Day two was smaller than the 25- to 30-foot waves of day one, with waves of 15 to 20 feet. I went a bit crazy on the smaller waves, having fun and pushing the limits because I now knew that the system worked. By day three, I was super confident. Maybe too confident.

But here is the strangest thing about surfing the biggest waves in the world.

I didn't hear them.

People ask me all the time what Nazaré sounds like. With hundreds of Olympic-size swimming pools' worth of water crashing down behind you, they assume it must be deafening. But I heard nothing. When I was on a wave, my brain filtered out everything except what I needed. The feel of the rail under my feet. The bumps and chop in the water. The sound of the whistle. Everything else vanished. The roar of the wave breaking behind me, the jet skis, my team hooting... none of it registered. I was in complete silence. At complete peace.

I was so focused that I didn't even realise my brain was filtering information without telling me. It was only keeping the data I needed to survive.

I only understood the silence on day three. We were waiting for my board to be recovered after a wipeout, and Lucas drove us down a 20- to 30-foot wave on the jet ski just for fun. I was just a passenger on the back—not focused, not in the zone. When the wave broke behind us, I heard it for the first time.

The boom. The violence. The sheer weight of the water detonating.

That was the first time I had felt scared in the water since day one. Hearing what the waves actually sounded like made me realise how much my brain had been protecting me. It had been running its own gate system, filtering everything I didn't need, creating silence in the middle of chaos.

If it can happen to them...

Dylan had almost died at Nazaré on a previous trip. It had made the global surf press. He got caught inside, washed toward the rocks and barely survived. After that, he promised his wife he would not surf on this trip. He was coming as my mentor, my board shaper, my safety. He would drive a ski. But he would stay off the boards.

It was day nine in Nazaré. The conditions were too messy for me to navigate blind, so I didn't surf. Dylan went out anyway, driving a ski for one of the cameramen to get footage of empty waves for the movie.

At some point — because surfers cannot help themselves, especially Dylan — he decided to catch a quick wave. He was riding my board. He hit some chop, slipped forward over the nose and the board ran over his head, splitting his scalp open. He needed eight stitches.

I was at the hotel when we got the call. My main guy, my mentor, one of the best big wave surfers in the world was lying in a Portuguese hospital with his head split open.

The forecast said day 10 would be the biggest and cleanest of the whole trip. It was my last chance before flying to the USA for the world championships. And my primary safety was in hospital.

We sat in the Red Bull hangar that night with Lucas, waiting for news, and then the doubt crept in. Dylan was one of the best in the world. He could see. He had decades of experience in these conditions. If that could happen to him, what might happen to me? I was a blind guy with so much less experience in heavy water. Something a lot worse could happen.

I thought about Bex back home. About Dylan's wife waiting for her phone to ring. Our poor wives. Both of us constantly risking our lives for fun, for the challenge. And they had to sit at home holding the fort, raising the kids, waiting for the news that might destroy their worlds.

Dylan was released overnight. The next morning, on day 10, he told me in the car on the way down to the harbour that he had decided to come out anyway.

He had eight stitches in his scalp and couldn't get them wet, so we took the shower cap from the hotel bathroom and duct-taped it to his head. I did the taping. There we were, in the dark, before the sun came up — a blind guy duct-taping a shower cap to his mate's head so he could go back into the biggest waves in the world. We put a beanie over the top because it was cold. He looked absolutely ridiculous.

That is how we roll. There are no gates for blokes like us. Only forward.

When the wave won't let you go

Thick fog covered the water that morning. Even sighted people had no gates. They couldn't see us from the shore. It was just us and the ocean.

I had caught about 25 waves over three days. The confidence was building. Maybe too much.

Stroggy's voice came over the radio from the headland: 'I think there's a big one coming.'

Lucas started towing me into position. 'Are you ready, Matt? Are you ready? Are you ready?' The familiar energy and excitement was in his voice.

Two other tow teams tried to go for the same wave, but Lucas waved them off. He had chosen this wave for me.

I felt the water lift beneath us as we went over the back of it. A big lump of ocean. Steep. Moving. About to break.

One blow of the whistle. I pulled the rope for acceleration and let go.

I dropped straight down the face. Down and down and down. The steepness was incredible. I could feel how big it was under my feet. Then I heard Lucas's whistle. I engaged my rail, tilting the board onto its edge so it cut into the wave face, which gave me grip and control instead of skimming flat across the surface.

I rode across the wave in silence. Pure silence.

I stayed too long; I was having too much fun, overconfident after 25 waves. I could feel the wave drawing up at the end. They call that section 'the Anaconda' at Nazaré — a big snake rearing up to swallow you whole. I heard the third whistle but knew it was too late.

I had no gate to escape through. I jumped off my board, trying to get under the power of the wave.

It absolutely annihilated me.

I got pushed down into the black. Deep. Violent. I knew I had to keep my arms and legs in so they didn't get dislocated — keep my core locked so my back didn't break. I went down, then up, then down again. I was getting dragged upside down, sideways. I didn't know which way was up.

After a while, I started hearing Dylan's and Lucas's voices in my head. 'Don't be a hero. Just pull.'

I pulled one tab on my vest. I felt it inflate, but it didn't do anything. I just kept getting dragged. I pulled the second tab. The canister squeezed around my chest with the explosion of gas.

Finally, the wave started to let me go. Slowly.

That first hold down lasted about 25 seconds.

When I came up, I could hear whistles in the distance. The boys were coming. But they were too far away. I was in the impact zone. And I could hear another wave coming.

The boys had promised I would never have to take two waves. 'Don't worry Matty, no matter what happens we have the best safety team in the world. You won't have to get a second one on the head.' Four jet skis. Best safety team in the world.

They weren't going to reach me in time.

I laughed. Actually laughed, floating there in my bright orange wetsuit. A kind of giggle. *Fuck you guys,* I thought. *You said you'd get here.*

My vest was inflated. I couldn't dive under the oncoming wall of whitewater — a 15-foot wall of whitewater coming at me like a freight train. I took the biggest breath I could and waited for the impact.

The second wave hit me harder than the first. I felt like an ant being hit by a garden hose on full. I got absolutely blasted and bounced and dragged. I locked every muscle in my body. Arms crossed over my chest. Legs crossed. Nothing to do but survive. The second hold down felt even longer than the first, although it probably wasn't.

When I finally came up, the jet skis were converging from every direction. But no one could see me in my bright orange wetsuit. I had four jet skis searching for me, with four cameras on land. A drone in the sky, and thousands of people on the headland.

And for long seconds, nobody knew where I was.

I had been dragged so far that I was out of the impact zone by the time they found me.

Lucas reached me first. 'Are you okay?'

'Yeah man. I'm cool.'

'We're done for today.'

'One more?'

'No way. No more.'

Forty years in one wave

The wave was measured at 51 feet. It was a Guinness World Record: the largest wave ever surfed by a blind person.

But here is what people miss when they see the footage.

They see a 51-foot wave. They don't see the esky lid.

They don't see the hundreds of waves caught on a bodyboard at age five, with Dad taking me out over and over again at Narrabeen to catch one more. They don't see me learning to hear the waves and feel them on my tummy before I ever stood up.

They see a world record. They don't see the bodyboard at five, the shortboard at 11, the wipeouts at 15 that taught me how to hold my breath when the ocean decided to teach me a lesson.

They see a blind man on a giant wave. They don't see Phil Shaw answering via a text message from a stranger's wife: 'No worries, I'll take him out.' They don't see the years of building capacity at home, surfing bigger and bigger waves with a mate who treated me like a surfer instead of a liability.

They see the Guinness certificate. They don't see my neighbours watching me walk around the block with piss on my shorts, holding my breath until my face turned purple, building the lung capacity that let me survive two consecutive giant wave hold-downs.

Forty years. From an esky lid to a 51-foot wave. Every wave I had ever caught, every wipeout I had ever survived, every system I had ever built — all of it was in that wave.

Dylan told me afterwards he had seen waves that big and a lot bigger at Nazaré. But he'd never seen one that big and clean and perfect. He was jealous. He had never caught one like that himself.

Back at the harbour, we had beers at a café by the water. Then we got in the car and drove to Lisbon. By that evening, I was on a plane to the USA. Two days later, I was competing at the ISA World Para Surfing Championships in Pismo, California.

Judged against everyone

In 2023, I was nominated for the Heavy Water Award at the Surfing Australia Awards. Not para surfing. Not adaptive. The open category. The best big wave surfer in Australia.

The Surfing Australia Awards is where the who's who of Australian surfing gathers. Legends. Champions. That night, Taj Burrow was inducted into the Hall of Fame. The room was packed with the heaviest names in the sport.

I couldn't believe I was even nominated. Then I found out I was a finalist. Top three. When they announced the Heavy Water finalists, they put all three of us up on the screen behind the stage, showing big edits for each finalist. My footage from Nazaré was being played alongside footage from the heaviest chargers in the country — men who dedicate their lives to the biggest, most dangerous waves on earth. Men who have every gate available to them. Men who can see.

I thought I had no chance of winning.

Vaughan Blakey was the MC that night. He read out all the finalists. And then he said: 'And the winner is Matt Formston.'

I couldn't believe it when I heard my name. An able-bodied award, not a para category. Not a special recognition. The actual award, judged against everyone. For the first time in my adult athletic career, I wasn't being recognised as a para athlete. I was being recognised as an athlete. Full stop.

I was sitting there holding Bex's hand. And then I had to work out how I was going to get up on that stage in a dark room without falling over, knocking things over, running into people and making an absolute fool of myself, as I usually do in those environments. But by this point I was comfortable using a cane, so I used it to get up on stage.

Ross Clarke-Jones handed me the trophy and interviewed me on stage about Nazaré. He's a big wave legend. One of the names I had grown up hearing about. And he was handing me an award that said I was the best in the country at what he had spent his life doing.

Bex was right there. The woman who had been my bedrock through all of this. Ten years earlier, in 2013, I had won my first world cup gold medal in cycling, and she had been there through all of it. Every training session. Every early morning. Every gold medal. Every record. Every sacrifice the family made so I could chase these dreams.

And now she was with me for this.

It felt like winning my first Best and Fairest trophy at the end of my Under 9s Narrabeen Sharks season. Back then, I wasn't being judged as a blind kid who did well for someone with a disability. I was being judged as the best player in my team. And I had won.

The delusion was never a delusion

Sighted surfers have gates. They can watch from the headland. They can assess from the channel. They can look down the face and decide. At every step, they can choose to say no.

I have no gates. I have only the systems I build and the people I trust and the one internal checkpoint that exists inside my own mind.

Fear tried to close that gate: the voices that had followed me since childhood, the media asking if I was going to die, the boogeyman in the closet. But I looked at the data. The boogeyman disappeared. I let go of the rope. I surfed a 51 foot wave blind.

And I came home to my children.

All those voices saying I didn't belong. All those years of mothers whispering that my mum was irresponsible for letting me play. All those media questions asking if I was going to die.

I had answered them all. Not with words, but with a 51-foot wave and an award that said I was the best in the country at what I did.

The delusion was never a delusion. It was just a goal that other people couldn't understand yet.

The Australian SAS selection course is designed to break candidates down to reveal their character. As a former commanding officer described it: 'Selection gives a good insight into the soul of the individual.' Of the 160 candidates who typically start, fewer than 36 finish. Research on these selections has found something counterintuitive: the soldiers who fail most often are not the weakest—they are the ones who have always succeeded. The naturally gifted athletes, the ones picked first, the ones who received constant praise, they quit at higher rates because the environment is foreign to them. The soldiers who pass are often the ones who were never the star, who had to grind their entire lives just to be average. For them, selection is simply an extension of what they have always experienced. They are used to operating without gates. Stanford psychologist Dr Alia Crum has spent her career proving the neuroscience behind this phenomenon. Her research demonstrates that what we believe about ourselves doesn't merely influence perception—it changes physiology, performance and outcomes. The delusion that gets you to the start line becomes the engine that carries you through. Belief converts to biological fact. The goal other people cannot understand is already real inside you. Your only job is to make the outside match the inside.

• • •

What gate are you hiding behind? And what would happen if you walked through it?

Chapter 21

The Cane

Own Every Hat

> You are not one person. You are many. Parent, athlete, businessman, mate, beginner, expert — each role requires a different version of you. It's not a mask; it's the real you, tuned for that context. The people who thrive aren't the ones with a single unshakeable identity — they're the ones who can shift between selves without losing the thread. Own every hat. Know when to wear each one. And know that the tool you've been refusing to use might be the one that helps you be your best when wearing any of the hats in your life.

I've been sitting in drawers for 25 years.

Not the same drawer: different drawers, in different houses, in different cities. Bedside tables. Closet shelves. The back corners of cupboards where things go when you don't want to look at them but can't quite throw them away. I'd get moved during relocations, wrapped in old shirts, placed carefully into boxes like I mattered. Then I'd be unpacked and shoved into a new drawer in a new house, where I'd wait again.

I'm a white cane, with an aluminium shaft. I have a white tip with a red strip at the end. I'm foldable for storage. I'm too long for him, actually—he didn't know about sizing when he bought me. He didn't want to know.

His canes now have suspension springs and swivels on the tips so they flex and don't get caught on things. I'm old school, stiff. A bit shit for walking, to be honest.

But I'm also the same cane he bought when he was 23 years old, back in 2002—standing in a store in Sydney, feeling like he was purchasing his own death certificate.

He didn't want me—let me be crystal fucking clear about that. He hated everything I represented. Every time he felt me in his hands, he felt the same thing—the thing he'd spent his whole life running from. Disability. Dependence. Being seen as less than.

So he kept me in drawers. A spare. Just in case his other cane broke while travelling. For years I'd been chucked in bags and taken on trips, but never actually been taken out. During 25 years of backup duty, I was never once unfolded.

Until Bali.

The beginning

You've already read about how Matt got me: the door-to-door electricity sales job he talks about in Chapter 8. The customers who couldn't trust a man who wouldn't look them in the eye. The manager who told him to get a cane or lose his job.

He bought me as a prop, not as an accessibility tool. He didn't know what size he needed. He just grabbed me off the shelf and hoped I'd solve his problem.

The first time he unfolded me was in Frenchs Forest. I could feel his heart pounding through his grip. He was terrified of what I meant. Of being seen.

And even then, he couldn't commit. He'd walk along the street with me folded up, tucked under his arm like a shameful secret. Only at a customer's gate would he unfold me — a costume he put on briefly for the performance.

But the moment he unfolded me, he realised that finding things became so much easier. He could feel the path, the steps, the obstacles. The tool he was ashamed of was the tool that actually helped. His sales increased exponentially. More people were saying yes. But instead of feeling proud, he felt sick. Were they signing because of his pitch? Or because they felt sorry for the blind guy at the door?

He quit that job. And I went into a drawer.

For the next 14 years, I was his only cane, even though I lived in a drawer.

The others

Around 2015, something shifted in Matt. He started owning his identity. Started accepting that he was a man with a disability, and that didn't make him less than anyone else.

That's when the other canes came into his life.

Shorter ones, with better technology. Canes that were the right length for his height. Professional, sleek canes that belong in boardrooms and on stages and in international airports.

Those canes got to do everything.

They walked him into corporate headquarters for executive meetings. They guided him through security at airports in Los Angeles, Singapore, London. They stood beside him on stages in front of thousands of people. They helped him navigate conference centres where he delivered keynotes about resilience and leadership.

One of them — not me — even got to walk him into Government House on the day he was awarded the Member of the Order of Australia.

I heard about it from the drawer: the ceremony, the Governor, the handshake. The moment when everything he'd built—the world championships, the world records, the business career, the community work—was formally recognised by his country.

One of those fancy new canes was there for that. I was wrapped in an old shirt in a cupboard.

I'm not going to pretend that didn't sting.

I'd waited for 25 years. I was his first. And I never got to be part of any of all the things he achieved in cycling, in surfing, on that wave in Nazaré.

He did all of that, and I sat in the darkness.

I understood why. I was too long. The wrong design. No suspension. I was a reminder of a version of himself he'd rather forget—the scared 23-year-old standing at a stranger's gate in Frenchs Forest, shaking with shame.

But understanding doesn't stop it hurting.

The question

After Nazaré, people kept asking Matt the same thing.

'So, what's next?'

It always made him laugh a little.

But still the question came, every time: 'What's next?' As if everything he'd done needed to be justified by whatever came next.

His breath capacity had come up in interviews, so people started suggesting freediving. He was comfortable in the ocean, able to stay calm when everything around him was trying to kill him.

Matt currently holds the record for the biggest wave surfed by any blind person. That box is ticked. The next box: the deepest dive by any para freediver. Not the deepest dive by a blind freediver, but *any* para freediver. Any disability. Any category.

He thought about holding both records at the same time.

I don't think anyone's ever done that. And Matt likes doing things no one's ever done.

People always point out that freedivers can close their eyes underwater and feel relaxed. But closing your eyes sometimes is very different to being blind. You can open your eyes again if something doesn't feel right. Matt can't — he has to do the whole thing with his eyes closed, essentially. Just darkness from start to finish.

So, in September 2025, Matt went to a place called Amed on the northeast coast of Bali.

He'd found a coach: Dan Parsons, one of the best freediving coaches in Australia, maybe the world. Dan runs a business called Freediving Central. He spends more time overseas than at home, training people at depth in perfect conditions around the globe.

And it turned out Dan lived only a couple of suburbs away from Matt when he was in Australia.

Matt had never freedived before — not once. He'd done more than 300 scuba dives. He'd built his breath capacity for big wave surfing. But swimming down as deep as he could on a single breath just to see how far he could go? He'd never attempted that.

Ten days later, he hit 108 feet.

And then he hit a wall.

There's a tiny piece of tissue at the back of the throat called the vocal fold. At extreme depth, you have to use it to move air from your lungs and into your sinuses to equalise the pressure. It's called reverse packing, and it's incredibly technical. And at 108 feet, under pressure, upside down in complete darkness, Matt couldn't make it work.

His lungs were fine. His air was fine. His mental state was calm. He had no pain in his ears or anywhere. But that tiny piece of tissue wouldn't cooperate. He couldn't go any deeper.

Most people take years to reach 100 feet; he'd done it in 10 days. But he was frustrated. He could feel the ceiling, and he couldn't break through it.

The problem

Dan and Matt were trying to figure out how he could swim freely in the ocean rather than just going up and down a fixed line. The line was safe but limiting. He wanted to explore — swim over reefs and around structures and through the open water.

The problem was navigation.

In scuba diving, Matt follows the light bouncing off his buddy. Bex was often his dive partner, and at slow speeds she could pull him out of the way of sharks and stingrays and other things he couldn't see. But in freediving, there's no time to be slow. You have one breath. You have to move efficiently. You can't waste time being tentative.

They sat down and talked through options — the way Matt does with everything. Two gears. Planning first.

Pool noodles? Too flexible. Matt could end up swimming too high or too low.

They kept brainstorming. And then Matt said it.

'What about this old cane I've had forever? The one I've never used?'

I'd been brought along on this trip as a backup, just in case his good cane broke. Same as every other trip. Same role I'd had for 25 years — sitting in a bag, waiting for something that never happened.

But now Matt was pulling me out, wrapping tape around my joints.

Packing tape. Stiff and rigid so I couldn't extend or fold — until I was locked straight like a pipe.

And I was perfect.

I wasn't perfect despite being the wrong cane but *because* I was the wrong cane.

Too long? That meant I fit perfectly between Dan and Matt — the right distance for two bodies swimming in unison. Dan holds the ball at my tip. Matt holds my handle at the back. They're an arm's length apart, with room to move — but close enough to stay connected.

Too stiff? That meant Dan could rotate his wrist and I'd transfer the movement directly to Matt. No flex. No lag. Instant communication through pressure and direction.

No suspension springs? No swivels? That meant I wouldn't absorb the subtle steering inputs. Every adjustment Dan made, Matt would feel immediately.

His fancy canes — the ones that walked into Government House, the ones with the springs and swivels and the perfect length and the sleek design — they would have been useless for this. Too short. Too flexible. Too sophisticated.

I was built for walking on land. Turns out I was actually built for navigating shipwrecks on a single breath.

I'd spent 25 years in a drawer. And the thing that made me wrong for everything else made me right for something none of those other canes could ever do.

The shipwreck

The USAT *Liberty*, a cargo ship torpedoed by the Japanese in 1942, sits just off the beach in Amed. The shipwreck is one of the most famous dive sites in Indonesia. The boat has spent more than 80 years underwater, encrusted with coral, home to thousands of fish.

Dan had been through it himself many times. He'd mentioned to Matt that they might swim through the torpedo hole — the gap blown through the hull nearly 100 years ago.

The plan was simple. Swim along the outside of the wreck — Dan holding the ball at my tip, Matt holding my handle. A cameraman named Jimbo was sitting at about 30 feet to get shots for a new documentary about Matt's freediving journey.

Then Dan made the call.

'I reckon we can swim through the hole.'

I thought about what Matt had told me about the *Adelaide*, a shipwreck off the coast near his home. Seven years earlier, in 2018, he'd been scuba diving inside that wreck when his torches went out. Complete darkness, not the reduced vision he lives with every day. Absolute blackness. He was surrounded by metal that could slice through his air hoses if he bumped into it wrong. He thought he was going to die.

He remembered thinking, *If you don't stay calm right now, you die. This is where you die, Matt, if you don't keep your head on your shoulders.*

He'd survived that one. Whacked the torch until it flickered back on. Swam out.

This was different. There was no tank this time. No torch. One breath. If something went wrong inside that wreck, there'd be no time to fix it.

But Matt had Dan. And Matt had me.

'Why not?' he said.

They took long, slow breaths, filling their lungs completely. Then they took their last breath, and down they went.

I've never felt anything like it: the pressure of the water closing around me; the pull of two bodies swimming in perfect unison; Dan's hand firm on the ball at my tip, guiding us through the darkness; Matt's hand firm on my handle, trusting me completely.

We went through the torpedo hole.

Inside the wreck, I could feel the water change. It was so still. We were enclosed. The temperature was slightly different. There was metal all around us that Matt couldn't see — that he had to trust wasn't going to cut him open or trap him or end his life.

But he didn't panic; he didn't let go. He held me and swam and trusted.

We came out the other side, about 36 feet down. Surfaced with air to spare.

Dan looked at Matt. 'That felt pretty easy. How about we go under the whole bottom of the boat?'

He didn't give much warning. Didn't tell Matt how deep it was. Just said it like it was the obvious next step.

And I thought: *Oh fuck. How did I get myself into this situation?*

For a moment, I was terrified. Underneath the entire hull of a shipwreck? Sixty feet down? One breath? Metal everywhere?

But then something else hit me.

I'd been stuck in a drawer for 25 years. Safe, unused, forgotten. And now here I was, being asked to do something that mattered. Something dangerous. Something real.

This was the opposite of a drawer. This was living.

After 25 years of sitting in darkness, I had a chance to actually be part of something. To help. To matter. To go somewhere those fancy Government House canes would never go.

Why the fuck not.

Matt didn't hesitate either. 'Let's go.'

Jimbo the cameraman didn't know where we'd gone. He was sitting at 30 feet getting shots, and suddenly we'd vanished.

We swam underneath the entire hull of a Second World War shipwreck on a single breath. Sixty feet down. The deepest free swim Matt had ever done without the freediving line.

Dan navigating by sight; Matt navigating by trust. Me connecting them.

Then we just popped up on the other side of the wreck.

If Matt had let go of me and panicked, he would have swum straight into the side of the boat. Perhaps cut himself open on 80-year-old metal. Drowned inside a shipwreck with no air.

But he didn't let go. He held on. He trusted.

I'd waited 25 years for this, in drawers, in darkness. I'd always been the thing he was too ashamed to carry. And now I was the one helping him do something that no one had ever done before — diving under a shipwreck blind.

Those fancy canes? They could never.

The mantas

They also took me to swim with manta rays.

Nusa Lembongan, another island near Bali. The mantas come through on the current, enormous creatures with wingspans wider than Matt is tall. Ancient and graceful, gliding through water their kind has owned for 20 million years.

We went down about 30 feet on a single breath, Dan steering and Matt following, with me between them.

The mantas swam above us. Matt couldn't see them clearly — they were just dark shapes against lighter water. He couldn't feel the water displacement as they passed. But he could feel their presence — the same resonance he picks up in boardrooms, the energy that tells him who's engaged and who's checked out before anyone speaks. Sighted people read faces; Matt reads frequencies. It's how he's navigated sporting arenas and executive tables his whole life.

Matt has a tattoo of three manta rays on his back and shoulder. They symbolise him and his parents — the foundations they gave him to take off and fly. Their initials and birth years are inked into the design. He got that tattoo the year before he met Bex.

That's one of the gifts of freediving. You're not intruding on the ocean with tanks and bubbles and mechanical noise—you're just bodies in the water, holding your breath, moving quietly. The animals don't flee: they accept you as part of their world.

I was part of that world now too. Not a symbol of disability. Not a mark of shame. A tool for wonder.

Three titles

At the end of 2025, Matt entered his first pool freediving competition. He'd been training for only a few months. He was the newest person in the sport. A complete beginner by any measure.

He won three Australian titles. And he wasn't far off setting para freediving world records.

In 2026, he'll compete at the world championships in both pool freediving and depth freediving. He says he's planning to become a world champion in both disciplines. He says he's planning to set world records in both.

He hasn't looked up what the current records are. He doesn't want to know. He doesn't want his brain to decide that a certain number is the limit because someone else stopped there.

He'll just train to be the best version of himself. Push until he can't push anymore. And trust that when he does that, it'll probably be enough.

This time next year, he says, he'll be a world champion in three sports: cycling, surfing, freediving.

I believe him. I've watched him for 25 years from the darkness of my drawer. I know what he's capable of when he decides something is going to happen.

Every hat

Here's what I've learned about Matt in these months of finally being used.

He doesn't own just one version of himself. He becomes different people depending on what the situation requires.

With his mates, he's one person. Rough. Takes the piss. Gives as good as he gets. At work, he's another. Professional. Strategic. Direct. With his children, he shifts between gentle and firm, and they know both versions of their father. As a keynote speaker, he's confident and commanding — the man who's done impossible things and earned the right to tell people about them. As a freediver, he's humble and eager to learn. He's a beginner comfortable with not knowing, who's willing to fail and fail and fail until he figures it out.

These aren't masks. They're all genuinely him. Different aspects of the same person, brought forward for different contexts, tuned for different relationships and challenges.

He calls this owning every hat — giving each role the right version of yourself. The right mindset, the right behaviours, the right energy.

The speaker on stage is useless in the water. The humble beginner is useless on stage. The rough mate is useless with his kids. The strategic businessman is useless in a pub fight.

Same person. Different hats. Each one authentic. Each one necessary.

I think I understand this now.

For 25 years, I represented something he couldn't afford to be. But I didn't stop existing. I just waited in a drawer until Matt was ready to see how his blindness is woven through every hat he wears.

And it turns out that the tool that was wrong for walking was exactly right for diving. When he realised I could be useful, I became a symbol of him visibly accepting how his blindness is part of him.

I'm still a white cane — but I'm not what I used to be. Or rather, I'm exactly what I always was, but Matt is the one who's changed. He's one of the toughest and bravest people on the planet, but his true bravery doesn't come from his ability to lock out pain or charge 50-foot waves.

His true bravery comes from his ability to be vulnerable. To let things in.

He wasn't always like this. He was a coward — too scared to show people all aspects of himself. He was physically tough but emotionally unavailable. And that stopped everything — creativity, growth, connection. He couldn't find solutions because he couldn't admit he needed help. He was too much of a coward to be vulnerable and show his true self to everybody.

Now that he's emotionally open, everything's different. He has the humility to accept that without me, he couldn't have done the shipwreck swim. There's no way he could have navigated that dive without some kind of tool connecting him to Dan.

Twenty years ago, he would have found a way to prove he didn't need help. His pride would have killed the possibility.

But now that he's accepted who he is — *all of who he is* — he's become a better version of himself.

I didn't change. He did. What he was willing to let me mean changed.

For 25 years, he was ashamed of me. He saw me as a symbol of everything he was running from. Now he takes me into shipwrecks on a single breath. Now he uses me to swim with manta rays. Now he holds me in the darkness at 60 feet and trusts me to connect him to the person who will bring him safely back to the surface.

If I could speak, I'd tell him this: 'I was never the thing you were afraid of. I was just a piece of aluminium with a white tip. You were afraid of what I meant. What people would think. What it would say about you.'

But meaning isn't fixed. It changes when you change. To Matt, I used to mean disability; now I mean capability. I used to mean limitation; now I mean connection. I used to mean shame; now I mean something else entirely.

And now that Matt owns every element of himself, and is brave enough to be vulnerable, I think he would agree.

For 25 years, he was ashamed of me. Now I help him stay alive in the deep.

And next year, when he stands on a podium as a world champion in three sports, I'll be there too. Taped up. Ready. Waiting to go deeper. Because that's what we do now.

We go deeper.

Yale psychologist Patricia Linville spent her career studying what she called 'self-complexity'—the degree to which people see themselves as having multiple distinct roles and identities. Her research found something counterintuitive: people with greater self-complexity are more resilient to stress and setbacks. When one aspect of their identity is threatened—a job loss, a failed relationship, a physical limitation—the other aspects remain intact. They have eggs in multiple baskets. The people who struggle most are the ones who've built their entire identity around a single thing. When that thing fails, everything fails. Matt spent decades building different selves—athlete, husband, parent, speaker, coach, businessman. Each one genuine. Each one distinct. And in a drawer, waiting for 25 years, sat a valuable tool that became a symbol for accepting how blindness was part of every hat he wore. The tool he was ashamed of became the tool that connected him to the next version of himself. Self-complexity isn't about being fake. It's about being complete.

• • •

How many versions of yourself do you have? Do you know the strengths and weaknesses of each one? And is there a helpful tool sitting in a drawer somewhere—something you've been too ashamed to use—that might be exactly what you need for where you're going next?

Chapter 22

The Eighth Standard

Trust

> Trust is the eighth Hard Standard — the one I told you we'd have to build together. Not because I was holding it back, but because trust can't be taught — it can only be earned. Trust is both the foundation and the amplifier of everything else. Without it, the other seven standards are just ideas. With trust, the Hard Standards become a system that can take you anywhere.

Sixty feet down, eyes closed, while descending along the hull of a Second World War shipwreck, I started to feel doubt.

Dan was taking us down the side of the wreck, towards the ocean floor. The plan was to go under the hull, through a hole in the bottom, and up through the centre. A route he'd mapped. A route I couldn't see. One breath. No tank. No safety line. Just trust.

Then the thought arrived: *Can I hold my breath this long?*

My diaphragm was starting to pulse — an involuntary twitch that tells you your body wants air. It's not yet desperate, but it's asking. Soon it would be demanding.

The second thought came fast: *Let go of the cane. Swim for the surface. Get out.*

I didn't know how far down we were, or if we'd passed under the hull yet. I was uncertain whether the shipwreck was above me or still beside me. If I swam up now and the wreck was above me, I'd hit steel. Hospital or dead. Those were the options.

And then came the thought that mattered most: *I trust Dan. I made that call before we went under. Now I have to deliver that trust with my actions.*

So I held on. I kept my grip on the cane and kept kicking. I kept my breath locked in my chest while my body screamed for air.

Seconds passed. Each one felt like a minute.

Then we went through a hole in the bottom of the hull, right on the sea floor. We flattened out. We started swimming horizontally through the belly of the wreck. Dan was navigating by memory and feel while I followed blindly, trusting that he knew where the exit was.

Then we started ascending. Rising through the centre of the wreck. My lungs were burning but holding.

We broke the surface in open water, the wreck behind us. I breathed. Felt the sun on my face. Mount Agung — Bali's active volcano, the same one that pushed this ship into the sea 60 years ago — towered above us on the shore.

I was smiling. It felt amazing.

That's what trust looks like when you've already made the decision to put your trust in someone. The only question is whether you'll honour that trust when everything in your body is screaming at you to break it.

If I'd let go — if I'd panicked and swum blind for the surface — I'd be dead. Or I'd have surfaced alone, having abandoned my cane, having abandoned Dan, having proven that my word means nothing when it costs me something.

If I'd let go, I wouldn't just have broken my trust with Dan: I'd have broken his trust in me. The next time we tried something innovative, something at the edge, he'd hesitate. He'd remember the guy who panicked at 60 feet. He'd factor that into every decision.

Trust is a bank account. Every kept promise is a deposit. Every broken one is a withdrawal. And some withdrawals close the account forever.

We've got plans, Dan and I. Crazier than a shipwreck. Maybe diving under ice. Maybe something no one's thought of yet. Those plans only work if the trust account stays full. If we both know, without question, that when it matters most, we'll deliver.

I held on.

That's the standard.

Being open to trust

There have been significant betrayals along the way: people I trusted deeply who broke that trust in ways that cost me financially and emotionally. I cut ties with every one of them. Rebuilding trust with someone who has broken it requires extraordinary consistency and proof, and in most cases that won't be possible. So, I didn't try. They were gone from my life and my family's life.

Even so, I chose to keep trusting other people. That was the harder path. The easier path would have been to close off, assume everyone was the same, build walls. But walls don't just keep bad people out — they also keep good people out. Without trust, you can't build elite teams, you can't perform at the highest level and you can't have the relationships that make any of it worthwhile.

The choice to stay open to new people after betrayal took more courage than I expected. But every meaningful thing I've built since — in sport, in business, in my family — has been built on trust with the people I choose to let in.

Building trust in myself

If you've read this far, you know about my lost, floating years: the drinking, the fighting, the violence that nearly put me in jail or in the ground.

What I haven't named until now is what was actually missing.

Trust.

I didn't trust anyone. And no one was trustworthy.

I remember leaving the Hotel Steyne at Manly one night. While walking along the road in the dark, running my hand along the wall because I couldn't see, I bumped into someone and it ended in an altercation. Then, while I was waiting in the taxi line, the same guys kept coming back for more.

That was my life. Feeling my way along walls; ending up in fights because I was operating from fear. I never knew if someone would help me get home or leave me to figure it out alone.

What I didn't understand back then was that I couldn't trust anyone else because I couldn't trust myself.

When you're lost and don't know what you want, how do you know what your standards are? I would let standards slip — turn up late, not do a job to the best of my ability, react badly when I should have stayed calm. Every slipped standard eroded trust. My trust in myself.

The rebuild started there — with becoming someone I could trust.

The chin-up bar I talk about in Chapter 10 was the first grain of sand in this rebuild. Every time I walked through the door, I did at least 10 chin-ups.

I walked in and out of that room 10 times a day or more. That's 100 chin-ups before I'd even thought about training.

There was no twisting the story. I either did them or I didn't. If I walked under the bar without doing the chin-ups, I broke the promise. No excuses. No negotiations. No moving the goalposts.

Then it became getting out of bed at the same time every day. Then training before work, no matter what. Then controlling my reactions in situations that used to make me explode.

Grain by grain, the mountain grew.

I started to trust that I would do what I said I would do — that I would hold my own standards even when no one was watching. I began to trust myself and to know how I'd show up. I'd become consistent — I'd built self-trust.

Once you build enough trust, it starts building itself — just like the Hard Standard 'The Hard Way Is the Easy Way'. The early deposits are hard — showing up when you don't feel like it, keeping promises no one would notice if you broke, doing the 10 chin-ups even when you're running late — but stack enough grains of sand and the mountain develops its own gravity. People start trusting you before you've proven anything to them personally, because your reputation arrives first. Opportunities come to you instead of you chasing them. Partners want to work with you because they've heard you deliver.

In your professional life, this is everything. Turn up early to meetings — not just on time, but early. Deliver what you promised when you promised it. And when you can't deliver, tell people before they have to chase you. I started telling people, 'You're third in line right now.' That way, they know I will get to them soon. This kind of transparency builds trust even when the news isn't good.

If you break something, you can build trust by getting in front of it falling on your sword early, simply saying, 'I stuffed this up. Here's what happened. Here's what I'm doing about it.' When you're honest, even in failure, it tells people they can rely on you to tell the truth.

The compound interest of trust is real, but you can tear it all down with one bad decision. Years of deposits, wiped out by a single withdrawal. That's why consistency matters more than heroics. The mountain is built grain by grain, yet it can collapse in an avalanche.

Judgement versus accountability

An athlete will never judge you for working out. A millionaire won't judge you for starting a business. A musician won't judge you for trying to sing a song.

It's always the person going nowhere who has something to say.

The people who judged me during those floating years — the ones who said 'How many fingers?', the ones who made comments about my blindness, the ones who tore down instead of built up — they weren't above me. They were threatened by me. I wasn't better than them, but my existence highlighted something they didn't want to face about themselves.

Judgement tears down, while accountability builds up. Judgement comes from people who are threatened; accountability comes from people who are invested.

Bex holds me accountable. Dan holds me accountable. My parents held me accountable. They'll call me out when I'm wrong but they're doing it because they want me to be better, not because they need me to be smaller.

The first time Bex called me out, we were at a kid's birthday party on Narrabeen Lake. I was with a few mates, being rowdy, just carrying on the way we'd always carried on — a bunch of blokes being loud at a party. It didn't feel unusual to me.

Later that night, when it was just the two of us, she said: 'I'm not a hundred per cent cool with that type of behaviour.'

I wasn't even conscious we'd been too rowdy. But that was the point — I'd been on autopilot, and she'd held up a mirror. From that moment, I was more conscious.

That's what good accountability looks like. It doesn't tear you down — it makes you aware.

Trust goes both ways

Every partnership in this book ran on trust. But the trust had to go both ways.

Lucas didn't just trust me when he towed me into that wave at Nazaré. He trusted that I would execute because if I didn't, he was in danger too.

Mick didn't just trust me on the back of his tandem. He trusted me to hold my line at 100 kilometres an hour. One wrong move from either of us and we're both dead.

Dan arrived in Bali already knowing who I was. He'd seen *The Blind Sea*. That reputational trust opened the door, but it only got us to the first conversation. The week of training that followed was him validating that reputation through personal experience.

That's how I ended up 60 feet down, holding my cane while Dan held the other end, trusting him to navigate a shipwreck I couldn't see. And he trusted me not to panic.

Trust goes both ways. You have to be worth trusting to receive it.

If you die

People ask what it was like saying goodbye to Bex before Nazaré.

The truth is less dramatic than they want it to be.

I was already in Portugal. The swell was coming. I FaceTimed her from my apartment — they could see me, I couldn't really see them, but that's how we always do it. The kids were around somewhere. She was doing whatever she was doing.

I was excited. Genuinely excited. The waves were coming and we were going to get out there.

She said: 'Good luck. Be safe.'

Then she said: 'If you die, I'll curse your spirit.'

That's Bex. That's us. We don't lean into the headspace of not coming home. We don't write letters to be opened in case of death. We trust the process. Trust the preparation. Trust the safety team. Trust each other.

The most dangerous part of that whole trip was probably the car ride from Lisbon airport. More people die in car accidents than big wave surfing. But nobody writes dramatic goodbye letters before getting in an Uber.

Hard and soft

I'm physically hard as rock. You know that by now.

But emotionally, I'm as soft as a marshmallow. And I'm proud of that.

Bex and I watch TV sometimes after the kids go to bed. If something emotional happens on screen — usually something happy — I have to leave the room. Something gets caught in my eye.

Bex says, 'Oh, here he goes again.' She thinks it's hilarious.

The Biggest Loser gets me every time. When people have massive physical transformations and that unlocks something emotional with their loved ones, I'm done. And don't get me started on *Marley & Me*. The dog dying is too much. I have to leave the room.

So I can do monster days in the gym, make hard calls in meetings ... then cry over a reality TV show.

Once it happened enough times, I realised: it's actually bravery to not hide it — to be completely emotionally available with the people who matter.

It's a contrast — like the Hard Standard 'Two Gears, One Engine'. Build it. Own it. Don't shy away from it.

Rock hard. Marshmallow soft. Both — on purpose.

The Hard Standards

I've watched teams — sports teams, business teams, all kinds of teams — built on bravado, where everyone is posturing and nobody is willing to admit their weaknesses. Those teams lose to teams where people bring their true selves — where vulnerability is allowed and different perspectives are welcomed.

The team that can say 'I don't know' will always beat the team that pretends to know everything. The leader who can say 'I was wrong' will always outperform the leader who never admits their mistakes.

Trust is what makes that possible.

Every Hard Standard I've given you in this book runs on trust.

Two Gears, One Engine? You can't commit fully without trusting the process. Standards Without Consequences Are Just Wishes? No one believes you'll enforce your standards unless they trust your consistency. The Bullshit Audit? You can't be honest with yourself without trusting the truth won't destroy you. The Hard Way Is the Easy Way? You won't invest in preparation unless you trust it will pay off. The Future Is Already Real? Belief requires trust. Empathy Is a Superpower? People won't let you in unless they trust your intentions. Own Every Hat? You can't shift between selves without trusting each one will be accepted.

Trust is the eighth standard: the one that makes the other seven work.

My formula for building trust

I use a simple formula for trust. I've tested it in boardrooms, in the ocean and in every relationship that matters to me:

Trust = Standards × Consistency × Time

The multiplication sign is the whole point. If any variable is zero, the entire output is zero. You can't shortcut trust. You can't fake it. You can't announce your way to it. You have to do the work.

Standards are the commitments you refuse to lower, regardless of pressure. They're not the ones on the wall in your company's reception area; they're the ones you actually hold yourself to when no one's watching. The chin-up bar. The 10 reps every time you walk through the doorway. The promise you made to yourself that you'd stop making excuses. If your standards aren't observable and don't carry real consequences when broken, they're not standards — they're suggestions.

Consistency is showing up the same way every time. It's the multiplier that either amplifies your standards into trust or exposes them as performance. One bad day doesn't destroy trust. But a pattern of inconsistency tells people you're unreliable — and once that signal is sent, people stop investing in you. They protect themselves instead of committing to you.

Time is the compounder. It's sustained demonstration that turns behaviour into reputation. Trust cannot be hacked or accelerated beyond a certain point. Dan and I built trust in a week in Bali, but only because both of us brought the reputations we'd built over decades. The time had already been invested. When Dan watched me train for a week and saw that my standards and consistency matched my reputation, trust compounded fast. When Mick and I rode together for years, trust compounded through thousands of hours of shared delivery at 100 kilometres an hour.

The formula works everywhere. It works in a marriage — Bex and I have built compound trust over more than a decade of consistent standards. It works in business — every corporate relationship I've built has followed the same pattern. It works in elite sport — every pilot, every spotter, every safety crew member earned my trust through the same three variables.

And it breaks the same way everywhere too. When someone's standards collapse, or their consistency fractures, the formula resets to zero. That's why the betrayals I've experienced have been so devastating — and why I cut those people out of my life rather than trying to rebuild. Time is the compounder, but it works in reverse too. Years of trust deposits can be wiped out by a single withdrawal.

So, choose carefully when you choose who to trust. But *do* choose to trust.

Because the alternative — closing yourself off, building walls, refusing to be vulnerable — that's not protection. That's a prison. And you'll serve your sentence alone.

My most important clients

I'm an executive coach. I help leaders get clarity and make hard decisions.

But my most important clients live in my house. They're seven, 10 and 12 years old.

When I parent my children, I'm not thinking about the child standing in front of me. I'm thinking about the 30-year-old adult they'll hopefully become. Every decision Bex and I make is aimed at that future person — not the tantrum, not the homework battle, not the short-term discomfort.

I'm parenting for the 30-year-old adult, not the seven-year-old child.

If my children become good humans — happy, healthy, able to contribute to the world — I'll have done the hardest job in the world well. That will be my greatest achievement. Not the records. Not the championships.

Three people who know how to build trust, who can recognise when it's breaking, who understand that some withdrawals close the account forever.

That's what I'm building now. Not with grand gestures but with a chin-up bar in a doorway. With bedtime words spoken every night. With consequences that don't move. With a marriage that solves problems and moves on without keeping score.

Grain by grain. Day by day. Year by year.

The mountain

I started this book as a five-year-old strapped to a machine, electrodes under my eyelids, feeling like a crash test dummy while doctors told my parents to lower their expectations. 'He'll never play sport. Never get a decent job. Never have many friends.' The world had already written my future before I could hold a pen.

I end it 60 feet underwater, eyes closed by choice, holding on to a white cane I was once ashamed of, trusting a man I'd known for a week to guide me through a shipwreck in the dark.

The distance between those two points isn't talent. It isn't luck. It's trust. Built one grain of sand at a time.

It's trust in myself — knowing who I am and how I'll show up, even when no one's watching.

It's trust in the right people — partners who call me out without tearing me down, who stay when it's hard, who solve problems and move on without weaponising the past.

It's trust that staying vulnerable, even after being hurt, is the only path towards everything worth having.

You can build trust quickly — I let Dan in within a week. But trust erodes even faster. And once it's broken, rebuilding trust takes longer than starting fresh. It may take forever.

The question isn't whether you're capable of building trust. You are.

The question is whether you'll add the first grain of sand today. Whether you'll hold on when everything in you wants to let go. Whether you'll do the 10 chin-ups when no one's watching. Whether you'll stay open after you've been hurt. Whether you'll parent for the 30-year-old adult instead of the child standing in front of you.

That's the Hard Standard. The real one. The one we had to build together.

Trust.

I started this journey as a five-year-old in a steel helmet. I'll finish it as an old man watching my children raise their own kids — seeing the seeds we planted bloom in ways I can't yet imagine.

That's the mountain. That's the investment. That's the longest game.

Rock hard. Marshmallow soft. Both, on purpose.

Why not you?

Why not now?

Afterword

From Rebecca Formston

It's 6.12 am. I'm standing in the kitchen in my dressing gown, packing three lunchboxes, trying to find a clean sports sock and telling someone to brush their teeth properly. The dog is barking. One child can't find their hat. Someone else has forgotten they have cross country. The kettle has boiled three times and I still haven't made tea.

That's a normal Tuesday.

It's loud and chaotic and busy. I start early, get the kids ready for school, get myself ready for work. I'm a preschool educator, so there's no easing into the day. It's on from the second I open my eyes.

Matt is usually there. He works from home a lot. He'll make breakfast. He'll likely be talking about some new idea while I'm trying to find a library book. But he can't help with the driving. So every school drop-off, every sport pick-up, every birthday party, every last-minute dash because someone's left their homework at home — that's on me.

When he's away, which happens more than people probably realise, I'm in charge of everything. Three kids. Work. Dinner. Washing. Sport schedules. Notes from school. The pool pump that's making a weird noise. All of it.

Other families' mornings probably look similar to ours. Except there are two people who can drive.

That one detail changes a lot.

People outside our house wouldn't guess how full-on he is. He's intense. Every day is go go go. If he finishes something big, his brain immediately moves to what's next. There's rarely a time where he just rests. Even when the doctors told him to rest, he didn't really want to. I had to be the one saying, 'You need to stop.'

He's very goal-driven. That's one of the things that attracted me to him in the first place. I liked that he had direction. I liked that he didn't drift. But living with it can be exhausting. I'm often thinking, *Oh my goodness, what is next and what do I need to keep up with now?*

He'll be mid-conversation about school fees and then casually drop in that he's thinking about a world record.

It's a lot.

At the same time, he is extremely loyal, faithful and committed. He loves us fiercely. I know everything he does is for us and to better our lives. That doesn't mean I don't roll my eyes sometimes. It just means I understand where he's coming from.

Day to day, his vision means I'm the only one who can read the homework properly, or the fine print on a school email, or the instructions on a medicine bottle. If we're at a restaurant, I read the menu. If there's a form, I fill it in. It can be exhausting.

But he's the one with the disability. I remind myself of that regularly, especially when I'm on my third sports club run of the afternoon and someone has spilt yoghurt in the back seat.

I do forget he's blind. Quite a lot.

He's so capable and so determined. He does everything a sighted person can do except drive. In my eyes, he sees a lot more than he actually can. I forget his limitations because he rarely leads with them.

The times I really notice are when a pattern changes. If I leave a cupboard door open in the kitchen, which I do, and forget to close it, he will walk straight into it. Because in his memory, that cupboard door is always shut. The kitchen exists in his head in a certain way. If I mess with that system, he pays for it.

There's a very specific thud that tells me I've left something where it shouldn't be.

I'll say, 'Sorry,' and he'll say, 'Cupboard?'

Yes. Cupboard.

Watching him build things still makes me laugh sometimes. He built all the retaining walls around our house. Proper, heavy, back-breaking work. He maintains the pool. He fixes taps. He installs shelves. He does IKEA flatpacks without the instructions.

Occasionally, I might have to read out a step. Usually, he's already worked it out by feel. The only thing he really needs me for is the measuring tape.

That capability is one of the reasons I married him. I was brought up with fairly stereotypical role models. The man does the handy jobs. That mattered to me. He can do all that. And he does it better than most sighted people we know.

Our division of labour just looks different. I drive. He builds retaining walls.

I remember our first date at Manly. We walked to Shelly Beach, then went to the Manly Wharf Bar for a beer. It was a sunny afternoon. I knew he was visually impaired before I met him, but I didn't know how visually impaired he was.

When he said he couldn't read the menu, I was a little bit stunned. I thought, *Oh wow.*

But it was an 'okay, cool' moment. I read the menu out loud and we progressed from there. It didn't feel dramatic. It was just information.

What I remember more clearly is wondering if he actually liked me. He seemed a little bit off. A little bit distant. He finished the date quite quickly with a quick peck on the cheek and dashed off home. I walked away thinking, *well, that's that. Perhaps he's not into me.*

Later he admitted he was extremely hung over from a big night.

Very romantic.

The Nazaré period was different to how people imagine it. I didn't overthink it. I didn't sit around catastrophising. I don't see the point in fretting over something that hasn't happened, especially when I knew he had trained well. He was the best prepared he could be and had the best team around him.

On the day itself, he was in Portugal. I was at home. There were school lunches to make. Shoes to find. A WhatsApp message from a kids' sports team.

Life doesn't pause because your husband is about to surf a giant wave.

We don't do big emotional goodbyes. We don't lean into the headspace of not coming home. I have never once been concerned that he wasn't going to come home to us. He throws himself into huge adventures, yes. But he prepares. He does the work. At the end of the day, we are his main priority. Whatever he's doing, he has prepared to the best of his abilities to make sure he can come home safe.

That's enough for me.

He writes that I never complained. That's generous.

I do complain.

I wouldn't be human if I didn't. The lifestyle can be extremely frustrating and tiring and financially straining. There are plenty of times when I've said, 'Can we just have a quiet year?' Sometimes I wonder what life would be like if we just led a normal life without big adventures and big projects.

It would probably be pretty dull.

But don't tell him I said that.

What does get to me is his generosity. He has such a kind heart. He wants to give lots of his energy and time to people. Sometimes those people are not very kind back. Sometimes they take advantage.

When someone has ripped him off, it's been awful — not just financially, but emotionally. Watching someone exploit that kindness is hard.

My life does take a backseat at times. His dreams and ambitions are time-consuming. We don't have much family support close by. My parents are in London. His family is hours away. Childcare falls on me a lot of the time.

That's what I chose. I knew what I was getting into.

I love being a mother. If I could, that would be my full-time role. At the same time, the lifestyle he provides for us is incredible. I am extremely grateful for his endeavours that enable us to lead such an amazing and exciting life.

It's a trade-off. I drive more than I'd like. I also get to watch my children see what commitment looks like up close.

The most annoying reaction I've heard is when he says to a stranger, 'I'm legally blind, can you tell me what you're pointing at?' And the response is a chuckle and, 'Oh I'm blind too, I should really wear my glasses more.'

It's usually innocent. Not meant in malice. But it minimises something that shapes every single day of our lives.

Not every disability is visible.

When he told me about the freediving world record, I probably rolled my eyes and said, 'Oh God, here we go again, another adventure.'

I realised years ago this was going to be our life. He will always chase the next extreme danger or crazy world record. I have learned to accept that and support him as best I can.

Do I trust him?

Yes.

I 100 per cent trust Matt with my life. He would never do anything to hurt us. He can be full-on, exhausting and bossy at times. But he has our best interests at heart. He has always had my back. From very early on when we met, I felt loved, respected and cared for.

When he says he'll be home for dinner, I believe him. If he says a competition is safe, I believe him. If he's doing something crazy, I know he has worked extremely hard to be the best he can be for that crazy endeavour.

That doesn't mean I don't sigh when the calendar fills up again.

If you're reading this and thinking he sounds like a lot, you're right.

He may come across as a bit intense, a little politically incorrect and sometimes a bit too much. He is. He talks big. He dreams big. He sometimes forgets to sit down.

But he's got so much to give. You can learn a lot from how he goes about his day-to-day life and all his crazy endeavours.

At home, he's the man who builds retaining walls by feel and then asks me to check the measuring tape. He's the dad who can't see our kids' faces clearly but somehow notices immediately if something is off in their voice. He's the husband who will throw himself into a freezing ocean on the other side of the world and then come home and fix a fence without being asked.

He is a pretty special freak of nature.

Though please don't tell him I said that. His head is big enough already.

References

Chapter 1

Navy SEALs 'Slow is smooth, smooth is fast'

SEALFIT (no date) *Slow is smooth, smooth is fast*. Available at: https://sealfit.com/slow-smooth-smooth-fast/ (Accessed: 28 April 2026).

USMilitary.com (no date) *Slow is smooth, smooth is fast*. Available at: https://usmilitary.com/slow-is-smooth-smooth-is-fast/ (Accessed: 28 April 2026).

Chapter 2

Toyota Production System and Kaizen

Toyota Motor Corporation (no date) *Toyota production system*. Available at: https://www.toyota-global.com/company/vision_philosophy/toyota_production_system/ (Accessed: 28 April 2026).

Lean Enterprise Institute (no date) *Toyota production system*. Available at: https://www.lean.org/lexicon-terms/toyota-production-system/ (Accessed: 28 April 2026).

Liker, J.K. (2021) *The Toyota Way: 14 management principles from the world's greatest manufacturer*. 2nd edn. New York: McGraw-Hill.

Chapter 3

British SAS Selection Process

Military.com (2020) 'This is what makes SAS selection the toughest in the world', Military.com, 24 April. Available at: https://www.military.com/off-duty/2020/04/24/what-makes-sas-selection-toughest-world.html (Accessed: 28 April 2026).

Men's Health (no date) *SAS training and selection*. Available at: https://www.menshealth.com/uk/fitness/a36379046/sas-training-selection/ (Accessed: 28 April 2026).

Chapter 4

Harvard Business Review on Standards and Accountability

Bregman, P. (2016) 'The right way to hold people accountable', *Harvard Business Review*, 11 January. Available at: https://hbr.org/2016/01/the-right-way-to-hold-people-accountable (Accessed: 28 April 2026).

Seppälä, E. (2014) 'The hard data on being a nice boss', *Harvard Business Review*, 24 November. Available at: https://hbr.org/2014/11/the-hard-data-on-being-a-nice-boss (Accessed: 28 April 2026).

Chapter 5

Alexander, B.K., Coambs, R.B. and Hadaway, P.F. (1978) 'The effect of housing and gender on morphine self-administration in rats', *Psychopharmacology*, 58(2), pp. 175–179. doi:10.1007/BF00426903. Available at: https://link.springer.com/article/10.1007/BF00426903 (Accessed: 28 April 2026).

Gage, S.H. and Sumnall, H.R. (2019) 'Rat Park: How a rat paradise changed the narrative of addiction', *Addiction*, 114(5), pp. 917–922. doi:10.1111/add.14481. Available at: https://onlinelibrary.wiley.com/doi/10.1111/add.14481 (Accessed: 28 April 2026).

Chapter 6

French Foreign Legion Anonymat Tradition

French Foreign Legion Information (no date) *Joining the French Foreign Legion*. Available at: https://foreignlegion.info/joining/ (Accessed: 28 April 2026).

Wikipedia (no date) *French Foreign Legion*. Available at: https://en.wikipedia.org/wiki/French_Foreign_Legion (Accessed: 28 April 2026).

Chapter 7

Carol Dweck Growth Mindset Research

Dweck, C. (2016) 'What having a "growth mindset" actually means', *Harvard Business Review*, 13 January. Available at: https://hbr.org/2016/01/what-having-a-growth-mindset-actually-means (Accessed: 28 April 2026).

Dweck, C. (2014) *The power of believing that you can improve* [TED Talk]. Available at: https://www.ted.com/talks/carol_dweck_the_power_of_believing_that_you_can_improve (Accessed: 28 April 2026).

Chapter 8

Brené Brown Shame and Vulnerability Research

Brown, B. (2010) *The power of vulnerability* [TED Talk]. Available at: https://www.ted.com/talks/brene_brown_the_power_of_vulnerability (Accessed: 28 April 2026).

Omadeke, J. (2022) 'The best leaders aren't afraid to be vulnerable', *Harvard Business Review*, 22 July. Available at: https://hbr.org/2022/07/the-best-leaders-arent-afraid-of-being-vulnerable (Accessed: 28 April 2026).

Chapter 9

Neuroscience of Emotional Pain and Avoidance

Erickson, K.I., Voss, M.W., Prakash, R.S., Basak, C., Szabo, A., Chaddock, L., Kim, J.S., Heo, S., Alves, H., White, S.M., Wojcicki, T.R., Mailey, E., Vieira, V.J., Martin, S.A., Pence, B.D., Woods, J.A., McAuley, E. and Kramer, A.F. (2011) 'Exercise training increases size of hippocampus and improves memory', *Proceedings of the National Academy of Sciences*, 108(7), pp. 3017–3022. Available at: https://www.pnas.org/doi/10.1073/pnas.1015950108 (Accessed: 28 April 2026).

Psychology Today (2025) 'How physical and emotional pain overlap', *Psychology Today*, August. Available at: https://www.psychologytoday.com/us/blog/your-body-has-something-to-tell-you/202508/how-physical-and-emotional-pain-overlap (Accessed: 28 April 2026).

Chapter 10

Angela Duckworth Grit Research

Duckworth, A. (2016) *Grit: The power of passion and perseverance.* New York: Scribner. Available at: https://angeladuckworth.com/grit-book/ (Accessed: 28 April 2026).

Duckworth, A. (2013) *Grit: The power of passion and perseverance* [TED Talk]. Available at: https://www.ted.com/talks/angela_lee_duckworth_grit_the_power_of_passion_and_perseverance (Accessed: 28 April 2026).

Chapter 11

Kahneman, D. (2011) *Thinking, fast and slow.* New York: Farrar, Straus and Giroux.

Chapter 12

Cal Newport — Deep Work research, Georgetown University

Newport, C. (no date) *Cal Newport*. Available at: https://www.calnewport.com/ (Accessed: 28 April 2026).

Newport, C. (2016) *Deep work: Rules for focused success in a distracted world*. New York: Grand Central Publishing. Available at: https://www.amazon.com/Deep-Work-Focused-Success-Distracted/dp/1455586692 (Accessed: 28 April 2026).

Chapter 13

Google Project Aristotle — Psychological Safety Research

Google re:Work (no date) *Guide: Understand team effectiveness*. Available at: https://rework.withgoogle.com/guides/understanding-team-effectiveness/ (Accessed: 28 April 2026).

PsychSafety (no date) *Google's Project Aristotle*. Available at: https://psychsafety.com/googles-project-aristotle/ (Accessed: 28 April 2026).

Chapter 14

Neuroscience of Motor Imagery and Mental Practice

Eisenberger, N.I. (2012) 'The neural bases of social pain: Evidence for shared representations with physical pain', *Psychosomatic Medicine*, 74(2), pp. 126–135. doi:10.1097/PSY.0b013e3182464dd1. Available at: https://www.ncbi.nlm.nih.gov/pmc/articles/PMC3813498/ (Accessed: 28 April 2026).

Pillay, S. (2014) 'To reach your goals, make a mental movie', *Harvard Business Review*, 5 March. Available at: https://hbr.org/2014/03/to-reach-your-goals-make-a-mental-movie (Accessed: 28 April 2026).

Chapter 15

Australian Institute of Sport — Overtraining and Recovery

Australian Institute of Sport (no date) *Position statements*. Available at: https://www.ais.gov.au/position_statements (Accessed: 28 April 2026).

Australian Institute of Sport (no date) *Nutrition*. Available at: https://www.sportaus.gov.au/ais/nutrition (Accessed: 28 April 2026).

Chapter 16

K. Anders Ericsson — Deliberate Practice and Expert Performance

Ericsson, K.A., Prietula, M.J. and Cokely, E.T. (2007) 'The making of an expert', *Harvard Business Review*, 85(7–8), pp. 114–121. Available at: https://hbr.org/2007/07/the-making-of-an-expert (Accessed: 28 April 2026).

Ericsson, K.A., Krampe, R.T. and Tesch-Römer, C. (1993) 'The role of deliberate practice in the acquisition of expert performance', *Psychological Review*, 100(3), pp. 363–406. doi:10.1037/0033-295X.100.3.363. Available at: https://psycnet.apa.org/record/1993-40718-001 (Accessed: 28 April 2026).

Scientific American (no date) *The expert mind*. Available at: https://www.scientificamerican.com/article/the-expert-mind/ (Accessed: 28 April 2026).

Chapter 17

McKinsey & Company — Diversity Wins: How Inclusion Matters

McKinsey & Company (2020) *Diversity wins: How inclusion matters*. Available at: https://www.mckinsey.com/featured-insights/diversity-and-inclusion/diversity-wins-how-inclusion-matters (Accessed: 28 April 2026).

McKinsey & Company (2018) *Delivering through diversity*. Available at: https://www.mckinsey.com/capabilities/people-and-organizational-performance/our-insights/delivering-through-diversity (Accessed: 28 April 2026).

McKinsey & Company (no date) *Diversity and inclusion*. Available at: https://www.mckinsey.com/featured-insights/diversity-and-inclusion (Accessed: 28 April 2026).

Chapter 18

Formula 1 pit strategy analysis

Formula 1 (no date) *Strategy report*. Available at: https://www.formula1.com/en/latest/article.strategy-report (Accessed: 28 April 2026).

Wikipedia (no date) *2021 Abu Dhabi Grand Prix*. Available at: https://en.wikipedia.org/wiki/2021_Abu_Dhabi_Grand_Prix (Accessed: 28 April 2026).

Chapter 19

Jim Collins and Jerry Porras — Built to Last and Core Values research

Collins, J. (no date) *Preserve the core/stimulate progress.* Available at: https://www.jimcollins.com/concepts/preserve-the-core-stimulate-progress.html (Accessed: 28 April 2026).

Collins, J.C. and Porras, J.I. (1996) 'Building your company's vision', *Harvard Business Review,* 74(5), pp. 65–77. Available at: https://hbr.org/1996/09/building-your-companys-vision (Accessed: 28 April 2026).

Chapter 20

Australian SAS Selection and Character

SOFREP (no date) 'SAS selection in Australia: A lesson in perseverance'. Available at: https://sofrep.com/specialoperations/sas-selection-in-australia-lesson-in-perseverance/ (Accessed: 28 April 2026).

Stanford University Marine Biological Laboratory (no date) Stanford MBL. Available at: https://mbl.stanford.edu/ (Accessed: 28 April 2026).

Chapter 21

Patricia Linville Self-Complexity Research

Linville, P.W. (1987) 'Self-complexity as a cognitive buffer against stress-related illness and depression', *Journal of Personality and Social Psychology,* 52(4), pp. 663–676. doi:10.1037/0022-3514.52.4.663. Available at: https://pubmed.ncbi.nlm.nih.gov/3572732/ (Accessed: 28 April 2026).

Linville, P.W. (1985) 'Self-complexity and affective extremity: Don't put all of your eggs in one cognitive basket', *Social Cognition,* 3(1), pp. 94–120. doi:10.1521/soco.1985.3.1.94. Available at: https://guilfordjournals.com/doi/10.1521/soco.1985.3.1.94 (Accessed: 28 April 2026).

Printed and bound by CPI Group (UK) Ltd, Croydon, CR0 4YY

20/07/2026

14925137-0003